The Australian Economy

The Australian Economy
The essential guide

Edited by Peter Kriesler

ALLEN & UNWIN

For Teresa, who does not believe that economists can speak English

© Peter Kriesler 1995

This book is copyright under the Berne Convention.
No reproduction without permission. All rights reserved.

First published in 1995
Allen & Unwin Pty Ltd
9 Atchison Street, St Leonards, NSW 2065 Australia

National Library of Australia
Cataloguing-in-Publication entry:

The Australian economy: the essential guide.

  Bibliography.
  Includes index.
  ISBN 1 86373 758 8.

  1. Australia—Economic conditions—1990– . 2. Australia—
  Economic policy—1990– . I. Kriesler, Peter.

330.994

Set in 10/11 pt Sabon by DOCUPRO, Sydney
Printed by McPherson's Printing Group, Maryborough

10 9 8 7 6 5 4 3 2 1

Contents

Tables	viii
Figures	x
Contributors	xii
Preface and acknowledgments	xiii
Glossary	xv

1 What is this thing called 'the Australian economy'?
  PETER KRIESLER   1
  • *Economic growth* • *Inflation* • *Unemployment* • *The balance of payments and international debt* • *Fiscal policy* • *Monetary policy* • *Microeconomic reform* • *The public sector* • *Environmental policies* • *Conclusion*

2 Economic growth: recent history and prospects
  STEVE DOWRICK   15
  • *Australia's growth performance—trends and cycles* • *The labour force's contribution to growth* • *The contribution of physical investment to growth* • *The contribution of technical progress to growth* • *International comparisons of GDP levels and growth rates* • *Concluding comments*

3 Inflation BILL JUNOR   36
  • *A definition of inflation* • *Measurement of inflation* • *Australia's inflation experience—a broad brush* • *The*

causes of inflation • Causes of inflation in Australia since 1960 • The costs of inflation • The costs and benefits of anti-inflation policies

4 Unemployment in Australia   TREVOR STEGMAN   61
• The costs and measurement of unemployment
• Australia's unemployment experience • The causes of unemployment • Labour market flows • Current policy

5 The balance of payments and international debt
COLM KEARNEY   80
• The balance of payments accounts • Australia's foreign indebtedness • The debt debate: does the current account matter? • Economies of scale
• Current Australian trade policy • Summary and conclusions

6 Fiscal policy in Australia   JOHN NEVILE   101
• How fiscal policy works • Crowding out • National savings and the current account deficit • Structural deficits • Fiscal policy in Australia

7 Money and monetary policy   ROSS MILBOURNE   119
• Prudential regulation • Credit creation and monetary policy • The theory of monetary policy • The transmission mechanism of monetary policy • Policy prescriptions • Australian empirical evidence • Recent Reserve Bank of Australia policy

8 Microeconomic reform   DAVID CLARK   142
• What is microeconomic reform? • Why microeconomic reform is unavoidable
• Microeconomic reform—an overview • The industry policy revolution • Labour market reform • Public sector reform • Barriers to further microeconomic reform • Microeconomic reform not a simple panacea for all of Australia's economic ills

9 The public sector: trends in Australia and other OECD countries   PETER SAUNDERS   170
• The Australian public sector in the 1980s
• Developments in other OECD countries • Other trends in the public sector • Marketisation • Summary

10 The environment: the role of economic instruments
ANTHONY OWEN   191
• Internalising externalities • Economics of emission control • The taxation approach • Tradeable permits

• *Combined taxes and permits* • *Applications*
• *Efficiency of economic instruments* • *Social welfare aspects of economic instruments* • *Australian experience*

Bibliography	214
Index	223

Tables

2.1	Annual growth of labour force and population	22
2.2	Weekly hours worked per person aged 15–64	24
2.3	Annual growth of labour force and working age groups relative to total population	25
2.4	Productivity growth and its components in the non-farm market sector	30
2.5	Economic development 1950–90 in a selection of OECD and East Asian countries	32
3.1	Consumer Price Index by categories	42
3.2	Indicators of labour market performance before and after the Accord	50
3.3	Sacrifice ratios for Australia	58
4.1	The Australian unemployment record	64
4.2	Unemployment rates by age and sex	66
4.3	The composition of changes in unemployment	69
5.1	The current account 1992/93	82
5.2	The capital account 1992/93	83
5.3	Australia's historical balance of payments	84
5.4	Australia's foreign indebtedness	85
5.5	Australia's debt interest payments and service ratios	85
5.6	Composition of main country groups and trade associations	97
5.7	Australia's current industry and trade policy	98
6.1	Budget deficits and interest rates in Australia, 1973/74 to 1992/93	108
6.2	Government expenditure in twelve OECD countries, 1986–88	110
6.3	The structural deficit and its components in Australia, 1973/74 to 1993/94	115
7.1	Major financial deregulations	121

7.2	Balance sheets of the banks and RBA as at January 1994	123
7.3	The transmission mechanism of monetary policy	128
8.1	The pros and cons of greater enterprise bargaining	156
9.1	Movements in Commonwealth budget and public sector outlays in Australia in the 1980s	175
9.2	Trends in general government outlays, 1980 to 1992	178
9.3	The changing structure of government in the 1980s	181

Figures

2.1	Index of real output (per capita) 1950–93	17
2.2	Growth of real output (per capita)	19
2.3	Annual growth rates in Australia and the UK	20
2.4	Australian population and labour force	21
2.5	Labour force participation and population structure	22
2.6	Women in the labour force	23
2.7	Men in the labour force	23
2.8	Public and private investment	27
2.9	Growth of productivity in the non-farm market sector	29
2.10	GDP growth and GDP levels	33
3.1	Australia's inflation rate 1960–94	40
4.1	Australia's unemployment	65
4.2	Labour market flows	76
6.1	Budget deficits and interest rate spread	106
6.2	Budget deficits and short-term interest rates	107
6.3	Government revenue as percentage of GDP, 1992	111
6.4	Structural deficits as a percentage of GDP and unemployment, Australia, 1973/74 to 1992/93	116
7.1	Terms of trade and the exchange rate	133
7.2	Four-quarter growth in GNE and M3	134
7.3	Money velocity	135
7.4	Four-quarter growth in real private investment and the interest rate	136
7.5	Four-quarter growth in the CPI and M3	136
7.6	Private consumption expenditure (real) and personal credit	137

7.7	Growth in business investment (real) and business credit	138
8.1	Why productivity must rise	147
8.2	Productivity expected to rise	152
8.3	GBE efficiency improves net rates of return on capital invested	159
8.4	Port productivity still poor	167
9.1	Longer term trends in Commonwealth budget outlays, 1953/54 to 1992/93	173

Contributors

DAVE CLARK is in the Economic History Department at the University of New South Wales and is Director of the Centre of Community and Business Education.

STEVE DOWRICK is in the Economics Department of the Research School of Social Sciences at the Australian National University.

BILL JUNOR is in the Economics Department at Macquarie University.

COLM KEARNEY is in the Department of Economics and Finance at the University of Western Sydney, Macarthur, and is Director of the Centre for Innovation and International Trade.

PETER KRIESLER is in the Economics Department at the University of New South Wales.

ROSS MILBOURNE is in the Economics Department at the University of New South Wales.

JOHN NEVILE is in the Economics Department at the University of New South Wales.

ANTHONY OWEN is in the Econometrics Department at the University of New South Wales and is Director of the Centre for Applied Economic Research.

PETER SAUNDERS is the Director of the Social Policy Research Centre at the University of New South Wales.

TREVOR STEGMAN is in the Economics Department at the University of New South Wales.

Preface and acknowledgments

As Australia approaches the end of the twentieth century its economy is balanced precariously. Some of the important economic variables—such as inflation—are at historically low levels, while others—like unemployment—are at historically high ones. Perhaps as a result, economics has come to dominate political discussion and public debate, and seems to make front-page news almost daily. Certainly the 'economisation' of politics is a relatively new phenomenon. In the past, policies on the economy represented only part of a party's overall agenda, which used to be much more broadly based. Now, most issues are judged from an economic perspective. The significance of economics was demonstrated in the last few federal elections which were fought on almost purely economic grounds. For the first time the leader of a major political party, albeit one in opposition, was a professional economist who campaigned on an almost exclusively economics-based platform. Major issues, such as immigration, work practices, health and education are increasingly being judged on the basis of economic criteria. The importance of economics, though not of economists, has never been higher.

Nevertheless, most non-professional economists (barring the media) are hesitant in joining the debate on economic issues, and have difficulty following it despite the fact that it has profound effects on all Australians, who are well aware of its daily impact. Much of this is due to the language and jargon which economists use, and their reticence in even attempting to speak to non-economists. This book attempts to overcome that problem. It represents an endeavour to outline the key features of the Australian economy in a way that is intelligible to the layperson. The authors of the various chapters are academic economists who have a commitment to make their area understandable to the non-economists. The chapters cover the main aspects of the Australian economy. In order to understand the significance of what has been happening, it is necessary to place it into context. To achieve this, discussion of the Australian experience has been combined with an introduction to the relevant economic theory in order to enable comprehension of both.

There are many terms which are bandied about quite readily, but whose precise meaning is unclear. To facilitate communication, certain key words and terms are presented in the Glossary at the beginning of the book. Many key economic variables, such as unemployment and inflation, are not capable of precise measurement; and, as a result, can be measured in many different ways. It is important to attempt to understand how each of these is measured, and why different measures may be used at different times. As a result, some attention is paid to the problems associated with measurement.

It is the sincere hope of all associated with the book that it will help raise the level of economic awareness in the country by making key issues accessible.

Many debts were incurred in the production of this book. In particular, most of the editing was completed while I was on leave at the Department of Economics, Macquarie University, and at the Social Policy Research Centre, the University of New South Wales. I appreciate the support I received from both institutions. In particular, I am indebted to George Matheson of the SPRC for his computational help. In addition, Peter Saunders and John Nevile both made many fruitful suggestions that helped raise the quality of the final product. I would also like to thank Sandra Escobar for help with compiling the index.

The support I received from Allen & Unwin was, as always, way beyond the call of duty, and I would like to thank Rebecca Kaiser for her patience and advice, and particularly Elizabeth Weiss who calmly read each chapter, and was instrumental in turning the ramblings of economists into the lucid text you have in front of you, with only minor damage to her sanity.

I am indebted to Moir of the *Sydney Morning Herald* for permission to reproduce his cartoon 'the experts'.

The debt I owe my wife, Teresa, for her support and encouragement is overwhelming. Her tolerance in listening to the ravings of economists at many a dinner party finally led her to ask the question which inspired this book, 'Why can't economists speak English?'. It is to her that this book is dedicated with love.

Glossary

ACCORD: A prices and incomes policy resulting from agreement between the Federal Labor government, the trade union movement and representatives of employers.

APEC: Asia Pacific Economic Cooperation. A trade association of nations, members of which are listed in Table 5.6.

APPRECIATION/REVALUATION: An increase in the value of $Aus against other currencies. Appreciation refers to a floating exchange rate regime, where the currency market sets the value of the $Aus. Revaluation refers to the fixed exchange rate regime where the value of the currency was set by the Reserve Bank.

ABS: Australian Bureau of Statistics. A federal bureau charged with gathering and processing all major economic, social and other statistics on Australia.

CAIRNS GROUP: A trade association consisting of primary producing countries. Member nations are listed in Table 5.6.

CONSTANT RETURNS (to scale): This occurs when all inputs into a production process are increased by the same proportion and output also increases by that same proportion.

CPI: Consumer price index. The most cited measure of inflation, this index is based on the price of a basket of consumer goods. Defined on pp. 38–9.

CROWDING OUT: The idea that an increase in government expenditure will reduce (crowd-out) private expenditure so that the increase in total expenditure is less than the increase in government expenditure.

DEPRECIATION/DEVALUATION: A reduction in the value of the $Aus against other currencies. Depreciation refers to a floating exchange rate regime, while devaluation refers to the fixed exchange rate regime.

DEREGULATION: The removal of controls and government regulation over an industry. During the 1980s financial markets and the setting of the exchange rate were both deregulated in Australia.

ELASTICITY: The responsiveness of the changes in one variable as a result of changes in another. For example, price elasticity measures the responsiveness of changes in demand to changes in price.

GATT: General Agreement on Trade and Tariffs.

GDP: Gross domestic product. The main measure, from the National Income Accounts, of the level of aggregate current domestic production.

INCREASING RETURNS (to scale): This occurs when all inputs into a production process are increased by the same proportion, but output increases by more than that proportion.

INDIRECT TAXES: These are paid by the producer or the seller, rather than 'directly' by the income earner.

INDUSTRY COMMISSION: A body established by the Federal Parliament to inquire into the operation of industries in the private and/or public sector. It reports to Parliament.

INTERMEDIATE GOOD: A good which is not itself consumed, but is used in the production of other goods. Examples include raw materials and machinery.

J-CURVE: The idea that things have to get worse before they get better; applied to the balance of trade (exports minus imports) as the result of a depreciation.

NAIRU: Non-accelerating inflation rate of unemployment. The level of unemployment which is believed to have a neutral impact on inflation; also called the natural rate. It has been argued that unemployment below this rate will tend to accelerate inflation, while unemployment above it will lead to inflation decelerating.

NRH: Natural rate hypothesis. See non-accelerating inflation rate of unemployment (NAIRU).

NEW CLASSICAL MACROECONOMICS: A theory which believes in perfectly functioning markets and rational expectations, so that the effects of changes in policy variables occur extremely rapidly (in theory, instantaneously).

NOMINAL VALUES: Money values of economic variable, influenced by actual changes in those variables and changes in their price.

OECD: Organisation for Economic Co-operation and Development. A forum for discussion of policy, a think-tank for new ideas and an agency for collecting international economic statistics. Member nations are listed in Table 5.6.

OPEC: Organisation of Petroleum Exporting Countries. Member nations are listed in Table 5.6.

RATIONAL EXPECTATIONS: The idea that people do not make persistently biased (incorrect) errors in their expectations in the long run, or, more strictly, the idea that expectations are formed on the basis of the best economic theory extant.

REAL VALUES: Actual changes in the money values of variables corrected for price changes. Real values are calculated by correcting nominal values (or current prices) for inflation.

TERMS OF TRADE: The ratio of export prices to import prices.

1 What is this thing called 'the Australian economy'?
Peter Kriesler

What are the main economic problems facing the Australian economy as we move towards the end of the century? What explanations have been given for these problems? What are the most appropriate policy instruments for dealing with these problems, and how has the efficacy of the instruments been changed by changes in the economic environment?

These are questions of great importance and have serious repercussions for all Australians. In order to begin answering them, some knowledge is needed of both the Australian economy and of the economic theory which tells us how the 'bits fit together'—and it is the purpose of this chapter, and indeed of the book as a whole, to answer some of these questions.

However, before even beginning to look at these issues, it is important to clarify exactly what is meant by 'the Australian economy'. Although most people have some idea what this means, to answer with any degree of precision is extremely difficult. The concept of 'Australia' is not so difficult, although with the increased internationalisation of the world, especially the world economy, the relevance of national boundaries is in a state of flux. What is embraced by the term 'economy', on the other hand, is not as clear. One way to overcome this problem would be to list all the components which comprise the Australian economy. This would include a vast and complex array of people, institutions, firms and objects engaged in various activities and transactions. One common factor which they share is that, at some stage, a transaction in monetary terms is involved. At least, this is the way in which the national accounts measure the economy, in terms of the total value added within the economy. This criterion, then, would reduce the economy to being related to money and market transactions, though clearly there is more to the economy than just a series of markets. It includes relations between people and 'things', between people and institutions, and between people and other people in the spheres of production, consumption or exchange. Moreover, there are many transactions which are not related to money and which we would still wish to include within the confines of what is meant by the 'economy'.

One of the major criticisms of economists is that they have ignored many of the important non-market relations and transactions. The value of the household and the depreciation of the natural environment are just two examples of activities which have been traditionally excluded from economic calculation. This shows that the borderline between 'economic' and 'non-economic' is unclear and is continually being redrawn, either as a result of new knowledge, or as the result of pressure from outside (for example, by feminists and environmentalists) being brought to bear on economists and politicians.

Notwithstanding a degree of 'fuzziness' as to exactly what is meant by 'the Australian economy', it is clear that the size of the economy, as traditionally measured by the national income accounts, and how fast it is growing have important impacts on the level of our well-being and our standard of living, although the areas which have traditionally been excluded, like the environment and the household, will also impact on those areas. As a result, any study of the Australian economy needs to look at certain specific areas if it is to cover the issues which influence well-being and, therefore, are of interest. Just as the economy changes and evolves over time, so do the areas of importance and the policies which influence them. The importance of some of these areas seems unlikely to diminish. In particular, the importance of economic growth in improving living standards and generating employment, and the importance of employment itself, appear to have extremely significant direct consequences on well-being (although the environmental movement is suggesting major rethinking of both).

The importance of inflation, the international sector and the public sector, on the other hand, is more indirect. As Junor suggests in chapter 3, although inflation may well involve major costs to the economy, policies to reduce inflation may well involve an even greater cost. It cannot be denied that certain sectors of the economy seem to see inflation as the major problem, and its reduction is perceived as a policy priority. However, whether it is really of significance to the economy as a whole or only to those sectors is not clear. If the latter position is correct, then the 'fight inflation at all cost' arguments advocated by certain sectoral interests cannot be seen as being in the best interests of the economy as a whole, particularly in the light of the significant costs of fighting inflation identified by Junor.

The question of whether or not the balance of payments position should be regarded as a problem for the Australian economy is also a controversial one. The importance of international trade to the Australian economy cannot be denied. However, the question of whether the current account and foreign debt impose any sort of constraints on the economy, much less indicate our movement towards a 'banana republic' as a former treasurer once suggested, is not so clear, and needs to be examined in detail. Similarly, there are important sectors of the Australian economy which believe that the smaller the role of government, and hence the smaller the size of the public sector in the economy, the better. Others believe the exact opposite. Debate about the optimal size of the public sector is a relatively recent phenomenon, but it has played a very important part in policy decisions of the 1980s and 1990s. As it provides the justification for much of the privatisation and corporatisation of the public sector, it represents an issue well worth exploring.

This leads us to an evaluation of the major policy instruments available to the government to influence the economy. These also have been in a state of change over the last two decades. In particular, the role of monetary policy, fiscal policy and microeconomic policy have been subject to major revisions as a result of changes to the economy. As a result, their traditional roles can no longer be taken for granted. Nevertheless, they are the most important tools with which the government can hope to influence the future of the economy and, therefore, the well-being of the nation.

The environment has been largely neglected both by economists and by policymakers until relatively recently. However, increasingly there is an appreciation that environmental issues have important implications both for our well-being and for that of future generations. Part of the reason for the traditional neglect of environmental issues, as well as the reason for overexploitation of the natural environment, lies in the fact that it is treated as a 'free good'. This has led to overexploitation and depletion of environmental capital. The 1980s has seen increased worldwide concern with these issues. As a result a number of international agreements on environmental protection have been signed. These have had, or will have, important consequences for national economies, including Australia's. The government has a range of economic instruments for achieving environmental goals. These have different implications for environmental protection, as well as varied impacts on the economy.

Much of this discussion would be relevant to most 'developed' economies. However, the distinguishing feature of the Australian economy is that it is a small open economy. Open because almost everything which is produced or consumed in the country has a tradeable component. Even things which we take for granted as being only for domestic consumption, such as our weather or our views, are increasingly being enjoyed by tourists and hence contribute to our export earnings. Since the First Fleet, European Australia has been dependent on the economic well-being of the rest of the world for its own economic health. Although Australia is very much influenced by what happens in the rest of the world, the converse is not true. In other words, Australia does not have a very significant impact on the world economy, except in the markets for a few products, such as wool. This is what is meant by calling it a 'small' economy. We are 'small' because we do not have a significant effect on the rest of the world, and 'open' because the rest of the world has a significant effect on us. Our smallness can be judged by the fact that our Gross Domestic Product (GDP) is smaller than that of some American cities. So, due to that smallness, and to the composition of exports and imports, Australia is largely influenced by factors over which it has little control.

The foreign sector is now, and has always been, vital to the health of the Australian economy—a large proportion of total economic activity and in particular a very large proportion of capital needed to carry out investment comes from abroad.

The degree to which Australia is influenced by the rest of the world increased dramatically as a result of the major changes to the economy in the 1980s: 'The most influential economic decisions of the 1980s were the floating of the Australian dollar and the deregulation of the financial system' (Kelly 1992, p. 77). Before these deregulations, the government of the day exerted direct control over both financial markets and the exchange rate. Since then, however, the value of the Australian dollar has been set by currency markets, while both money and banks have been free to move into and out of the country at will.

The net effect of this has been to change the fundamentals of the economy. It has influenced both the ways in which the government can affect the economy, and the responsiveness of the economy to policy. To understand this, it is appropriate to look at recent developments in the economy, and the present Government's response to them.

We can distinguish two general types of economic policy, macroeconomic and microeconomic policy. Macroeconomics is concerned with the economy as a whole, so macroeconomic policy is concerned with trying to influence economy-wide aggregates, such as the rate of economic growth, the inflation rate, the level of unemployment, the balance of payments and so on. In other words, macroeconomic policy is about trying to influence the size of total output, employment and prices. Microeconomic policy, on the other hand, is aimed at specific sectors and industries. It does not attempt to influence the total size of output, but rather the composition of output—in other words, what is produced, and the way it is produced.

The emphasis of government policy has, until relatively recently, been with macroeconomic policy. Until the breakdown of the Keynesian consensus, in the mid-1970s, many policymakers and economists believed that the government could influence the major macroeconomic variables of economic growth, inflation, unemployment and the balance of payments by concentrating on the use of macroeconomic policy, particularly fiscal and monetary policy. Since the mid-1970s one of the major debates in economics has been about the efficacy of the various arms of macroeconomic policy. This has resulted in greater importance being placed on microeconomic policy. In Australia, microeconomic reform has been an explicit part of policy since the 1980s, and has been broadly interpreted to include discussion as to the optimal size and composition of the public sector, and debate as to the appropriate policies to deal with the natural environment.

In order to evaluate these issues, it is useful to briefly survey the changes in Australia's recent record on economic growth, inflation, unemployment and the international sector, before looking at the changes in policy these have induced.

Economic growth

Although economic growth has traditionally been associated with improvement in living standards, and therefore with welfare, this has been increasingly regarded as problematic. In particular, the usefulness of conventional measures of economic growth as indicators of welfare has been challenged. Many, including the environmental movement, have pointed to non-measurable benefits, as well as the costs incurred in order to achieve growth (especially to the environment) as mitigating the usefulness of economic growth, in terms of growth in measured output, as an indicator of well-being. Notwithstanding this, growth in output appears to be necessary to allow reasonable levels of employment and to give greater access to consumer goods.

Since the 1950s Australia has averaged about 4 per cent growth in real GDP per annum. In terms of output per person (as measured by real GDP per capita) the record, although not quite so good, is still acceptable. Given Australia's high population growth, it is not surprising to find that increases in the labour force are one of the main causes of economic growth. The labour force has been growing not only due to increased population, but also due to demographic changes, the most important of which is the increased participation of women since the 1960s. The other important change to the labour market has been the increased share of part-time work in total employment. These issues are explored at length in chapter 2.

As well as increased labour force, economic growth is also influenced by the productivity of those workers. Productivity will, in turn, be determined by investment and by the productivity of that investment, which is dependent on technical progress. Total investment consists of investment by the private sector and by the public sector. Dowrick shows that, up to the 1990s, private sector investment varied between 20 per cent and 24 per cent of GDP. However, since 1990 it has fallen quite significantly to under 18 per cent, and has played an important role in the economic recession. Public investment, after falling fairly slowly since its 1960s' level of 8 per cent, fell sharply in the late 1980s to 5 per cent. These falls in investment have important implications for the economy, not only in terms of our ability to produce but also in terms of our ability to compete internationally. Investment is an important determinant of productivity and, therefore, of costs. Without investment in the newest techniques, international competition, especially for the manufacturing sector, becomes extremely difficult.

Inflation

Inflation is something that nearly everyone talks about, but few people know exactly what it means, or how it is measured, much less what causes it or even why it is considered to be a problem. Economics is very useful both in giving a precise definition of inflation, and in telling us how it is measured. It is not quite so clear on identifying causes. One area of great debate in economics is the causes of inflation, and different economists have advocated various causes. The fact that economists often have many different theories of inflation (among other things), and that they rarely seem to agree, is one of the important factors explaining the low public opinion of them. It has led to all sorts of jokes, such as the comment that if one has ten economists in a room, then we can be sure of at least twenty opinions. However, this sort of perception is not well founded. We have to bear in mind the extreme complexity of the economy, which means that most of the important economic variables have many complex causes. In other words, the reason that economists seem to have so many theories about inflation, unemployment and so on, is not because one theory is correct and all the others are wrong. Rather it is because inflation and unemployment are elaborate phenomena, and have many different causes. As a result, all the theories may contain part of the explanation. However, at any one particular time, one account may be a better explanation of the causes than the others. In chapter 3 Junor demonstrates exactly this point. After considering the main explanations of inflation, he identifies where and when each has played a role in initiating Australia's inflation.

Unemployment

Whereas Australia's recent record on inflation has been creditable, the same cannot be said for unemployment, which has recently reached its highest level since the Great Depression. Figure 4.1 shows that, after being relatively stable at around 1.6 per cent up to the early 1970s, the unemployment rate rose quite dramatically, peaking in 1983 at about 10 per cent, and then fell fairly steadily before a sharp climb to record levels at the end of the 1980s.

Unlike inflation, the costs of unemployment, both to the individual and to the economy, are uncontroversial and readily identifiable. However, like the inflation rate, there is some difficulty with precise measurement of the unemployment rate, mainly due to the problem of identifying exactly who is to be included in the labour force. Changes in the number of people in the labour force also mean that both employment and unemployment can increase at the same time, so that any meaningful discussion of unemployment must include an analysis of demographic factors affecting the size of the labour force.

The question of what causes unemployment is even more controversial than the causes of inflation, and as with the discussion of inflation, this is at least partly due to the many different influences on unemployment. Here it is important to differentiate the factors determining the size of the labour force from those determining the level of employment. The main factors considered to influence the level of employment are the level of demand for final goods and services, as determined by the economy's growth rate, and the 'cost' of labour or the wage rate, as well as structural and frictional factors. It is also important to note that the incidence of unemployment does not fall evenly on all groups. In particular, since the mid-1980s unemployment has fallen most heavily on males previously employed full time. Over the same time there has been an increase in the proportion of long-term unemployed.

The significance of unemployment to the economy both in terms of the social costs borne by the individual and the lost opportunities to the whole economy make policies aimed at alleviating it imperative. Stegman examines the Government's recent attempts to do so, including recent policy statements.

The balance of payments and international debt

The importance of the international sector to the Australian economy has been stressed throughout this chapter. Its importance can be gauged by the fact that the economic recession of the late 1980s was induced by contractionary fiscal and monetary policy as a response to the deterioration in Australia's current account, mainly caused by income payments on foreign debt.

Although the current account of the balance of payments has always been of some concern to policymakers, the nature of the problem changed quite substantially during the 1980s. Traditionally, Australia has had a deficit on the current account financed by capital inflows, which also helped finance domestic investment. The main cause of the current account deficit was the deficit on the balance of trade, that is, the excess of imports of goods and services over exports. Since the 1950s, this deficit has been mainly due to the services component. Since the mid-1980s the difference between the trade balance and the current account balance has been growing, due to the increase in the income balance. This is the result of the substantial increase in our foreign debt, as shown in Tables 5.4 and 5.5, with the increase in income flows abroad, which are recorded in the current account and represent payments servicing that debt. The value of total net external debt has increased from 6.2 per cent of GDP in 1980/81 to 42.9 per cent in 1992/93. At the same time the cost of servicing that debt has increased from 5.4 per cent of GDP to 16.9 per cent, peaking at 26.3 per cent in 1990/91. It was concern with the size of Australia's foreign debt that led to the tightening of government policy which, in turn, led to the 1990s' recession. The costs incurred by the economy as a result have stimulated debate as to whether the balance of payments should be a target of economic policy, and whether in fact foreign debt, or indeed current account deficits, matter. Kearney surveys this debate in chapter 5.

One of the reasons why both the current account and foreign debt have been seen as problems is that since the deregulation of both the exchange rate and the financial system the government has lost much of its ability to set the value of the exchange rate and to control international capital flows. As a result, the value of the exchange rate is no longer directly controlled by government policy, but rather, is indirectly influenced by it. Prior to its deregulation in December 1983, the exchange rate, which determined the value of the $A, was set by the Reserve Bank. After that time its value was 'floated' and was determined in foreign exchange markets by market forces. In the short run the main factors influencing the value of the exchange rate are speculation as to its likely future value and the difference between Australian and foreign interest rates. This has meant that the rate of interest has increasingly been used as a policy instrument to control the value of the exchange rate.

This helps illustrate, as does the cartoon at the beginning of this chapter, the important principle that not only do most economic phenomena have many causes (as was argued above), but most causes impact on the economy in many different ways with very different degrees of desirability. Take the argument of the cartoon. An increase in the value of the $A will have mixed effects on the economy. It will increase the price of imports, which may reduce the quantity of goods imported—which is a good thing—but will also feed through to increase the inflation rate (as discussed in chapter 3)—which is a bad thing. The government may increase domestic interest rates to try to protect the value of the dollar. This is likely to have contractionary effects on the domestic economy and, if successful, will lead to an increase in the dollar's value. This in turn will make imports cheaper and exports dearer which, while being good for inflation, will make imports more attractive and exports less competitive. And so on . . .

As an ex-prime minister once said, 'Life was not meant to be easy', and this is certainly true if one is attempting to understand the economy. It is because the economy itself is so complex, with every element effecting every other element in a milliard different relationships, that there is no such thing as a simple correct answer. Despite this, the government still needs some direction in order to implement policy, though this is further complicated by the fact that the efficacy of many of the traditional arms of policy have been changing in the last two decades. In particular, the ability of fiscal and monetary policy to alleviate balance of payments problems has been blunted. Kearney suggests that microeconomic policy, with particular emphasis on trade policy, may be more potent, especially if part of an overall rationalisation of policy.

This leads us to the evaluation of government economic policy, considering first the traditional arms of fiscal and monetary policy, before looking at microeconomic policy in general and then its specific application to the public sector and to the environment.

Fiscal policy

Fiscal policy involves changes to government expenditures and revenues. For most of the postwar period the Keynesian consensus gave to fiscal policy the main role for economic stabilisation. A government budget deficit was seen as an injection of aggregate demand into the economy, and so was regarded as providing an appropriate stimulus during a recession.

For all the postwar period, until the late 1980s, Commonwealth governments ran budget deficits. Since 1987/88 these became budget surpluses, but these have disappeared in the last few years, with deficits again being the normal state of play.

To understand the reasons for these turnarounds, we need to distinguish between what are called the structural and the cyclical components of the budget deficit. This distinction is based on the fact that the government budget deficit both affects the economy and is, in turn, affected by it. For example, consider the effect on the size of the budget deficit of a downturn in economic activity, in other words, of economic growth falling. In this case, we would expect an increase in unemployment and a decrease in business turnover. Both of these would reduce taxation revenues and lead to increases in government expenditure in the form of increased social security payments. As a result, there will be an increase in the size of the government budget deficit notwithstanding the fact that there has not been any change in government policy. So, in order to understand the stance of fiscal policy we need to be able to distinguish between these cyclical effects and intentional discretionary changes in fiscal policy.

Clearly, given the substantial increase in unemployment and the downturn in business activity as illustrated by falling GDP, it would be reasonable to assume that the cyclical factors have played an important role in the change in the budgetary position since the late 1980s. Nevile calculates the structural deficit for Australia from 1973/74 to 1993/94 in Table 6.3. From that table we see that the structural budgetary position was in surplus for most of the early 1980s and 1990s.

Given that we have record levels of unemployment, we may ask why the Government doesn't expand fiscal policy. Why doesn't it spend more? The reason is that the Government and some sectors of the Australian economy are very worried about the size of deficits. The perceived problem with an increase in government spending is that it would lead either to the equivalent *crowding out* of private expenditure or else would lead to a deterioration in the current account. Crowding out is seen by some economists as being the inevitable consequence of an increase in government expenditure, and occurs when private expenditure is 'crowded out' by the increase in government expenditure. Under these circumstances, total output and employment will not change as a result of an increase in government outlays—all that happens is a shift in its composition between the private and public sectors. These arguments for the impotence of fiscal policy represent the main criticisms of Keynesian economics and are examined in great detail in chapter 6.

Monetary policy

Traditionally, monetary policy has been seen to operate through either the rate of interest or the money supply, as well as by the setting of the exchange rate. The 1960s, 1970s and early 1980s saw considerable debate among the various brands of monetarists and Keynesians, about what was the best way to operate monetary policy. During that period, the Reserve Bank, which was the central government authority, tried to set either the interest rate or money supply, as well as the value of the exchange rate, that is, the value of the Australian dollar. Nowadays, the Reserve Bank implements monetary policy indirectly through its influence on interest rates. The mechanics of how this is done is outlined in chapter 7.

The way in which the Reserve Bank's influence on interest rates feeds through to the rest of the economy is yet another area of controversy among economists. The controversy, which Milbourne surveys, can be summarised by concentrating on two main channels. First, monetary policy has a direct impact on the level of domestic expenditure, as interest rates may influence both consumer and business spending, and investment. In other words, by affecting aggregate demand it will influence output, employment and prices. Second, as the cartoon at the beginning of this chapter illustrates, higher interest rates make it more attractive for overseas investors to invest in Australia. This, other things being equal, leads to inflows of international capital, which cause an appreciation of the currency; in other words, the increased money coming into Australia increases the value of the Australian dollar. This may reduce inflation by reducing the cost of imports, and at the same time makes domestic import-competing industries less competitive.

As has been shown above, in the late 1980s, worried about the size of the current account deficit, the RBA tightened monetary policy, which, in addition to the fiscal contraction, precipitated the 'recession that we had to have'. However, due to financial deregulation, monetary policy has become a rather blunt instrument, and it did contribute to making the recession both more severe and more prolonged than was intended.

Microeconomic reform

As mentioned above, the 1980s saw an increase in the importance of microeconomic policy. In chapter 6 Kearney discusses the necessity of the Government rationalising policy with respect to industry and trade policy. Given the importance of the external sector, it is clear that microeconomic policy needs to be aimed at enhancing international competitiveness. The problem is that the structure of investment is not providing us with an industrial base which is internationally competitive so as to allow us to export more and reduce our reliance on imports. The problem with our exports is that they are heavily weighted towards a narrow range of commodities for which the terms of trade are extremely variable. We need to broaden our export base and move into new areas with better long-term prospects while with respect to our imports, we need to encourage domestic import substitution. This means that while maintaining our international competitiveness we need to restructure our economy in order to alleviate the constraint on domestic economic activity imposed by the external sector.

Currently there seems to be a confusion based on the mistaken view that microeconomic reform is simply privatisation of the public sector and deregulation of the private sector. Microeconomic policy needs to extend beyond this. No one, for example, denies the need to reform the tax system, even though the exact nature of the desired changes is much more controversial. Certainly something needs to be done about a system which provides disincentives for investment in areas which enhance capacity and productivity. Clark outlines the controversy which also exists about the nature of labour market reform with various advocates championing enterprise bargaining, complete deregulation and various positions in between. Similarly, chapter 8 looks at the public sector—an arena in which much hot air has been spent. Few would doubt the necessity of making the public sector more efficient. However, this does not mean acceptance of the privatisation and corporatisation of large parts of it, just because there is a belief that rationalisation and efficiency can only be achieved in the private sector.

The public sector

The debate about the role of the public sector in microeconomic reform highlights the major re-examination in the perception of the public sector's role in the economy since the 1970s. As noted above, since the Second World War, the Keynesian policy consensus amongst most 'developed' economies was associated with a focus on the absolute size of the government budget deficit as the main macroeconomic policy instrument for influencing the economy. As such, there was little concern with the size or composition of the public sector, or with government expenditures and receipts. With the breakdown of that consensus in the 1970s, more attention was paid to both the size of government involvement in the economy, and with its composition. For various reasons, some of which were discussed in the section on fiscal policy above, there seems to be an association between reduction in the size of the public sector and enhanced economic performance. Interestingly, as Saunders shows in chapter 9 (and Nevile in chapter 6) this is not a purely Australian phenomenon, and comparisons with other OECD countries are fruitful.

Environmental policies

As a result of increasing pressure, both external (in the form of international treaties and other agreements) and internal, the Federal Government has made various commitments towards the achieving of environmental goals. An important example is the commitment to certain targets for the emission of greenhouse gases. The implementation of these policies will have enormous impacts on the Australian economy, at both the microeconomic and macroeconomic levels. There is a wide range of instruments available to the Government to achieve its environmental objectives, though they will have significantly different impacts on the economy. As part of microeconomic policy it is important to evaluate the potential policy instruments for achieving environmental objectives, at the same time realising that these should only form part of an environmental policy.

Conclusion

There is an ancient Chinese curse 'May you live in interesting times'. Certainly, with respect to the Australian economy, we are living in such times. Many of the traditional economic relationships have been reshaped, both domestically and in the world economy. Financial markets, labour markets, the role of policy, international trade and currency markets are all in a state of flux. Australia is still to find its place in the world economy. The rest of this century promises much for the Australian economy. Those looking back from the early years of the next century will see the seeds of their economy being planted in what we are currently doing. Given the uncertainty of economic relations, all we can do is to try to be informed, and then do our best.

Annotated recommended reading

Australian Treasury, *Economic Indicators*, Australian Government Publishing Service, Canberra. A good source for up-to-date statistics on the Australian economy.

——, *Economic Roundup*, Australian Government Publishing Service, Canberra. Another good source for up-to-date statistics.

Centre for Applied Economic Research, *The Economic and Labour Relations Review*, University of New South Wales, Sydney. A regularly published journal with accessible articles.

Clark, D. (published annually), *Economic Update*, Financial Review Library, Sydney. Contains graphs and discussions of important economic statistics.

Economics Society of Australia, *Economic Papers*. Another regularly published journal with much relevant material.

Foster, R.A. and Stewart, S.E. 1991, *Australian Economic Statistics 1949–50 and 1989–90*, Occasional paper no. 8, Reserve Bank of Australia. A single volume containing 40 years of statistical data.

INDECS 1992, *State of Play 7*, Allen & Unwin, Sydney. An overall discussion of the Australian economy.

The Reserve Bank Bulletin, Reserve Bank of Australia, Sydney. A monthly bulletin with up-to-date statistics.

Stegman, T. and Junor, B. 1993, *Introductory Macroeconomics*, Harcourt Brace Jovanovich, Sydney. A good Australian macroeconomics textbook.

2 Economic growth: recent history and prospects
Steve Dowrick

A remarkable feature of economic development since the Second World War has been the huge increase in the output of goods and services. Measured economic growth has seen the output of the Australian economy increase fivefold since 1950. The population has doubled over the last four decades, but economic growth has been sufficient to more than double the quantity of goods and services available to the 'average' Australian.

One of the ironies of popular economic commentary is that despite this unprecedented bonanza in economic production it is commonly accepted that Australia's economic performance has been poor. For instance, when the Federal Government's Industry Commission (IC) submitted its annual report to the Treasurer in September 1991 it claimed that Australian economic performance was so poor that many of the Asian economies were outstripping us, and in particular that the standard of living in Japan was by now some 66 per cent higher than that in Australia.

Such criticisms of Australia's growth performance are commonplace in the media from commentators who wish to argue that particular policies or institutions need to be reformed. In fact, however, a proper measurement of living standards—one that takes account of the different prices faced by consumers in Australia and Japan and the greater opportunities for leisure enjoyed by Australians—shows that the higher standard of living is probably to be found in Australia. Moreover, much of the rapid economic growth of the East Asian region is a phenomenon of catching up with the technologies of the advanced capitalist economies.

Economic growth is neither the magic cure-all that some of its more enthusiastic advocates claim it to be, nor the malign despot its critics sometimes try to caricature it as being. Naive exhortations for economic growth portray it as the be-all and end-all of economic policy—the cure for unemployment, poverty and social malaise. This simplistic prescription for economic ills can, however, fail to take account of important side effects such as the costs of environmental degradation and the value of non-market activities such as raising children or enjoying leisure. On the other hand, opponents of economic growth characterise it as the destroyer of natural resources and lifestyles, but these equally naive views often ignore the fact that technical and economic changes can lead to the development of new technologies and new sources of supply which can enhance access to both natural and manufactured resources for everyone.

Economic growth as it is usually measured is not necessarily the same thing as economic welfare. An ideal social accounting would measure economic growth with full weight given to non-tangible benefits and costs. As it stands, however, we are reliant for most purposes on a national accounting system which is driven largely by the quantities and values of market transactions. As long as we realise that these market-based accounts relate to only a part, albeit an important part, of our economic activities, then we can argue that measured economic growth is an important indicator of social welfare.

Other things being equal, economic growth yields greater access to goods and services and should allow more choice. While it allows access, for those who want them, to home computers and air travel, it does not prevent those who prefer to grow their own vegetables and weave their own clothes from doing so. Of course the 'other things' are not necessarily kept equal. For example, a full social accounting of economic progress should take account of the noise pollution of aircraft and any inequality of incomes which may result from the revolutions in transport and information technologies.

Accepting these limitations to the measurement of economic growth, this chapter examines Australia's growth record from two perspectives. First, we examine how our growth has changed over time, and the major factors which account for our growth performance. Then we look at international comparisons of economic development in order to assess our comparative success and failure. These two approaches enable us to then make some predictions for the future path of Australian economic growth.

Australia's growth performance—trends and cycles

Figure 2.1 displays the path of real output between 1950 and 1993,

Figure 2.1 Index of real output (per capita) 1950–93

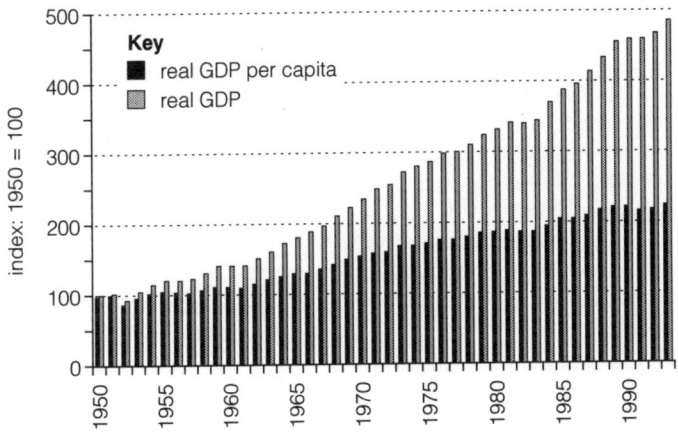

Source: ABS National Accounts accessed via DX for 1960–93, Summers and Heston (1993) for 1950–60.

both in terms of aggregate output and in terms of output per head of population. Our measure of output is the standard national accounting definition of real Gross Domestic Product (GDP) based on the figures produced by the Australian Bureau of Statistics (ABS). GDP is measured in 'real' terms. In order to discount the effects of price inflation, the goods and services produced in 1950, or in any other year, are valued at the prices which prevailed in 1990, with due allowance for changes in quality.

For graphical presentation, real GDP is indexed to 100 in 1950. The upper line shows that the output of goods and services in the Australian economy doubled between 1950 and 1967, doubled again by 1985, and is now five times as high as it was four decades ago.

Sustained economic growth of nearly 4 per cent per year (actually 3.8 per cent) over four decades has been a remarkable achievement. Much of this growth is attributable to a rapidly expanding population. A measure which is a better indicator of living standards is real GDP *per capita*, that is, output divided by the total population. The lower line in Figure 2.1 indicates the path of goods and services available to the 'average' Australian. The index reached 229 by 1993, representing an average annual growth rate of 2.0 per cent since 1950.

If we want to explain the growth path of the economy, an important initial consideration is to distinguish the short-term fluctuations of the business cycle, typically consisting of booms and recessions over a five-year or six-year period, from the longer term trends. Trend growth can then be explained in part by the contribution of labour, in part by the contribution of capital, and then in terms of underlying technical progress.

Visual inspection of the path of real GDP or real GDP per capita shows what are apparently minor and temporary blips where the growth of the economy falters or even falls for one or two years before resuming its upward progress. These recessionary episodes are evident as negative per capita growth at approximately five-year intervals in 1951–52, 1956–57 and 1961. For the next fifteen years per capita GDP rose continually, until the recurrence of recessionary years in 1977, 1982–83 and 1990–91.

From the long-term perspective suggested by Figure 2.1, these fluctuations of the economic business cycle appear to be relatively minor. It may not appear to matter much if there are temporary falls in output as long as the trend growth rate of the economy is strongly upwards. In practice, however, these short-term movements in economic activity tend to dominate public policy debate. The cyclical fluctuations are emphasised in Figure 2.2, which displays annual rates of growth rather than levels of both output and output per capita.

This graphical representation of the business cycle displays a very pronounced tendency for economic activity to decline and then recover over cycles of approximately five years. The amplitude of the fluctuations was reduced in the 1960s and early 1970s when economic downturns were characterised by positive growth rates. Since 1975, however, downturns have produced negative growth, at least in GDP per capita, for one-year or two-year periods.

There are good reasons for public policy debates to be concerned with business cycle movements, particularly as the labour market tends to display a pronounced asymmetry with respect to output fluctuations. It was particularly evident in the last decade that the downturn of 1982–83 caused unemployment to rise rapidly, but it took six years of sustained growth to bring unemployment rates back down to their previous levels.

From the point of view of the unemployed, it may be the business cycle rather than the longer term trends which are paramount. From the perspective of politicians facing elections every two to three years, a preoccupation with the short term is certainly understandable. Indeed, the greatest part of research and public debate in macroeconomics has, over the last few decades, been focused on the cycle. Debate has raged, and continues to rage, over the question of whether and how governments can usefully intervene to reduce the fluctuations of the cycle, though they appeared to do so successfully during the long boom of 1960–73 in Australia and in most advanced capitalist economies.

Other chapters in this book deal with monetary and fiscal policy and their relation to cyclical fluctuations in the economy. Here it is

ECONOMIC GROWTH

Figure 2.2 Growth of real output (per capita)

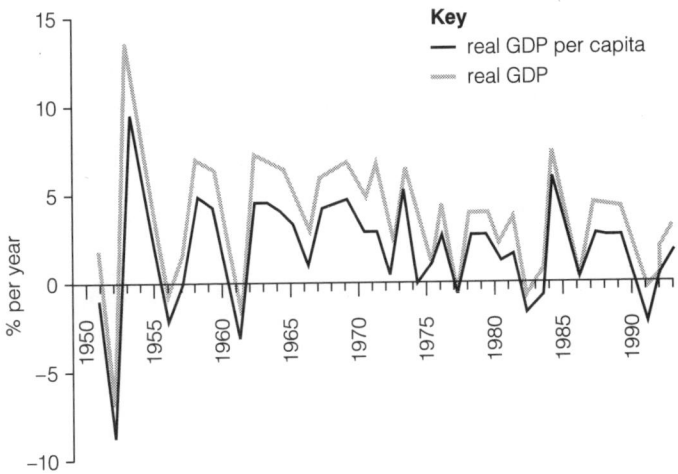

Source: ABS National Accounts accessed via DX for 1960–93, Summers and Heston (1993) for 1950–60.

relevant to point out that these cycles are not just a domestic phenomenon. All of the advanced industrial economies have, for instance, experienced a severe recession in the first few years of the 1990s and are only just, like Australia, beginning to recover. Indeed, Figure 2.3 shows that business cycles in Australia and the UK have followed remarkably similar patterns over the past four decades. The timing of booms and recessions has sometimes been out by a year, but the common cycles are very evident.

This evidence could be taken to suggest that cyclical activity in the Australian economy is governed largely by the state of the world economy and is therefore outside of our control. This view is probably too extreme, because suitably timed fiscal and monetary policies almost certainly can moderate cyclical fluctuations. Nevertheless, there are good grounds for arguing that the focus of research and public policy debate should concentrate on the determinants of the longer term trends in economic growth. This is the purpose of the following sections.

The labour force's contribution to growth

The biggest single reason for economic growth in Australia is the rapid rise in population. Australia has had the fastest growing

Figure 2.3 Annual growth rates in Australia and the UK

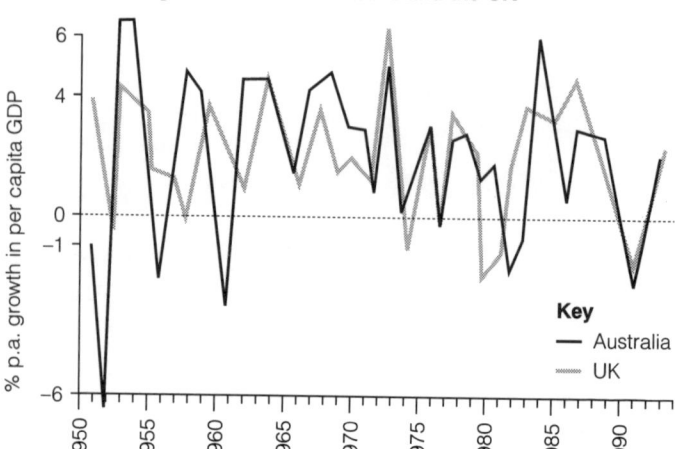

Source: ABS National Accounts accessed via DX for 1960–93, Summers and Heston (1993) for 1950–60.

population of all the advanced industrial economies in the postwar period. Population growth has been fuelled by the substantial program of immigration, but it is also due in part to a sustained baby boom. Population has grown by an average of 1.7 per cent per year over the last four decades, although this rate of growth has slowed considerably in recent years as the natural rate of increase has slowed and, particularly, as immigration was cut in the wake of the recession of the early 1990s. The data are displayed in Figure 2.4 and summarised in Table 2.1.

A fast-growing population will, other things being equal, lead to a rapidly growing labour force which will generate economic growth by expanding employment and its associated output. Indeed, if the capital stock grows at the same rate as the labour force, and if there are constant returns to capital and labour in production, then we can say (loosely) that population growth accounts for 1.7 per cent per annum growth in GDP since 1950—nearly half of the actual growth rate of 3.8 per cent per annum. On the other hand, if we ignore the impact of population growth on the development of the nation's capital stock and assume that a 1 per cent increase in labour input will raise output by 0.7 per cent (a fairly typical estimate of the output–employment elasticity) then the contribution of population growth is 1.2 per cent per annum, which is still a very substantial contribution of one-third of the growth which has actually occurred.

The raw population figures actually understate the demographic

ECONOMIC GROWTH

Figure 2.4 Australian population and labour force

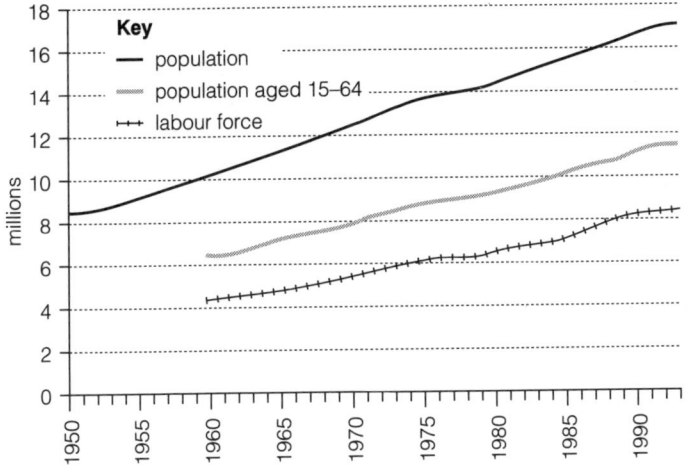

Source: ABS National Accounts accessed via DX for 1960–93, Summers and Heston (1993) for 1950–60.

contribution to the labour force. In the 1950s Australia had, as a result of the postwar baby boom, a high proportion of its population under the age of 15. As the baby boomers have moved into the adult age group, so the potential labour force has expanded faster than the total population (see Table 2.1). This 'baby boom effect' has added around 0.2 to 0.3 percentage points to the annual growth of the potential labour force.

The story does not end there. The proportion of the working age group who choose to participate in the paid labour force has also been steadily increasing. In 1960, 67 per cent of the population aged between 15 and 64 years were in the labour force. By 1993, that proportion had risen to 74 per cent and would have been higher still if high unemployment had not discouraged several hundred thousands of potential workers from actively seeking employment. This rise in participation comes despite the fact that young people are increasingly choosing to continue their education well beyond the minimum school leaving age and that many older people are taking the option of early retirement in their early 60s or late 50s.

These trends are illustrated in Figure 2.5. The uppermost line shows how participation has increased amongst the working age population. The middle line shows how the population has been increasingly made up of 15 to 64-year-olds. The bottom line shows the product of these two trends, a very substantial rise in the proportion of Australians who choose to join the labour force.

Table 2.1 Annual growth of labour force and population

Period	population growth % p.a.	population 15–64 growth % p.a.	labour force growth % p.a.
1950–60	2.23		
1960–70	1.30	1.46	1.64
1970–80	1.37	1.76	1.94
1980–90	1.48	1.78	2.32
1990–93	1.10	1.09	0.74

Source: ABS National Accounts accessed via DX for 1960–93, Summers and Heston (1993) for 1950–60.

This rise in participation reflects a revolution in Australian social and economic life, namely the movement of hundreds of thousands of women into the labour force. Figure 2.6 illustrates the substantial increase in participation by women over the last fifteen years alone. The proportion of the female working age population in the labour force increased from 50 per cent in 1978 to over 60 per cent by 1993 and is still increasing. Although the largest increase has occurred amongst women working part-time, it still remains the case that the majority of women are working full-time.

In considering the relative participation rates of men and women, it is important to take account not only of numbers of people employed but also of hours of work. The trends here are rather different. In fact, the trend level of aggregate hours of labour supplied by adult men—taking total hours worked divided by the population

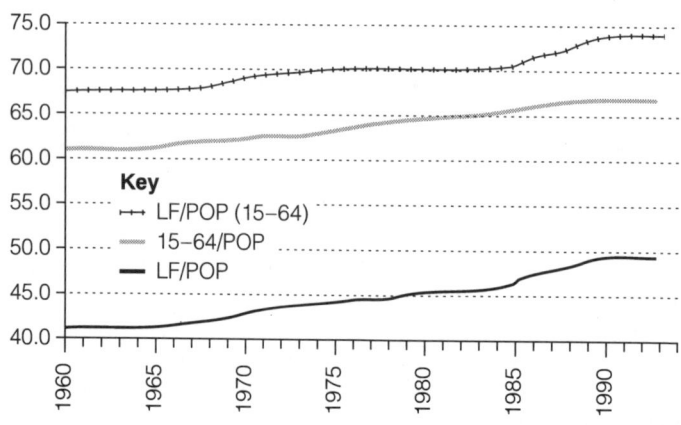

Figure 2.5 Labour force participation and population structure

Source: ABS National Accounts accessed via DX for 1960–93, Summers and Heston (1993) for 1950–60.

Figure 2.6 Women in the labour force (% of population 15–64)

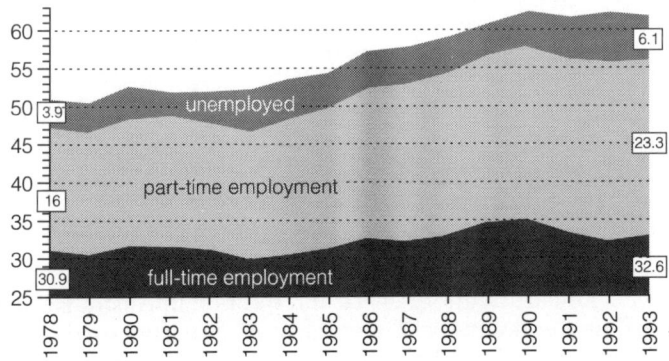

Source: ABS Labour Force Statistics, via DX.

Figure 2.7 Men in the labour force (% of population 15–64)

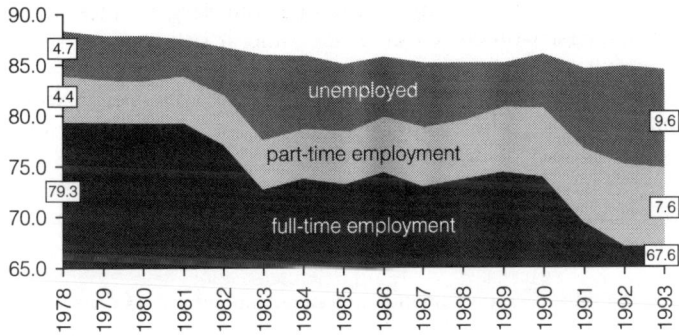

Source: ABS Labour Force Statistics, via DX.

of men aged between 15 and 64—has hardly declined over the past fifteen years. On average, men aged 15 to 64 supplied 33 hours of work per week in 1978 and 32 hours per week in 1990. During the recent recession male hours worked per head of population fell to the level experienced in the recession of 1983—and that decline is clearly due to a drop in demand rather than any substantial fall in the supply of labour. Selected data on men's working hours are displayed in row 1 of Table 2.2 (p. 24).

The lack of a downward trend in hours of male labour supply appears to contradict the evidence of a substantial decline in male participation rates over the same period. The reconciling, and less well known, fact is that for those men in full-time employment there has been a steady increase in average hours of work (see line 4 of

Table 2.2 Weekly hours worked per person aged 15–64

			1978	1980	1983	1990	1993
1	men 15–64	hours per man	33.6	33.5	30.6	32.3	30.5
2	women 15–64	hours per woman	14.2	14.5	13.9	17.0	16.4
3	female share of total hours worked	%	29%	30%	31%	34%	35%
4	full-time men	hours per worker	41.4	41.5	41.0	42.6	43.4

Note: Hours of work are for employees, August of each year except June 1993.
Source: ABS 6203.0, 6204.0, 6101.0.

Table 2.2). Longer hours of work for those in full-time jobs have largely offset the decline in the number of men employed, at least up until the recession of 1991–92.

For employed women, on the other hand, average hours per worker have declined slightly as a result of the increase in part-time working. It follows that all of the increase in the supply of hours by adult women, up until the recession, is attributable to increased numbers in employment.

Despite the large increase in the numbers of women participating in the labour force, their contribution to total hours worked is still only half that of men. In other words, the supply of labour by women outside the home is increasing but the potential supply is still substantially unused.

Probably the biggest single driving factor in the continuing choice of women to join the work force is the improvement of access to schooling. The increase in female educational attainment across recent generations is remarkable. Only one-quarter of women born before 1938 have post-school qualifications, and two-thirds of that group left secondary education early. Of those born in the 1960s, however, one-half have post-school qualifications and only one-third left secondary education early. In other words, between successive generations the proportion of women leaving school early has halved and the proportion with tertiary education has doubled. For the current generation of labour market entrants, young women are on average at least as well educated as their male counterparts. Although young men are more likely to have a trade qualification, young women are more likely to have a tertiary degree.

The economic link between education and labour force participation is straightforward. Education increases potential earnings and therefore makes joining the labour force relatively more attractive compared to leisure, child-bearing and home production activities. As successive groups of highly educated women move through their life cycles, we can expect birthrates to decline and labour force participation to rise even higher.

ECONOMIC GROWTH

Table 2.3 Annual growth of labour force and working age group relative to total population

	pure participation effect	+ demographic effect	= growth of labour force relative to population
	labour force/ pop.15–64 (growth % p.a.)	pop.15–64/ total pop. (growth % p.a.)	labour force/ total pop. (growth % p.a.)
1960–70	0.18	0.16	0.34
1970–80	0.17	0.40	0.57
1980–90	0.54	0.30	0.83
1990–93	–0.35	0.00	–0.36

Source: ABS National Accounts accessed via DX for 1960–93, Summers and Heston (1993) for 1950–60.

The effect of more women working has substantially outweighed the withdrawal of younger and older people from the labour force. This participation effect, allied to the demographic effect of the baby boom generation, has produced a substantial increase in the proportion of the total population who are active in the labour force. The growth in this aggregate participation rate and its components are summarised in Table 2.3. The decline in participation over the first three years of the 1990s is entirely due to the fact that discouraged workers, particularly women, drop out of the labour force when jobs are scarce. Ignoring this recessionary effect, the trend rate of increase in aggregate participation is strongly positive: nearly one percentage point per year over the 1980s. If we take account of the fact that much of this increase in participation over recent years has been in the part-time sector, the supply of hours per head of total population has been somewhat slower at around 0.6 annual percentage points. This trend increase in labour supply makes a substantial contribution to economic growth of around 0.4 percentage points per year.

The contribution to measured economic growth of women moving from traditional domestic roles into the labour force probably overstates the true increase in economic activity. This is because national accounts fail to measure the contributions of both men and women to home child care, home maintenance, catering and so on.

Nevertheless, it is indubitably the case that the rapidly rising trend in labour supply has been the biggest single factor in driving up the measured output of the Australian economy over the last few decades. Measured output has grown at an annual average rate of 3.7 per cent, and labour supply probably accounts for nearly half of that growth, with a contribution of around 1.2 per cent from pure population growth and around 0.4 per cent from the increasing supply of hours of work coming in particular from the baby boom generation of well-educated women.

The contribution of physical investment to growth

While labour force growth can stimulate economic activity, it is not likely to be very productive unless workers are equipped with the tools and machinery and buildings which are necessary for modern production. Indeed, the rapidity of the growth of the Australian labour force makes new investment in capital equipment particularly important if productivity levels are not to fall behind.

Figure 2.8 shows levels of public and private investment over the last three decades. The left-hand scale refers to public and the right-hand scale to private investment, each expressed as a percentage of GDP measured at 1989–90 prices. Up until 1990, private investment had been quite consistently in the range between 20 per cent and 24 per cent of GDP, its fluctuations partly caused by and partly contributing to the economic cycle. The recent decline in private investment to under 18 per cent of GDP has undoubtedly contributed to the slow recovery of the economy from the 1990–91 recession. Nevertheless, in respect of the longer term trends, the relatively high rate of private investment in Australia has undoubtedly contributed substantially to long-term growth.

The progress of public investment (including both government investment and the investment of government enterprises) has been rather different. Starting at levels above 8 per cent of GDP in the 1960s, public investment fell slightly in the 1970s and then fell dramatically to 5 per cent in the late 1980s. The cuts in public investment helped to achieve the Government's aim of fiscal surplus in the late 1980s, but the impact on longer term growth may well be damaging.

Of course public investment (as with private investment) covers a multitude of both productive and non-productive projects: often bureaucratic white elephants and political pork-barrels are lumped together with vital investments in schools, hospitals, water and power supplies, roads and communications and the like. If only the former, non-productive categories were cut from public investment, then economic growth might actually be enhanced by reductions in wasteful expenditure. However, recent econometric evidence from the USA (Aschauer 1989; Munnell 1992) and from Australia (Otto and Voss 1994) suggests that, on average, public investment tends to be very productive. Quite apart from the direct benefits to consumers of better roads, schools and hospitals, these studies find that increasing

ECONOMIC GROWTH

Figure 2.8 Public and private investment

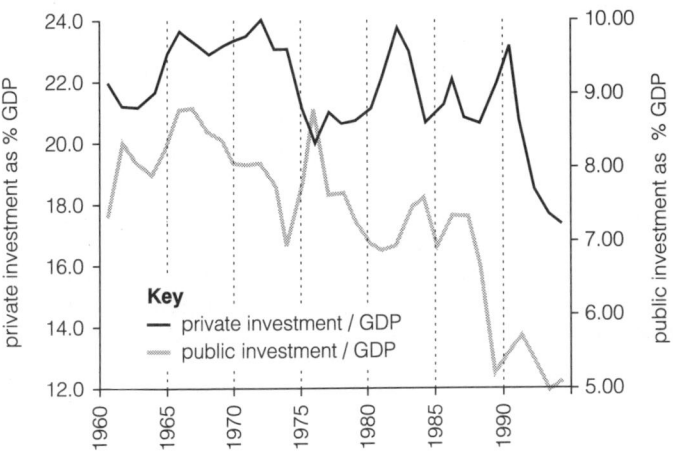

Note: Public investment is the sum of government investment and government enterprise investment.
Source: ABS via DX.

the stock of public capital actually increases the productivity of the private sector. Better public provision of transport and communications, or of healthier and more educated workers, does substantially reduce the costs of private production. Moreover, several studies suggest that although there is some crowding out of private investment in the short run, the enhanced productivity of the private sector causes private sector investment to increase in the longer run. It follows then that the decline in Australian public sector investment since 1985 may well have reduced the potential for future growth.

There is also some concern that private investment may overemphasise housing and office blocks at the expense of investment in machinery and equipment. International evidence from De Long and Summers (1992) suggests that investment in equipment is likely to bring substantial spillover benefits. Workers learn to use and adapt the new technologies embedded in new equipment and this acquired knowledge becomes a public good which stimulates productivity in other firms and sectors. To the extent that these spillover benefits are not captured fully by the firm making the investment, there is a tendency for private investment in equipment to be sub-optimal. If so, Australian tax and financial incentives, which tend to favour investment in housing and in tangible assets like offices, are perhaps misdirected.

The contribution of technical progress to growth

The previous sections have suggested the extent to which economic growth has been driven by: (i) cyclical fluctuations in economic activity; (ii) the growth of the labour force; and (iii) the growth of private and public capital stocks. After taking account of these contributions, it is usual to find that there is some residual component to growth which is not explained by a simple factor input model of production. This residual or unexplained growth is sometimes labelled technical progress. A more accurate description is, however, to label it 'multi-factor productivity growth' or 'MFP growth'.

Pure technical progress, new ideas or 'blueprints' about ways of satisfying human wants, is impossible to measure. Nevertheless, looking back over the history of human technology and civilisation we have a very strong presumption that such technical progress is at the heart of economic development. Rather naively, economists often identify technical progress with multi-factor productivity growth, although if pushed they will typically admit that this identification is really an expression of their ignorance about the other contributions to growth, that is, contributions other than the growth of capital and labour inputs.

In principle, we know that investments in education and training contribute to growth, improving the skill levels of the work force, and that the discovery (or depletion) of natural resources can also contribute. These contributions are, however, notoriously difficult to measure. So this section will concentrate on the rather easier task of identifying trends in multi-factor productivity—trends which represent some combination of true technical progress and the contribution of these other unidentified factors.

Before we can seriously measure productivity, the amount of output provided by one unit of inputs, we need to understand how we measure output itself. Up until this point, we have used the national accounts aggregate of GDP. Unfortunately, some outputs which are important components of GDP are not amenable to measurement—particularly the non-marketed services of government and some of the services of the financial sector. Lacking adequate measures of real output in these sectors, the Australian Bureau of Statistics (1989) reports that it values these services at the cost of their inputs. This procedure is tantamount to assuming zero productivity growth for these sectors. If we want to examine productivity, it is then important to use the statistics for those sectors of the economy where real output is measured directly. We also want to avoid fluctuations in output which are caused solely by random weather conditions. Accordingly, the following analysis of productivity is restricted to the output of the non-farm market sector of the economy.

ECONOMIC GROWTH

Figure 2.9 Growth of productivity in the non-farm market sector

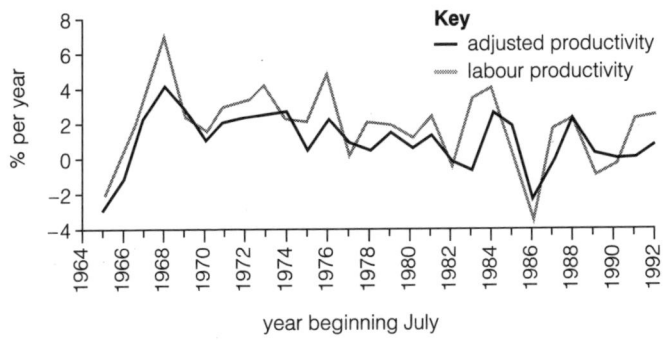

Source: ABS 5234.0, July 1993, Australian National Accounts: Multi-factor productivity, 1991/92, extended by author to 1992/93.

The dashed line in Figure 2.9 shows annual growth in labour productivity, defined as the ratio of real output to the number of hours worked in that sector. A strong cyclical pattern is evident. When the economy moves into recession, labour productivity tends to fall as firms hold onto overhead labour and hoard skilled workers who might be difficult to replace. If recession is prolonged, as in 1992, productivity may start to rise as low productivity firms go out of business and hoarded labour is discarded. Then, when the economy begins to recover, labour productivity can rise very fast as underutilised labour is put back to work.

Apart from these cyclical fluctuations, Figure 2.9 also suggests a trend decline in labour productivity. In the late 1960s and early 1970s, annual growth in labour productivity averaged nearly 3 per cent. This rate of growth declined to 2 per cent in the ten years after the watershed of the 1973 oil crisis, and has declined even further to just 1 per cent in the most recent ten-year period (see row 4 of Table 2.4).

This slowdown in the growth of labour productivity triggered widespread criticism of labour market institutions, particularly the centralisation of wage setting, which was set in place under the 1983 Accord between the incoming Labor Government and the Australian Confederation of Trade Unions. Partly as a result of this evidence, the first years of the 1990s have seen moves to deregulate the labour market and, in particular, to decentralise bargaining to individual enterprises.

As yet it is still too early to judge from national accounts data whether or not enterprise bargaining is delivering the improvement in productivity that is expected of it. But more pertinent to this analysis is to note that much of the evidence of a productivity

Table 2.4 Productivity growth and its components in the non-farm market sector

		1965/66–73/74 % p.a.	1973/74–83/84 % p.a.	1983/84–92/93 % p.a.
1	growth of capital stock	5.5	3.4	2.8
2	– growth of hours worked	2.4	–0.6	1.5
3	= growth of capital intensity	3.2	4.1	1.3
4	labour productivity growth	2.7	2.1	1.0
5	– contribution of capital intensity	1.0	1.2	0.4
6	– cyclical effects	0.2	–0.1	0
7	= cyclically adjusted MFP growth	1.6	1.0	0.7

Note: The contribution of capital intensity is calculated as the growth in the capital labour ratio x 0.3; the cyclical effect is the growth in output less the previous year's growth in output x 0.36.
Source: ABS 5234.0, supplemented by author for 1992/93.

slowdown has been misinterpreted. Part of the aim of the 1983 Accord was to encourage employment growth through wage restraint. To a substantial extent that aim has been successful, as evidenced by the data in Table 2.4 which indicates much stronger growth in hours worked in the ten years from July 1983 (1.5 per cent per year) compared with the decline in hours worked in the previous ten years (–0.6 per cent per annum).

One result of strong employment growth induced, in part, by wage restraint is that we expect firms to favour more labour-intensive methods of production. This in turn implies that output per unit of labour will not be as high as it would have been under higher wages and more capital-intensive production. This is not to say that wage restraint has been harmful for productivity, rather that labour productivity is a misleading measure. Instead, we should estimate the combined productivity of both labour and capital, that is, multi-factor productivity.

The way we do this is illustrated in Table 2.4. Subtracting labour growth from the growth of the capital stock gives a measure of the growth of capital intensity (the capital–labour ratio) which is reported in row 4 of the table. We then subtract from observed labour productivity growth (row 4) the contribution of increased capital intensity and the contribution of cyclical fluctuations. These contributions are estimated from the production–function relationship estimated by Dowrick (1990) on earlier data. The resulting measure of multi-factor productivity growth is given in the last row of the table. It is also illustrated as the solid line in Figure 2.9.

This preferred measure of underlying productivity growth tells a substantially different story from the crude measures of labour productivity. Almost all of the labour productivity slowdown after

1983 can be attributed to the much faster growth of employment and the consequent slower growth of capital intensity. The sharp decrease in productivity growth actually occurred from 1973, in line with the productivity slowdown in the USA and Europe. Any further slowdown in MFP growth since 1983 appears to be small (from 1.0 per cent to 0.7 per cent) and not statistically significant.

International comparisons of GDP levels and growth rates

It has become a habit amongst economic commentators to bemoan Australian economic performance, frequently citing faster growth rates of other Organisation for Economic Co-operation and Development (OECD) and Asian countries as evidence of their superior economic policies and institutions. What these comparisons ignore is that Australia is at a very different stage of development from most of the countries to which we are being compared. In particular, many southern European and East Asian economies have been able to capitalise in the postwar period on the 'advantage of backwardness', that is, the opportunity to catch up on the world's most advanced economies by importing or copying their products and technologies. As these countries catch up on the productivity levels and living standards of the advanced economies, so there is a strong tendency for their growth rates to converge.

Table 2.5 presents data on levels and growth rates of per capita GDP for a selection of countries. Amongst this sample, Australia began in 1950 as one of the richest economies, second only to the USA. Australian growth rates have in fact roughly equalled those of the USA over the four decades. By 1990, a number of countries had caught up with Australian levels of per capita GDP, namely Sweden, Japan and Hong Kong.[1] The latter two had experienced particularly fast growth of 7 per cent per year or more in the 1960s, but Japanese growth rates have been falling since 1970 and economic growth in Hong Kong growth rates has slowed since 1980. The southern European economies of Italy and Greece, which had been catching up on Australia in the postwar reconstruction period of the 1950s and 1960s, have slowed down in more recent decades. Some of the new East Asian 'tigers', such as Korea, Indonesia and China are now experiencing the rapid growth spurts which characterised Japan and Hong Kong several decades ago.

These observations suggest the possible existence of a consistent pattern whereby rapid growth is possible for countries which are entering into the process of industrialisation of previously underdeveloped economies. Once through this phase of economic

Table 2.5 Economic development 1950–90 in a selection of OECD and East Asian countries

	Level of per capita GDP $US 1990					Annual average rate of growth of per capita GDP % p.a.			
	1950	1960	1970	1980	1990	1950–60	1960–70	1970–80	1980–90
USA	8625	9776	12725	15097	18399	1.3	2.6	1.7	2.0
Australia	6771	7879	10917	12622	14304	1.5	3.3	1.5	1.3
NZ	6623	7920	9352	10260	11540	1.8	1.7	0.9	1.2
Sweden	5749	7492	10643	12290	14495	2.6	3.5	1.4	1.7
UK	5195	6548	7695	10028	13068	2.3	1.6	2.6	2.6
Italy	2803	4636	7669	10445	12557	5.0	5.0	3.1	1.8
Greece	1411	2088	4234	5895	6679	3.9	7.1	3.3	1.2
Japan	1492	3033	7500	10292	14836	7.1	9.1	3.2	3.7
Hong Kong		2210	4456	8801	14410		7.0	6.8	4.9
Singapore		1712	3155	6958	10965		6.1	7.9	4.5
Malaysia		1397	2117	3772	4904		4.2	5.8	2.6
Taiwan		1382	2387	4827	8510		5.5	7.0	5.7
Thailand	847	929	1508	2146	3532	0.9	4.8	3.5	5.0
Korea		907	1688	3123	6209		6.2	6.2	7.6
China			825	1241	2324			4.1	6.3
Indonesia		625	700	1252	1942		1.1	5.8	4.4

Source: Summers and Heston (1993).

acceleration, the growth performance of these economies comes to resemble the growth of the other advanced economies.

We can examine more closely this relationship between economic growth rates and level of development by plotting the decade average growth rates against the level of per capita GDP for each country at the beginning of that decade. Figure 2.10 displays the resulting scatter plot. There appear to be two strong relationships. Below $US3000 per capita, economic backwardness appears to be a handicap. The very poorest of these economies tend to grow slower than the richer—a phenomenon which is analysed in greater detail by Abramovitz (1986) and Dowrick (1992). Economic growth rates of around 7 per cent are quite common for economies at the $US3000 level, but as these economies grow richer there is a very pronounced tendency for their growth to slow down.

These tendencies are illustrated in the figure by an inverted V-shape which peaks at around $US3000. One of the most interesting features of this picture is that this pattern of growth applies across all four postwar decades and appears to hold as much for the advanced OECD economies as for the East Asian economies.

The Australia–Japan comparison is particularly interesting. The Japanese 'miracle' growth rates occurred in the 1950s and 1960s

Figure 2.10 GDP growth and GDP levels

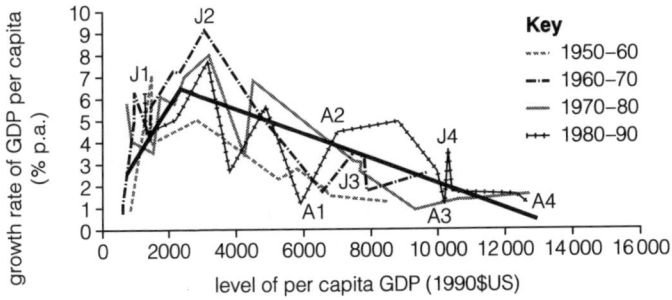

(marked J1 and J2 in Figure 2.10) when the Japanese economy was embarking on rapid industrialisation. In the 1970s and 1980s the Japanese growth performance (J3 and J4) was not dramatically better than the Australian performance in the 1950s and 1960s (A1 and A2) when Australia was at a similar level of economic development. Indeed, much of Japanese continued economic success relative to other advanced economies is due to their very high savings and investment rates rather than to any continued 'miracle' of technical progress.

This analysis tends to suggest that the Australian growth performance, since 1960 at least, has been pretty much what would be expected for an economy at the high end of the economic development scale. It cautions against the doomsayers who compare Australian growth to that of the Asian economies in order to bolster their contention that there must be fundamental flaws in Australian policies or institutions.

Concluding comments

Most of the above analysis is concerned with the proximate determinants of growth, particularly the inputs of labour and capital into production and technical change. This approach has not delved into the deeper determinants, the factors influencing people's decisions of whether to enter the labour market, whether to save, where to invest in physical capital, or when to invest in education or research. These more fundamental determinants of growth are presumably linked to both social and market institutions and also to culture.

There is a fast-expanding economics literature which is trying to develop adequate theoretical models of the growth process. Drawing on some of the insights of earlier economists such as Schumpeter and Kaldor (see Hanusch 1988), the 'new growth theories' of Romer (1986 and 1990) and others emphasise the importance of spillover benefits which can occur when a firm or individual makes investment decisions. Investment in research, or learning to use new equipment and techniques, can create new knowledge which is readily available to others and generates benefits which are not necessarily captured by the individual making the investments. So there may be an important role for government to use taxes and subsidies to encourage or provide socially beneficial investment in education and research as well as in public infrastructure. On the other hand, general taxation can also reduce the benefits from investment and hence inhibit private investment.

Culture and institutions also matter. A harmonious society characterised by warm personal relationships and trust may not only be more pleasant than an aggressive, cutthroat environment but also more conducive to economic progress. At the same time, a culture which values new ideas and institutions which encourage training and innovation are likely to promote growth.

The measurement and contribution to economic growth of these less tangible factors is, however, particularly difficult if not impossible to identify. Nevertheless, we can draw some tentative conclusions from the evidence which has been presented here and from the wider economic debate which is summarised in recent publications such as Sheehan (1992), Barro and Lee (1993) and Dowrick (1993).

First, comparative analysis of economic performance over the last 30 or 40 years suggests that Australian institutions and policies are not performing particularly badly. While there is no doubt much room for improvement, there is no justification for condemning our performance out of hand. The case for institutional or policy reform—whether of financial markets or the labour market or industrial policy—needs to be made in terms of detailed cost–benefit analysis rather than in terms of a blanket condemnation of past growth performance.

Second, we can expect an expanding labour force to continue to generate substantial economic growth over the next decade. Most of this expansion will come from a new generation of women seeking careers commensurate with their educational attainments. As the economy experiences a cyclical recovery, there will also be some return to the work force of older women who have been discouraged from seeking employment during the recession of the early 1990s. Indeed, the feminisation of work and the work force is likely to be the biggest single source of growth in the Australian economy.

Third, it remains to be seen whether the current reforms to labour market institutions, particularly the devolution of wage setting to the level of the enterprise, will increase productivity growth. The optimistic scenario is that it will usher in a new era of cooperative industrial relations with work force and management agreeing to share the benefits of more efficient and innovative work practices. A more pessimistic forecast is that trade unions and employers may well revert to the uncoordinated bidding up of wages and prices by craft and industry bargaining groups, as in the 1970s and early 1980s.

Fourth, low levels of both public and private investment do not augur well for medium-term productivity growth. Productivity should increase in the short term as the cyclical recovery enables better use of underutilised workers and equipment. But unless both government and firms direct more funds into appropriate equipment and infrastructural projects, strong growth is unlikely to continue beyond the recovery phase.

Note

1 We should be wary of concluding from these figures that these countries have actually surpassed Australian living standards. Dowrick and Quiggin (1993) demonstrate that, when account is taken of the comparatively large amount of leisure enjoyed in Australia, there is a strong presumption that Australian living standards are in fact higher—a proposition which is endorsed by much of the commentary emanating from Japan itself on their very long working hours and lack of leisure.

Recommended reading

Abramovitz, Moses 1986, 'Catching up, forging ahead and falling behind', *Journal of Economic History*, Vol. 46, pp. 385–406

Dowrick, Steve 1993, 'A review of new theories of economic growth: and their implications for Australian policy', *Economic Analysis and Policy*, Vol. 23

Romer, Paul 1990, 'Endogenous technological change', *Journal of Political Economy*, Vol. 98

3 Inflation
Bill Junor

'Inflation cuts wages—increases prices and profits'

Fading versions of this slogan, and others expressing similar views, adorn numerous railway cuttings and other vantage points in urban and rural Australia. For many of us, reading these maxims may well have been our first exposure to economic ideas. As it stands, this slogan embodies several propositions regarding inflation. First, there is a somewhat tautological definition of inflation ('inflation . . . increases prices'); second, there is an assertion regarding the effects of inflation, namely the claim that inflation redistributes income in a particular way ('inflation cuts wages—increases . . . profits'); and, third, there is an implied value judgment that inflation is undesirable. Missing from the slogan (not surprisingly given that it consists of only seven words) are any hints regarding the causes of inflation and any suggestions as to the nature of appropriate policies to control inflationary pressures. A convenient starting point for a discussion of these various aspects of inflation is with a definition of inflation.

A definition of inflation

Attempts to define inflation tend to fall into two broad categories. First, those which define inflation by reference to what are claimed to be its causes. Two examples of this 'causal' approach to a definition of inflation are 'too much money chasing too few goods' and 'money wages rising faster than labour productivity'. The problem with this approach to a definition of inflation is that it offers various (and often competing) explanations of the causes of the inflationary process, rather than a definition of inflation.

Falling into the second category are those definitions which focus on the effects of inflation. An example of this 'symptoms' approach is the particular definition that will be employed here: *inflation is upward movement in the general level of prices.*

Measurement of inflation

The notion of the general level of prices can be captured by a price index which weights the prices of the various goods and services covered by the index by their relative importance in a selected base year. This 'weighting' process ensures that the resulting index provides an adequate representation of the various price changes, positive and negative, that occur in a particular period of time. Inflation can then be measured as the percentage change in the price index:

$$P_t = \frac{(PI_t - PI_{t-1})}{PI_{t-1}}$$

where P_t is the rate of inflation in period t, PI_t is the value of the price index in period t, and PI_{t-1} is the value of the price index in the previous period $t-1$. Inflation is therefore expressed as a percentage change per unit of time, most commonly per quarter or per year.

The Australian Bureau of Statistics (ABS) publishes many different price indexes—they differ on the basis of their method of construction and on their coverage. There are two basic approaches to the construction of price indexes. The Base Weight (or Laspeyres) Index employs a base period 'basket' of goods and services to compare the current period value of the basket (using the current period prices of the goods and services in the basket) to the base period value of the same basket (using base period prices). The use of the same (base period) basket for both base and current periods ensures that any change in the index reflects *only* price changes between the two periods. The index for the base period must be equal to 100 since, in that period, base prices and current prices are identical. The value of the index for the current period indicates therefore the percentage increase in prices that has occurred between the base and current periods, that is, on our definition of inflation, the rate of inflation for that period. By contrast, the Current Weight (or Paasche) Index uses a current period basket of goods and services to compare the current period value of the basket to the base period value. As with the Base Weight Index, the value of the index in the base period is 100 and the current period index indicates the rate of inflation over the period. However, unlike the Base Weight Index, which is a fixed basket index (until such time as the basket is revised), the composition of the basket of goods and services in the Current Weight Index changes each period; it is therefore a variable basket index.

Ignoring for the moment the coverage of the index, there are deficiencies in both Base Weight and Current Weight Indexes as measures of inflation. In Base Weight Indexes the composition of the basket of goods and services (the 'regimen') is revised periodically but remains fixed between revisions. Such indexes therefore tend to become less representative the longer they are unrevised, because changes in the pattern of demand induced by relative price changes are not reflected in the regimen. Current Weight Indexes are always representative of current period demand patterns; such indexes therefore not only measure the inflation rate but also reflect changes in the composition of goods and services.

As well as compositional changes, the quality of goods can vary over time. If these quality changes are associated with price movements, they will be reflected by variations in the particular price index being used. Strictly, such price changes should not be included in the price index. To the extent that this type of price change is present in the price index, the 'true' measure of inflation is distorted.

A further deficiency of price indexes as measures of inflation relates to the extent of coverage of such indexes. Some cover a relatively narrow range of goods and services, for example the Price Indexes of Copper Materials and Price Indexes of Materials Used in Coal Mining. Clearly such narrow coverage indexes, although measuring changes in the prices of the specific goods to which they apply, are of little value in measuring changes in the *general* level of prices.

It is the broad coverage indexes that are relevant to the measurement of inflation. These include the Consumer Price Index (CPI) and the implicit price deflators for Gross Domestic Product (IGDPD) and for Domestic Final Demand (IDFDD). The CPI (a base-weighted index) is perhaps the best known measure of inflation. There are several reasons for its popularity: the CPI is usually published within one month of the end of the quarter to which it refers; it is widely (though incorrectly) regarded as an index of the 'cost of living'; it has been used as an input into wage and salary adjustments and was used as the basis for wage indexation; and it is used currently for indexation of social security benefits. Notwithstanding its wide popular recognition as *the* measure of inflation, the CPI is somewhat limited in this regard, largely because of its coverage. The CPI measures quarterly changes in the prices of goods and services that represent a high proportion of the expenditure of metropolitan wage and salary earner households. This means that while the CPI includes price changes of all those domestically produced and imported consumer goods and services that form part of the 'basket', price changes of investment goods and exported goods are not explicitly included.

The various implicit price deflators (so named because they are not measured directly, but rather are derived from the current and constant price estimates of the National Accounting aggregates to which they apply) are also used as measures of the inflation rate. The IDFDD reflects price changes for Domestic Final Demand, the components of which are current and capital expenditures by both private and public sectors, including expenditure on imported goods and services. By contrast, the IGDPD captures movements in the prices of final goods and services, including exported goods, produced in Australia.

The preceding discussion suggests that, while several broad coverage price indexes are available, none can provide an estimate of *the* rate of inflation. Rather, they provide somewhat imperfect measures of the rate of change of the prices of goods and services that come within their ambits. This qualification partly explains why many economists, even those who argue that inflation imposes significant economic costs, stop short of arguing for zero inflation as a goal of macroeconomic policy.

Australia's inflation experience—a broad brush

The path of Australia's inflation since 1960 is shown in Figure 3.1 by the rates of change of the Consumer Price Index and the implicit Domestic Final Demand deflator. In a recent comprehensive survey of inflation in Australia between 1950 and 1991, Stevens (1992) employed the implicit deflator for private consumption expenditure from the National Accounts in preference to the CPI. The latter series is rejected by Stevens (1992, p. 183, n. 1) in order '. . . to avoid measurement difficulties . . . which have affected the short-term reliability of the published CPI as an indicator of prices for current consumption goods and services'. While it is true that the revised Medicare arrangements in 1984 and the introduction of mortgage interest charges in 1986 gave rise to 'measurement difficulties', it is also true that the CPI, despite its limitations, remains the most closely watched indicator of inflation. It is for this reason that a CPI-based inflation rate, together with one based on Domestic Final Demand

Figure 3.1 Australia's inflation rate 1960–94

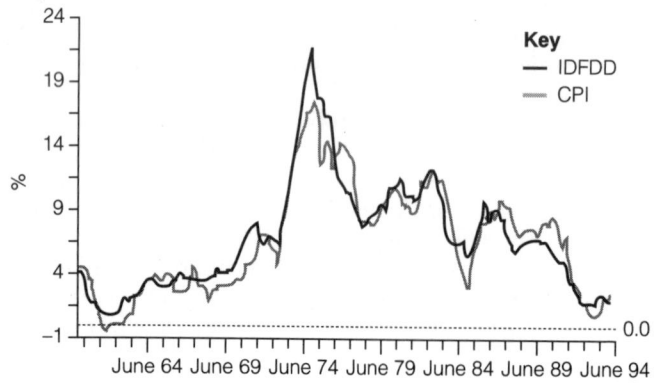

Source: ECONDATA.

(which is free of the particular limitations noted by Stevens) is employed here.

The time period chosen, from 1960 to the present, is sufficiently long for a wide range of inflation experiences to be observed.

The first point to be made is that although there have been episodes, both of accelerating and decelerating inflation, when the two indexes have diverged, they have for the most part moved together. That is, notwithstanding the differences in coverage, these two indexes are telling essentially the same story about inflation over the period 1960 to 1994.

Second, three inflationary sub-periods can be discerned:

- the period 1961 to 1972 when inflation increased from an annual rate of less than 2 per cent in 1961 to around 4 per cent in 1964, stabilised at this level until the end of 1969, and then accelerated again to around 7 per cent;
- the period 1972 to 1986 which was characterised by marked volatility in inflation rates with peaks in 1975, 1982 and 1986, and troughs in 1978 and 1985. Inflation rates, as measured by the IDFDD, varied between a high of 21.6 per cent in 1975 and a low of 5.2 per cent in 1985;
- the period 1986 to the present which has seen inflation rates fluctuating around a downward trend to stabilise at around 2 per cent in 1992.

Third, Carmichael (1990), using the growth of the CPI as his measure of inflation, characterised the 1970s as the decade of high inflation and the 1980s as the decade of steady inflation, and suggested that '[b]y mid 1988, hopes of a continuing steady decline in inflation . . . had been dashed'. With the advantage of several additional years of data, we can see that Carmichael's pessimism was not warranted. Inflation, whether measured by the CPI or IDFDD, fell sharply after the March quarter 1990. However, as can be seen in Figure 3.1, the CPI-based inflation rate diverged from the IDFDD-based rate in 1986, and from the June quarter 1989 until the March quarter 1990 the two measures moved in opposite directions. This suggests that Stevens's concern regarding the 'short-term reliability' of the CPI—arising in this instance from the inclusion of mortgage interest charges in the post-1987 regimen—may be well placed.

One attraction of the CPI is that the ABS publishes a decomposition of the overall change in the inflation rate into rates of change for the various expenditure categories. Table 3.1 shows the quarterly percentage change in the CPI, expressed as the weighted average of the eight capital cities, for the eight major categories.

As might be expected when annual rates of inflation are below 2 per cent, the quarterly percentage changes for the expenditure categories are a mixture of positive (inflation) and negative (deflation) figures. A striking feature of Table 3.1 is the extent to which the relatively large positive *and* negative changes for the individual categories are the *direct* result of the budgetary policies of the Commonwealth and State governments and of monetary policy. Categories most susceptible to these influences over the period since March 1992 are housing (via the monetary policy effect on housing interest charges) and tobacco and alcohol (via Commonwealth excise on tobacco and State licence and franchise fees) and health and personal care (via changes to the Pharmaceutical Benefits Scheme).

As a consequence of falling mortgage rates, housing, with a weight of 15.90 per cent in the latest CPI, has been an important source of deflationary pressure, with falls in six of the last ten quarters. Over the same period, tobacco and alcohol, with a weight of 7.475 per cent, has been the single largest contributor to inflationary pressure in five of the quarters.

The impact of government policy changes on the CPI has led to calls for the reporting of the underlying (or core) rate of inflation, that is the inflation rate corrected for the effects of these policy changes. However, the exclusion of particular items depends on whether the CPI is intended to serve as a general measure of inflation or as the basis for adjusting wages and social security benefits. In its 1992 review of the CPI, the ABS noted that income compensation has been the major traditional use of the CPI, and for this reason an 'All groups' index based on outlays was judged appropriate. The ABS currently reports the change in the CPI for 'All groups', 'All groups excluding housing', and 'All groups excluding tobacco and

Table 3.1 Consumer Price Index by categories—weighted average of eight capital cities. Percentage change between current quarter and previous quarter

Category	1992				1993				1994	
	March	June	Sept	Dec	March	June	Sept	Dec	March	June
Food	0.6	0.3	-0.4	0.7	2.2	-0.9	0.7	0.6	0.3	-0.3
Clothing	-0.2	0.5	-0.2	1.1	-0.3	0.6	-0.9	-0.3	-0.5	0.1
Housing	-2.3	-1.9	-1.7	-0.6	0.4	0.8	-0.3	-1.4	0.1	0.7
Household equipment and operation	-0.3	0.6	-0.6	0.1	-0.6	0.5	0.1	-0.1	0.5	0.3
Transportation	0.0	-0.4	1.8	0.0	0.4	0.7	1.0	0.3	-0.3	1.8
Tobacco and alcohol	0.4	1.1	3.2	2.7	2.2	1.5	2.2	1.8	1.1	1.3
Health and personal care	4.7	-3.9	-0.2	1.1	2.4	0.6	0.1	0.4	2.9	0.9
Recreation and education	-0.1	-0.1	0.5	1.0	1.1	0.5	0.3	1.1	0.2	0.8
All Groups	0.0	-0.3	0.1	0.5	0.9	0.4	0.5	0.2	0.4	0.7
Annual inflation rate All Groups*	1.7	1.2	0.8	0.3	1.2	1.9	2.2	1.9	1.4	0.7

Note: * current quarter over same quarter in previous year.
Source: ABS, *Consumer Price Index*, Catalogue No. 6401.0, various issues.

alcohol', but has foreshadowed reporting of an 'All groups excluding mortgage charges and consumer credit' in the future (ABS 1992).

The causes of inflation

Economic theory suggests that both supply and demand factors should be evaluated in seeking explanations for inflationary processes. Identifying the source of inflationary pressure is important in the formulation of appropriate anti-inflation policies. Inflation generated by demand factors might be expected to respond to policies designed to reduce aggregate demand. If, on the other hand, supply factors are the source of the inflation, then policies which moderate demand, although leading to reduced economic activity, may not have any direct impact on inflation.

Two competing explanations of the inflationary process can be identified. The first nominates excess demand as the cause of inflation; the second nominates disturbances on the supply side which lead to cost increases as the cause of inflationary pressures. Before undertaking an explanation of the causes of inflation in Australia, a brief discussion of these competing explanations is necessary.

The common feature of the various theories of inflation which come under the general heading of demand-pull inflation is that the general level of prices is 'pulled up' by excess demand for goods and services. What distinguishes these theories from each other is the cause of the excess demand.

Keynesian demand-pull theory of inflation attributes inflationary pressures to the existence of excess demand for goods and services. This excess demand may originate from domestic sources (private or government demand) or from overseas (export demand).

What is meant by 'excess demand'? One approach is to define it by reference to the deviation of the actual rate of unemployment (taken to be a proxy for the state of aggregate demand) from the Non-Accelerating Inflation Rate of Unemployment (NAIRU). The NAIRU is the unemployment rate at which supply and demand pressures in the labour market are balanced and where, therefore, there is an absence of upward (and downward) pressure on money wages and prices. If the actual rate of unemployment is less than the NAIRU then money wage rates will begin to increase, and the associated increase in unit costs will put upward pressure on the general level of prices. The lower the actual rate of unemployment relative to NAIRU (the greater the excess demand), the higher will be the rate of inflation.

A variant of the Keynesian demand-pull theory of inflation divides the labour market into sub-markets for specific types of

A third variety of cost-push inflation is 'inertial' inflation. This arises in situations in which workers and producers expect inflation to continue in future income periods. Thus, even if income claims are consistent, inflationary pressures will be generated if the expectation of future inflation causes economic agents to attempt to adjust their money wages and prices in order to maintain their current relative position. Such an inflationary process is regarded as inertial because the inflation arises from an attempt to maintain, rather than increase, relative shares. If workers and producers expect an inflation of 10 per cent per year, then, if they do not attempt to increase their wages and profits by the same amount (assuming zero labour productivity growth), they are willingly accepting an expected reduction in their relative share.

The discussion above has been concerned with 'pure' varieties of demand-pull and cost-push inflation. A focus on 'pure' types of inflation is justified by the need to establish their essential characteristics. Two points, however, need to be made about such an approach:

- It is not suggested that hybrid inflation (mixed demand-pull and cost-push) does not exist. To the contrary, such an inflation type is likely to be the norm.
- In practice, it is difficult (if not impossible) to classify any real-world inflation as either demand-pull or cost-push. The inflationary process will be associated with both money wages and prices rising; it will be difficult therefore to establish a causal link from wages to prices or from prices to wages. What can be done is to point to the various influences on inflation, without attempting to apportion any particular rate of inflation between these influences.

Causes of inflation in Australia since 1960

When the inflationary pressures at work in Australia over the period from 1960 are observed, both supply and demand influences may be detected, although, for the reasons given above, it is not generally possible to disentangle their separate effects. Before proceeding to a closer examination of Australia's inflation experience, one general point should be made. This relates to the importance of foreign influences on Australia's inflation rate. Stevens (1992, p. 186) points to the close correlation between the inflation rate of Australia and the average inflation rate for the G7 economies, particularly over the period prior to the floating of the $A in 1983. This is not to argue that domestic influences, whether policy-induced or otherwise, have imports to rise. The resulting current account deterioration will, in a flexible exchange rate regime, generate pressures for an exchange rate depreciation. The relatively higher domestic inflation together with the current account deterioration, may lead to speculation of a depreciation. If this occurs, then a speculative capital outflow will add to the pressure for an exchange rate depreciation.

If a depreciation does occur, then it may exacerbate, rather than moderate, the inflationary pressures in the domestic economy. Clearly the domestic price of imports will increase as a result of the depreciation and, to the extent that the imports are final goods, this will impact directly on the domestic price level. Further, if the imports are intermediate goods or if money wages rise in compensation for the higher import prices, then domestic costs of production will increase. This will put further upward pressure on the general level of prices.

Unemployment

An increase in the general level of prices may cause a fall in the level of aggregate demand and employment and, therefore, an increase in the unemployment rate.[2] The main mechanisms by which inflation causes an increase in unemployment are an increase in interest rates, a reduction in real wealth, and a loss of international competitiveness.

Although the costs of inflation can readily be identified conceptually, it is, as Nguyen (1991) points out, very difficult to estimate these costs directly. For this reason most empirical studies attempt to estimate the costs indirectly, by considering the effects of inflation on either the level of real output or its rate of growth. In this context McTaggart (1991) identifies three possible effects of inflation: the rate of growth of real GDP falls; the level of real GDP falls but its rate of growth is unchanged; both the level and rate of growth of real GDP fall. If, therefore, inflation does impose costs then we should observe that an increase in the rate of inflation will be associated with a reduction in the level of real GDP and/or its rate of growth.

Studies which attempt to examine the impact of inflation on growth typically employ long-term averages for inflation and growth for a number of countries. For the most part these studies find that reducing inflation would increase the rate of growth, although Kyriakopoulos (1991) in a study of OECD countries, including Australia, finds no evidence of a relationship between inflation and growth.

The approach adopted by McTaggart (1992) to estimate the costs of inflation in Australia over the period 1970 to 1991 focuses on the impact of both the level and the variability of inflation on the level of output. McTaggart undertakes several 'back of the envelope' type calculations based on empirical estimates of the effects of the level and variability of inflation on investment and output over the period 1962/63 to 1990/91 in Australia. His calculations suggest that a 1 percentage point increase in the inflation rate causes a reduction of approximately one-quarter of a percentage point in real GDP in the long run. McTaggart, using an average inflation rate of 7 per cent per year, concludes that a zero inflation rate would cause the level of real GDP to be 1.75 per cent higher in each year. For 1993/94 this represented some $7.4 billion in current prices.

However, as noted earlier, so far the 1990s have been characterised by much lower rates of inflation than obtained in the 1970s and 1980s. Thus, if inflation were to be reduced to zero from its current annual rate of less than 2 per cent, then a rather more modest increase in GDP of one-half of one per cent, or $2.1 billion in 1993/94, would result.

Before concluding that simply because inflation imposes costs, an anti-inflation strategy is justified, it is necessary to consider the costs of disinflation as measured by foregone output and unemployment.

The costs and benefits of anti-inflation policies

The Natural Rate Hypothesis (NRH), formulated in the late 1960s by Milton Friedman and Edmund Phelps, has dominated thinking about anti-inflation policies for much of the subsequent period. In essence, the NRH states that there is a unique and stable rate of unemployment, the natural rate, at which the rate of inflation is also stable. If the actual rate of unemployment coincides with the natural rate, then there are no forces acting to change the ruling rate of inflation, whatever it happens to be. Conversely, if the actual rate of unemployment is greater than the natural rate, then the inflation rate will be falling; if it is less than the natural rate, inflation will be rising.

Reducing inflation in this framework requires that the policy authorities implement contractionary policies. In the New Classical version of the NRH, announcement of a credible policy (that is, a policy which economic agents believe will reduce inflation and expect the policy authorities to maintain) will reduce inflation without increasing unemployment above the natural rate. By contrast, in the Keynesian and Monetarist versions, the actual rate of unemployment must exceed the natural rate for a period of time (though the precise length of this period is a matter of dispute between the two versions) in order to reduce the inflation rate. The common feature of all these versions of the NRH is that, when equilibrium is restored, the actual rate of unemployment will again be equal to the natural rate and inflation will be stable at a lower, though not necessarily zero, rate.

In the context of the NRH model, the costs of anti-inflation policies can therefore be evaluated in terms of the increase in unemployment caused by these policies; similarly, the benefits of such policies can be evaluated in terms of the induced decrease in the inflation rate. To compare the costs and benefits of anti-inflation policies, however, the outcomes of such policies must be expressed, not in terms of unemployment and inflation, but in terms of a single measure. Real output, as measured by GDP, can serve as this measure.

It was argued previously that reducing inflation would increase real output. McTaggart (1992) estimated that, for Australia, a 1 percentage point decrease in the inflation rate would cause real output to increase by one-quarter of a per cent. But it is also the case that increasing unemployment will be associated with a policy-induced reduction in real output. Junankar and Kapuscinski (1992) have attempted to estimate the output costs of unemployment in Australia from 1981/82 to 1991/92. They employ three different methods to estimate such output losses and conclude that, based on the mean values generated by the three methods, a 1 percentage point increase in the unemployment rate will be associated with a 1 to 1.2 per cent decrease in the level of real output.

To form a judgment regarding the net benefit (or cost) of anti-inflation policies, in terms of real output, requires that we have evidence on the percentage increase in unemployment required to generate a 1 percentage point fall in the inflation rate, and on the time period relevant to the reduction in inflation and to the unemployment increase. In this regard, Schelde-Andersen (1992, p. 109) notes the existence of '. . . a general consensus that while the benefits of lower inflation are permanent, the costs associated with reducing inflation are only transitory, so that a cost–benefit analysis would always come down in favour of adopting a policy of price stability'. Clearly this consensus is based on the NRH; contrary to his assertion, however, it is not the case that a cost–benefit analysis will always favour disinflation. If, for example, the output gains from lower inflation are small relative to the output losses from the temporarily higher unemployment and if equilibrium is restored only slowly, then it is quite possible for the present discounted value of the output gains to be less than the discounted value of the output losses. Further, even though the output gains from lower inflation are permanent, if the discount rate applied to these gains is high, then their present value will be small.

Table 3.3 Sacrifice ratios for Australia

	GDP	Unemployment
Ball	1.00	n.a.
Schelde-Andersen	−0.15	6.00
Stevens	1.30 to 2.70	1.10 to 6.40

Source: Ball (1993), Schelde-Andersen (1992), Stevens (1992).

Empirical estimates of the relationship between the increase in unemployment (output loss) and the decrease in the inflation rate are presented as 'sacrifice ratios'. The sacrifice ratio is defined as the ratio of the cumulative rise in the unemployment rate (or the cumulative output loss) to the decline in the inflation rate over the same period. Three recent studies, Ball (1993), Schelde-Andersen (1992), and Stevens (1992) have estimated sacrifice ratios for Australia in terms of both cumulative output loss and cumulative unemployment increase. Table 3.3 below summarises their results.

The three sets of results are not strictly comparable because:
(a) Stevens and Ball examine particular episodes of disinflation, whereas Schelde-Andersen uses the same time period for all the OECD economies, and in the case of Australia this period embraces two disinflation episodes;
(b) the numerator in the sacrifice ratios of Stevens and Ball is the deviation of output (or unemployment) from trend, while Schelde-Andersen uses the deviations from the initial actual values; and
(c) Ball truncates the output losses by assuming that output returns to its normal growth path one year after the end of the disinflation, and this may have the effect of understating the sacrifice ratio.

Notwithstanding these differences, one clear conclusion does emerge from consideration of these sacrifice ratios, namely that the New Classical view that anti-inflation policy generates costless gains is not supported by Australian experience. Past episodes of disinflation have imposed output and employment losses.

The results of Ball and Stevens, based on a similar analytical approach, suggest that a reduction of 1 percentage point in the rate of inflation leads to a cumulative loss of real output of between 1 and 2.7 per cent. Stevens (1992, p. 234) sets the output loss slightly higher at between 1.5 and 3 per cent. If these results are combined with those of McTaggart (1992), then a permanent real output gain of 0.25 per cent per year (as a result of a 1 percentage point reduction in the inflation rate) must be set against cumulative transitory real output losses of between 1 and 3 per cent of GDP. Without details

Menon (1993) distinguishes three conduits by which exchange rate changes can feed through into domestic inflation—the direct and indirect effects discussed above, and an effect on the price of domestically produced goods that are close substitutes for imports. In his study of Australian imports of manufactured goods from 1981 to 1991, Menon finds that the 'pass-through' of exchange rate changes to the $A price of imported manufactures averaged about 70 per cent for final goods and a higher rate for intermediate goods. Further, he suggests that where domestically produced manufactures and imports are close substitutes, the price of the domestic good will track closely the $A price of the imported good. It would appear therefore that incomplete pass-through of exchange rate changes to the $A price of imports contributed to a moderation of inflationary pressures in Australia, although, to the extent that the third effect was important, even incomplete exchange rate pass-through would have had inflationary consequences. The modification of inflationary pressure was observable particularly during the period from 1984/85 to 1986/87 when the $A sharply depreciated and the average $A price of imported manufactures appears to have been smoothed relative to their full pass-through price (Menon 1993, p. 42).

No simple characterisation of inflation in this period, or sub-periods, as demand-pull or cost-push, is possible. Demand elements were present at different times, emanating from external and policy-induced sources. The predominant influences on the rate of inflation during this period were from the supply side, although, as was noted, there were marked inter-temporal changes in the relative importance of the various supply-side shocks.

1986 to the present

Attention may now be directed to the final period from 1986 to the present, when the inflation rate, as measured by the IDFDD, fell from 8.5 per cent in 1985/86, levelled off at 6.6 per cent from 1987/88 to 1988/89, and then fell sharply to stabilise at about 2 per cent in 1991/92.

With the exception of 1986/87 when a growth rate of 0.8 per cent was recorded, real Domestic Final Demand grew by more than 4 per cent per annum from 1985/86 to 1988/89. An improvement in the terms of trade in both 1987/88 and 1988/89 added external support to the overall growth in demand. Although fiscal policy was tight, monetary policy was eased in the first half of 1987 and further eased after the share market crash in October 1987. This was associated with a steady fall in the unemployment rate from 7.8 per cent in 1985/86 to 5.7 per cent in 1988/89. Despite the tightening labour market, money wage growth was relatively stable in a range between 5.9 and 7.4 per cent per annum from the opening of this period until 1990/91. As in the previous period, this atypical behaviour of money wage growth in the presence of an improving labour market can be attributed to the operation of the Accord.

During 1988, in response to the rising current account deficit, monetary policy was progressively tightened and interest rates rose sharply. Real demand growth slowed in 1989/90 and became negative in 1990/91. The unemployment rate increased to 8.4 per cent in 1990/91 and continued to increase to 11.0 per cent in 1992/93; the modest growth of real domestic demand in 1990/91 and 1991/92 was insufficient to prevent the unemployment rate from rising. Money wage growth fell to 2.9 per cent in 1991/92 and to 0.7 per cent in 1992/93. Since this fall in money wage growth over 1991/92 and 1992/93 coincided with an increase in the unemployment rate, the disinflation can be attributed, in part, to the policy-induced reduction in demand.

Although demand pressures were present for the first half of this period they were not translated into increases in the inflation rate. Stevens (1992) suggests that flexible exchange rates, which led to falling $A import prices when a monetary policy-induced appreciation of the $A occurred in the late 1980s, and the Accord, which restrained money wage growth when the unemployment rate fell, are jointly responsible for this atypical outcome. The sharp fall in inflation in the 1990s is attributable to the policy-induced contraction in demand initiated in the late 1980s.

This discussion of the causes of inflation in Australia since 1960 has identified the presence of both supply and demand influences and has highlighted the vulnerability of the economy to overseas inflationary shocks, whether deriving from the supply side or the demand side.

The costs of inflation

What are the effects of inflation and do they impose economic costs? We may consider these effects under several headings:

Uncertainty

It is argued that inflation (in particular, the variability of inflation) will give rise to uncertainty regarding the profitability of real investment because it makes it more difficult to form expectations about the future return on investment. Inflation will also increase uncertainty about the financing of such investment.

If producers become more uncertain about the future rate of

return on real investment, this may shorten investment horizons and lead to a preference for projects with a short payback period (that is, projects where the initial expenditure is recouped in a relatively short time). If inflation does lead to a bias against long-term projects, this will cause resources to be misallocated. Increased uncertainty may also cause the deferring of real investment projects in favour of holding financial assets with a high nominal return. To the extent that investment projects are deferred and/or resources are misallocated as a result of inflation, then economic growth will be adversely affected.

Increased uncertainty may also distort financing decisions. Firms may display a preference for borrowing short-term rather than risk being 'locked in' to high-cost long-term borrowings if interest rates fall subsequently. However, should nominal interest rates rise, whether as a result of increasing inflationary expectations or restrictive monetary policy, then this will entail higher refinancing costs.

Inflation-induced uncertainty might also have adverse effects on labour markets. To the extent that the expected rate of inflation is an element in the wage bargaining process, increased uncertainty may lead trade unions to prefer more frequent wage negotiations. This in turn leads to the possibility of an increased incidence of strikes, with adverse consequences for economic growth.

Redistribution of income

When inflation occurs, the money values of aggregate expenditure and aggregate income will both increase at the same rate (equal to the rate of growth of real expenditure and real income plus the rate of inflation). This (national accounting) fact does not mean that inflation does not entail costs, since the increase in income may be distributed in an arbitrary and inefficient way. For example, producers who sell their products in competitive markets, individuals on fixed nominal incomes, and workers unable to maintain their real wages by securing money wage increases in line with inflation will all experience a redistribution away from them. On the other hand, producers and workers who are able to exercise some degree of market power will achieve a redistribution in their favour. Inflation, therefore, redistributes income from the competitive and the economically weak towards the monopolistic and the economically powerful.

Redistribution of wealth

Creditors holding financial assets with fixed monetary values (for example, currency and bank deposits) will experience a redistribution away from them and in favour of debtors. This redistribution will be reduced to the extent that nominal interest rates increase in line with inflation. Similarly, wealth-holders with assets whose capital value increases in line with (or faster than) inflation will preserve (or increase) their relative wealth.

Higher interest rates

Inflation will tend to cause nominal interest rates to increase. A distinction should be drawn between Keynesian and Monetarist explanations of this phenomenon.

In the Keynesian view, an increase in the price level will reduce the real money supply while leaving unchanged the level of real expenditures and, therefore, the demand for real transactions balances. This excess demand for real transactions balances will cause interest rates to rise.

The Monetarist view emphasises the importance of inflationary expectations in the determination of the nominal rate of interest. The expected nominal interest rate can be defined as the sum of the ruling real rate of interest and the expected rate of inflation. If rising prices lead economic agents to increase their estimates of the expected rate of inflation then, given the real rate of interest, the expected nominal rate will increase by the same amount. If wealth-holders expect a higher nominal interest rate, then it follows that they expect a lower price of non-monetary financial assets in the future. The expected capital loss will reduce the demand for these assets and their market price will fall; therefore the nominal interest rate will rise.

Whether it is via the Keynesian or Monetarist routes that inflation affects nominal interest rates, the key issue from a cost of inflation perspective is the extent to which the inflation premium is incorporated into the nominal interest rate. If the inflation premium is fully incorporated then the real rate of interest is unaffected by inflation and so too will saving and investment decisions. If the nominal interest rate does not fully reflect the inflation rate, then the real interest rate will be distorted. On this point, McTaggart (1992, p. 60), after surveying the empirical literature, notes that '. . . it is not clear how real rates are affected, but we can be certain that real resource allocations are different in a world with inflation than in a world without'.

Balance of payments problems

If the domestic rate of inflation is higher than the inflation rates of our trading partners, this will render our exports less attractive to overseas and their exports more attractive to us. At the ruling nominal exchange rate, this will cause our exports to fall and our of the size of the annual output losses in particular disinflation episodes and of the appropriate discount rate, it is not possible to estimate the net present value of these output gains and losses. However, it is likely that for output losses at the upper end of the range, the present value of these transitory losses would exceed that of the permanent output gains. This suggests that anti-inflation policy is likely to impose net output losses, which is not consistent with the consensus view that a cost–benefit analysis would always favour lower inflation.

This conclusion is given further support when Stevens's estimates of the unemployment sacrifice ratio are combined with the findings of Junankar and Kapuscinski (1992) noted previously. Together these suggest that a permanent real output gain of 0.25 per cent per year should be set against cumulative transitory output losses of between 1.1 and 7.7 per cent of GDP.

Numerators in sacrifice ratios are usually calculated as deviations of actual output (or unemployment) from their potential or equilibrium level (or rate). If these equilibrium levels and rates are themselves affected by the anti-inflation policies, along with the actual levels and rates, then this should be taken into account in estimating the output costs of such policies. Consider an anti-inflation policy which causes the actual unemployment rate to rise; if the natural rate of unemployment is influenced by the actual unemployment rate, then the natural rate will also increase. This phenomenon, where the natural rate tracks the actual rate, is known as hysteresis. To the extent that hysteresis is present, then anti-inflation policies will result in a permanent increase in unemployment and therefore permanent, rather than transitory, output losses. Thus, to the extent that there is hysteresis in the natural rate, this will render the results of a cost–benefit analysis less favourable for any given disinflation policy.

On balance, the evidence is inconclusive on the relative output costs of inflation and unemployment, and therefore on the desirability of anti-inflation policy. In such circumstances, it is difficult to disagree with Norton (1992) when, in opening discussion on the paper by Shelde-Andersen (1992), he observed that '. . . now that inflation is down, the best policy is to not let it rise again'.

Notes

1 This is discussed in greater detail in chapter 7.
2 The relationship between inflation and unemployment is analysed in chapter 4.

Recommended reading

Fender, J. 1990, *Inflation: Welfare Costs, Positive Theory, and Policy Options*, University of Michigan Press, Ann Arbor

Frisch, H. 1983, *Theories of Inflation*, Cambridge University Press, Cambridge

Hall, R.E. (ed.) 1983, *Inflation: Causes and Effects*, University of Chicago Press, Chicago

Stevens, G. 1992, 'Inflation and disinflation in Australia: 1950–91', in A. Blundell-Wignall (ed.), *Inflation, Disinflation and Monetary Policy*, Reserve Bank of Australia, Sydney

Trevithick, J.A. 1980, *Inflation*, Penguin, Harmondsworth

4 Unemployment in Australia
Trevor Stegman

It is useful to see macroeconomic policy as a juggling act of goals related to the three major national economic problems of unemployment, inflation and the balance of payments position. While this chapter addresses the problem of unemployment, it is important to appreciate that, from a macroeconomic perspective, the three problems are interdependent, so the issues discussed in this chapter need to be understood in context with chapters 2 and 3. The three problems are interdependent because (as is explained below) they are all related to the fundamental issue of macroeconomics: the level and rate of growth of the nation's aggregate production of goods and services (Gross Domestic Product) discussed in chapter 2.

The nature of the interrelationships between the three problems, the causes and the appropriate policy responses, and the extent to which their interdependence requires policy trade-offs, are matters which provide the basis for much economic and political debate. The aim here is to provide some analysis of the problem of unemployment in Australia.[1]

The costs and measurement of unemployment

Since the level of unemployment is a reflection of the extent to which we are failing to fully utilise the nation's labour resources, there is an obvious general cost from unemployment in terms of foregone output, lower per capita income and lower national living standards. The existence of unemployment means that aggregate production of goods and services is less than the potential output of the nation: aggregate economic activity, and hence aggregate output and national income, are less than the economy is capable of producing.

In addition to this opportunity cost to the nation, there are well-known individual costs from unemployment borne by those who cannot find the paid employment necessary to provide for themselves and their families. Australian research points to unemployment being the major cause of poverty in this country (see, for example, Saunders 1992). Broader social costs linked to high levels of unemployment include rising crime rates, lower community health standards and social alienation.[2]

Transfers from those employed to those unemployed, through the taxation and social welfare systems, attempt to spread the costs of unemployment more evenly across society. However, rather than attempts to share out a reduced national economic 'cake' more fairly, the desirable solution to unemployment is to raise the level of employment, increase the level of productive activity of the nation up closer to its full-employment potential, and have a bigger national economic 'cake'.

The level of unemployment is usually measured as a rate: the unemployment rate is the percentage of the labour force unemployed—that is, not in employment for pay or profit. The labour force is defined as those of working age (15 years and older) willing and able to work.

While this definition of the unemployment rate seems clear, its measurement in practice provides many difficulties. The official unemployment figures come from a monthly survey of around 30 000 households by the Australian Bureau of Statistics (ABS).

According to the ABS definitions, a person is counted as employed if either they did at least one hour of work for pay or profit ('employed' includes 'self-employed') or they worked at least one hour unpaid in a family business or farm in the survey week. Those not counted as employed are classified as 'unemployed' only if they actively sought, and were willing and able to start, employment in the survey week. The remainder are classified as 'not in the labour force'.

Thus the ABS definition of unemployment is very strict, and may significantly understate the 'true' level of unemployment for two main reasons: it fails to take account of underemployment and the fact that job-seekers may become discouraged by their failure to secure a job.

First, the ABS figures make no allowance for workers who worked part-time in the survey week but would prefer more hours, or prefer full-time employment and were unable to find it. Neither can the official measure make any allowances for employed workers whose skills are currently underutilised because they are unable to find employment in jobs where their skills would be more productively used.

Second, since those out of work are not officially counted as unemployed if they have not actively sought work in the survey week, the ABS unemployment figures may omit many people who should be considered as genuinely unemployed. These are people who, although they want employment and are willing and able to start, have not actively sought work in the current week because they perceive that their chances of finding a job are currently poor. Because actively seeking work incurs costs in terms of time, effort and money, some genuinely unemployed may become discouraged from job-seeking until they perceive that the probability of being successful has improved. In the ABS figures these 'discouraged workers' will be counted as 'not in the labour force' rather than as unemployed.

When there is a downturn in the labour market and demand for labour falls, the 'discouraged worker effect' will mean that the official unemployment figures understate the extent of the deterioration, since those who give up actively looking for work, even temporarily, will be considered as having 'dropped out' of the labour force.

On the other hand, when the labour market recovers and demand for labour picks up, increased job opportunities will draw many people who were not actively seeking employment back into the labour force. This will weaken the impact of the recovery in demand for labour on reducing the official unemployment figures.

The extent to which the official figures underestimate 'true' unemployment (the degree to which the nation's labour resources are underutilised) is difficult to measure. Labour market research suggests that not only is 'hidden unemployment' a significant problem, but that it increases substantially when there is a recession in the labour market and demand for labour is depressed.[3]

The official figures for employment and unemployment are released on a monthly basis, but it is unwise to place too much emphasis on month-to-month variations, for two reasons: seasonality and sampling error.

The factors that determine changes in the unemployment rate (the size of the labour force and the number of people in employment) are subject to strong seasonal influences. For example, there is a surge of school leavers into the labour force in the period from December to February, and there is an increase in temporary and part-time employment opportunities in the retail industry in December. To take account of seasonal factors the ABS publishes estimates of 'seasonally adjusted' figures, but like all estimates these have a degree of imprecision. Alternatively, we may simply compare the

Table 4.1 The Australian unemployment record

At August	% of LF	Persons (000)	Average duration (weeks)
1973	1.8	106	9
1974	2.4	141	–
1975	4.6	278	13
1976	4.7	293	–
1977	5.7	359	–
1978	6.2	396	26
1979	5.9	374	–
1980	5.9	392	–
1981	5.6	377	35
1982	6.7	459	–
1983	9.9	684	42
1984	8.5	605	–
1985	7.9	571	–
1986	8.0	597	49
1987	7.8	602	–
1988	6.8	539	–
1989	5.7	469	44
1990	7.0	587	–
1991	9.5	806	–
1992	10.6	906	51
1993	10.7	916	–
1994	9.2	798	–

Note: Average unemployment rate for 1962–72 = 1.6%.
Source: ABS.

figure for a particular month in successive years in order to measure the trend movement in the unemployment rate.

The second reason why we should not read too much into month-to-month variations in the unemployment rate is that the figures are population estimates based on a sample. The sample is chosen to be representative and it is relatively large. However, in assuming that the labour market experience of the people in the sample gives unemployment rates that can be applied to the population as a whole, we can only be reasonably confident that the resulting estimates are 'about right'. Small variations in the official monthly unemployment rate may well be due to experiences peculiar to the people in the sample, rather than indicative of some general trend in the labour market.

Australia's unemployment experience

Table 4.1 presents the ABS figures for the unemployment rate for the last two decades (measured at August in each year). Australia's unemployment experience can be summarised as follows:

Figure 4.1 Australia's unemployment (% of labour force)

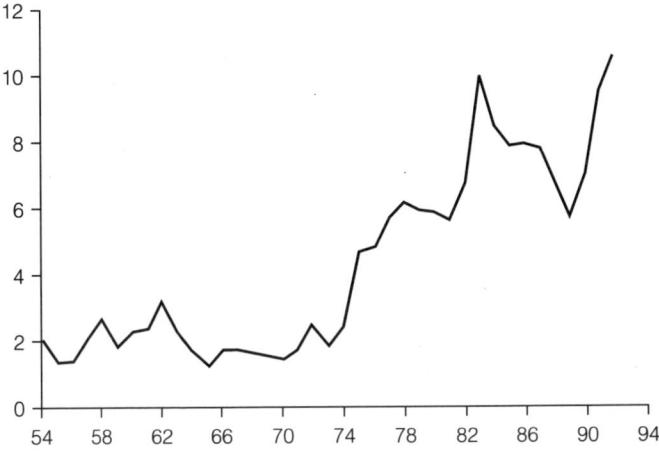

- From a fairly stable rate averaging around 1.6 per cent for the decade 1962–72, the unemployment rate rose significantly in the mid-1970s.
- The employment rate appeared to stabilise at the higher level from 1979 to 1982, but rose sharply again in 1982 and 1983.
- The unemployment rate fell slowly but steadily from 1984 to 1989 before climbing sharply again from 1989 to 1993.

This pattern is depicted in Figure 4.1.

Table 4.1 also provides the average duration in weeks of unemployment for selected years. It is significant that with the increase in the unemployment rate, the average duration of unemployment has also increased substantially. This is a reflection of the unequal incidence of unemployment, as can be explained by the following example: suppose the unemployment rate is constant over a year at one-twelfth of the labour force, or approximately 8.3 per cent—the Australian unemployment rate was around this level in 1986. If everyone in the labour force had an equal share of unemployment over the year then we would expect the average duration to be about one month. (Since one-twelfth of the labour force is unemployed over the year, equal incidence would mean everyone would get a spell of one-twelfth of the year in unemployment.) The fact that the average duration in 1986 was much higher, at 49 weeks, means that the burden of unemployment has fallen on only a minority of the labour force, and the majority of workers have been sheltered from experiencing unemployment.

Table 4.2 Unemployment rates by age and sex (August)

	15–19 years			20+ years		
	M	F	P	M	F	P
1973	4.6	4.9	4.7	1.0	2.3	1.4
1983	23.0	22.2	22.6	8.7	7.9	8.4
1985	19.3	17.1	18.2	6.8	6.7	6.7
1990	16.6	16.5	16.5	6.0	6.0	6.0
1992	25.1	24.8	25.0	10.2	7.9	9.3

Source: ABS.

The substantial increase in the average duration of unemployment, and the unequal incidence on particular social groups, also points to an increasing problem of long-term or 'hard-core' unemployment.

In August 1992 the proportion of the unemployed who had been unemployed for twelve months or more was 33.4 per cent (around 300 000 persons). By comparison, the figure in August 1981 was 20 per cent (around 70 000 persons).

Research clearly shows that the probability of finding employment falls with the length of unemployment (see, for example, Foster and Gregory 1983). With increases in the general unemployment rate comes an increase in the number of workers who have been unemployed for a long period of time and whose prospects of leaving the unemployment pool are poor. Even with a recovery in labour market conditions, the erosion of job skills and attractiveness to potential employers that results from a prolonged spell of unemployment means that these people remain disadvantaged. The new job opportunities are likely to be taken by new entrants to the labour force and by those with only a brief spell in unemployment. Even with a recovery in conditions generally then, the problem of long-term unemployment is likely to require special targeted policies to offset labour market disadvantages.

The unequal incidence of unemployment and the possible need for targeted assistance programs have led to considerable research into the labour market experience of particular social groups, such as migrants, women, youth, and middle-aged males.

Table 4.2 presents the unemployment rates by sex and age for some selected years. While the main feature of this table is the much higher rates of unemployment for youth than for adults (in August 1992 the adult unemployment rate was 9.3 per cent, but the youth rate was 25 per cent), a number of points about the youth unemployment rate need to be understood.

First, in 1992 only 51 per cent of the population aged 15–19 years were participants in the labour force—nearly half of the working age youth population are in full-time education and are not counted as either employed or unemployed.

Second, although youth has many inherent disadvantages in the competition for jobs (e.g. lack of experience, 'last in, first out' retrenchment policies), many first-time youth jobs are of short duration, interspersed with frequent, very short spells of unemployment, and represent job-sampling behaviour.

Third, although the youth unemployment rate in the current recession is about three times the adult rate, a comparison with previous periods reveals that the youth rate is always about three times the adult rate. For example, in the buoyant conditions of 1973, the adult rate was 1.4 per cent and the youth rate was 4.7 per cent. This suggests that the current high level of youth unemployment is not the result of some factor peculiar to the current youth labour market (such as current youth wage levels), but is the result of the high level of general unemployment and the perennial labour market disadvantages of youth. The best way to get youth unemployment down is to get the general level of unemployment down.

These qualifications should not decrease our concern about high youth unemployment. High youth unemployment today will mean future shortages of the labour skills acquired through on-the-job training. Future recovery in labour demand may run into shortages of skilled labour and result in inflationary pressure rather than reductions in unemployment.

While special targeted labour market programs to assist particular groups may be justified on the grounds of equity and efficiency, it must be remembered that if the economy does not generate sufficient growth in aggregate employment to more than match increases in the size of the labour force, such programs will do no more than redistribute unemployment. The relationship between unemployment (U), employment (E), labour force (LF) growth and GDP growth can be appreciated with the use of some simple arithmetic:

If we express the definitional equation for unemployment,

$$U = LF - E$$

in terms of changes, then

$$\Delta U = \Delta LF - \Delta E.$$

We can appreciate that unemployment will increase if employment falls (a negative change in E), or if employment increases but the increase in employment is insufficient to match any increase in the labour force. To stop unemployment and the unemployment rate from increasing we need to generate sufficient growth in employment to match labour force growth.

As shown in chapter 2, the size of the labour force is determined by the size of the working age population and the participation rate—the proportion of the working age population which is considered as being in the labour force, that is, counted as employed or as unemployed.

Population growth depends upon natural increase and net immigration. Changes in the age mix of the population will determine the proportion that are of working age. Australian research finds no strong relationship between these factors and short-term economic conditions, although the level of immigration has appeared to respond to the state of the economy, largely because of changes in government targets (see Kelley and Schmidt 1979).

Economic factors are much more significant in affecting the participation rate. In chapter 2 it was shown that trends in the participation rate largely reflect such factors as the work force behaviour of married women and students, school retention rates, and the average retirement age. In particular, it highlighted the long-term trend in Australia over the last two decades of increased participation by married women, which has been partially offset by longer school retention for teenagers and earlier male retirement. Over the last seven years the male participation rate has stabilised, while the female participation rate for females aged 30 years and over has continued to increase strongly.

In the short run the participation rate is strongly influenced by economic conditions. When the economy goes into a recession the participation rate falls due to the 'discouraged worker' effect. When the economy recovers, discouraged workers and other non-participants are drawn back into the labour force. Therefore the participation rate typically moves pro-cyclically in the short run.

Table 4.3 presents estimates for the last decade of the changes in the number of people unemployed, disaggregated into labour force and employment changes. Changes in the labour force are further disaggregated into changes resulting from the increase in the working age population and changes resulting from a change in the participation rate.

The pro-cyclical movement in the participation rate is clearly evident. For example, in 1982, 1983, and 1991, falls in employment were accompanied by falls in the participation rate which moderated the impact on unemployment. On the other hand, in 1986 there was very strong growth in employment (243 000 additional jobs) but increased participation added 111 000 persons to the labour force and with the natural increase in the working age population this

Table 4.3 The composition of changes in unemployment[a]

Year	ΔU	=	ΔLF From ΔPop	+	From ΔPR [b]	=		–	ΔE
1982	81		145	+	–73	=	72		–9
1983	225		144	+	–34	=	110		–115
1984	–79		126	+	20	=	146		225
1985	–34		142	+	36	=	178		210
1986	25		157	+	111	=	268		243
1987	5		152	+	26	=	178		173
1988	–63		160	+	38	=	198		261
1989	–70		162	+	143	=	305		375
1990	118		139	+	76	=	215		97
1991	219		146	+	–83	=	63		–156

Note: a All figures in '000 persons.
b This is the estimated change in the labour force that would have occurred if there had been no change in the participation rate from the previous year.

Source: ABS.

meant that the employment growth was not enough to match labour force growth and the number unemployed actually rose (by 25 000).

The data of Table 4.3 also indicate that Australia's dramatic increases in unemployment over the last decade cannot be attributed to any abnormal labour supply factors. We cannot blame an influx of married women or migrants into the labour force for the substantial increases in unemployment. In all the years that unemployment increased significantly, employment either fell or, compared to what might be considered normal labour force growth, the increase in employment was inadequate. We may conclude that Australian unemployment has increased so dramatically because the economy has failed to generate adequate growth in employment.

Since a growing labour force requires growth in employment to avoid any increase in unemployment, growth in aggregate production of goods and services in the economy (GDP) must be strong enough to create sufficient employment opportunities. The rate at which GDP needs to grow to stop the unemployment rate from increasing depends on *labour force growth* and *productivity growth*.

Each year the labour force grows (due to population growth and any changes in the rate of participation of the population in the labour force, as discussed above). So we need sufficient economic growth to generate sufficient extra jobs to provide for the increase in the labour force.

Additionally, output per person employed, a measure of Average Labour Productivity, tends to increase over time (due to the increased quantity and quality of the capital goods with which labour works, i.e. technological progress). Therefore to stop unemployment increasing we need sufficient economic growth to cover both increases in the labour force and in productivity.

The rule relating required output growth (for no increase in the unemployment rate) to labour force and productivity growth rates, is referred to as 'Okun's Law':

To maintain a constant unemployment rate, output must grow at a rate equal to the sum of the growth rates in the labour force and in the average productivity of labour.

Growth in aggregate production of goods and services must be sufficient to generate enough extra jobs to provide for a growing work force, and to provide for the fact that each worker can produce a higher volume of output. (This is not to imply that an appropriate cure for unemployment is to reduce productivity growth. The point is, that to avoid increased unemployment, productivity growth must be used to increase production of goods and services, rather than to save on the number of jobs.)

If output growth falls below the Okun's Law benchmark, the unemployment rate will increase. For a reduction in the unemployment rate, output growth is required to be greater than the benchmark rate.

Although both labour force and productivity exhibit trend increases over the long run, in the short term both are affected by current economic conditions. For example, as we have discussed above, the participation rate will fall in times of low aggregate economic activity if job-seekers become discouraged and drop out of the work force.

Average Labour Productivity, measured simply as output per person employed, is affected by changes in average working hours (say from a shift from full-time to part-time jobs), and by changes in the industrial composition of aggregate output (an increase in the relative contribution of capital-intensive industries like mining, at the expense of labour-intensive industries, would increase the average measure of labour productivity). Therefore the Okun's Law benchmark, while a useful 'rule of thumb', is subject to fluctuation.

On average over the last decade the Australian labour force has grown by approximately 2.5 per cent per annum (see Table 2.1). Productivity growth has been slow by historical standards (due mainly to an increased proportion of part-time employment and the relative growth of labour-intensive service sectors), averaging only approximately 1 per cent per annum (see Figure 2.9 and Table 2.4). On the basis of these figures the Okun's Law benchmark for GDP growth is approximately 3.5 per cent per annum.

Figure 2.2 depicted output growth for Australia for the period 1979 to 1992. Drawing an approximate Okun's Law benchmark at about 3.5 per cent, the correspondence between inadequate GDP growth in Figure 2.2 and the changes in the unemployment rate of Table 4.2 and Figure 4.1 is clear. In Figure 2.2, a line drawn across the graph of GDP growth generally identifies years in which the unemployment rate increased (GDP growth less than 3.5 per cent) and years in which the unemployment rate decreased (GDP growth greater than 3.5 per cent).

The fact that strong, consistent GDP growth is required just to stop the unemployment rate from increasing and, on present estimates, GDP growth well in excess of 3.5 per cent is necessary to make any substantial reduction in unemployment, highlights the main problems for unemployment policy. There are two constraints on the ability of the economy to sustain such growth rates. The first is the danger of inflationary pressures arising if policy seeks to generate increased growth through expansionary demand policies. In the face of shortages of particular types of skilled labour, and supply bottlenecks in particular industries, such policies may have their main effect as higher prices rather than higher employment.

The second constraint on growth concerns the balance of payments. The GDP growth required for reducing unemployment might result in a growth rate in imports (both consumer imports and imported inputs into production) which is not matched by adequate growth in Australia's exports. In these circumstances concern for the balance of payments, and the effect of current account deficits on the level of external debt, may mean that Australia cannot afford the GDP growth rates necessary to reduce unemployment significantly.

The causes of unemployment

The causes of unemployment have long been a matter of controversy in both economic theory and in policy debates. A full consideration of what economic theory has to say about the causes of unemployment is beyond the scope of this chapter. In this section we provide a brief summary of three main causal factors.

Depressed levels of aggregate demand for goods and services

Since the demand for labour is derived from the demand for the goods and services that labour produces, if growth in aggregate demand expenditure is too low to provide sufficient growth in employment, then unemployment will result.

Thus one principle of national economic management is to try and ensure an adequate, stable rate of growth in aggregate demand expenditure so as to maintain a high level of employment, through appropriate fiscal and monetary policy. However, government policy often finds it necessary to restrict the level of demand expenditure to counter inflationary pressures, or because the economy is growing too quickly for the balance of payments constraint. This dilemma for macroeconomic demand management policy may require a trade-off between the goal of low unemployment and other policy goals.

Frictional and structural unemployment

Frictional unemployment consists of 'job-searchers' temporarily unemployed between jobs. Although temporary for the individual, there will be an aggregate level of functional unemployment determined by the amount of labour turnover (the number of people changing jobs) and the time taken to match the appropriate worker with the appropriate job.

Structural unemployment is a more serious concern. It is a reflection of the extent to which those unemployed are inadequately or inappropriately skilled to take advantage of any employment opportunities. Structural unemployment arises because the composition of the demand for labour does not match the composition of the available supply of labour.

The level of unemployment resulting from frictional and structural causes is referred to by some economists as the natural rate of unemployment, or alternatively as the Non-Accelerating Inflation Rate of Unemployment (NAIRU). Note that to refer to frictional and structural unemployment as comprising the 'natural rate' of unemployment does not imply that this rate of unemployment is incapable of responding to policy initiatives. Policies can be undertaken to influence the levels of frictional and structural unemployment, for example, improvements to job information networks, retraining and reskilling schemes.

The point is that 'natural rate' unemployment does not represent an excess supply of labour to put downward pressure on wages (since those unemployed are either voluntarily unemployed or do not have the appropriate job characteristics). Furthermore, general increases in aggregate demand for goods and services will not have much impact in reducing unemployment if it is structurally based, and may lead to a surge in inflation due to skill shortages.

The extent to which Australia's high unemployment is caused by structural factors is difficult to quantify. Since productivity growth has been relatively low, it appears that 'technological unemployment' has not been a major cause. Unemployment is not just the result of machines having replaced people in producing goods and services. If this had been the case, output per worker would have increased significantly.

A crude measure of the 'mismatch' in the labour market, and the extent of structural unemployment, can be provided by the survey data that the ABS collects on unfilled vacancies.[4]

If U is the number unemployed and V is the number of unfilled vacancies, then the ratio U:V is a rough indication of the extent of structural unemployment. If U:V is less than or equal to one, then all unemployment can be considered as structural: there are sufficient job vacancies and the unemployed must therefore have inappropriate skills and characteristics for the available jobs. The higher the U:V ratio, the less important are structural imbalances in causing unemployment. The vacancy figures are notoriously unreliable, since many employers use informal networks in seeking labour, but taken at face value they imply U:V ratios which have been consistently much greater than one over the last decade in Australia. (In 1983 the U:V ratio was around 21. This would imply that even if we had been able to wave a magic wand over the labour force to make everyone appropriately skilled, for every person placed in a job there would still be 20 left over as unemployed.)

Despite the unreliability of the vacancy figures, the U:V ratio has been so high that it can safely be concluded that the main cause of Australia's increased unemployment has been 'not enough job opportunities' rather than 'inappropriately skilled workers'.

Inappropriate wage levels

The relationship between wages and unemployment is the most controversial issue in macroeconomics. Simple supply and demand analysis would imply that if unemployment reflects an excess supply of labour over demand for labour, then, in the familiar supply and demand cross diagram, the current 'price' of labour must be above its equilibrium. With normally sloped supply and demand curves, the cure is a fall in the price so as to equate supply and demand. Such simple analysis, however, can be quite misleading when applied to the aggregate economy and the question of general unemployment.

Since the demand for labour depends upon the demand for goods and services, and expenditure on goods and services is largely financed by the wage income of labour, it is not clear that a reduction in wages would increase the demand for labour. Lower wages might mean lower expenditure on goods and services. Employers would hardly increase their demand for labour if their sales of products were falling.

In analysing the relationship between wages and unemployment, it is useful to distinguish three concepts of wages (the 'price' of labour):

- money wages (also referred to as nominal wages). The general level of money wages is the average money wage per employee (per period, e.g. per week);
- real wages. This is the ratio of the average money wage to some measure of the average or general level of prices;
- relative wages. This is the ratio of the average money wage for one labour market group to the average money wage of other groups.

Changes in the level of money wages reflect movements in wages generally. If money wages rise, and the increase is greater than the increase in labour productivity (output per employee), then the labour cost of producing a unit of output will increase—and therefore 'unit labour costs' increase. Businesses could be expected to pass on this cost increase in higher prices—and the result is inflation. Since inflation results in a loss of international competitiveness, and less demand for domestically produced goods and services in relation to goods and services produced overseas, the result is unemployment. Additionally, wage-based inflation may provoke governments into imposing contractionary demand management policy in the belief that increased unemployment will cause a moderation in wage demands.

If employers are not able to pass on increases in money wages by raising prices, and real wages rise faster than labour productivity, then the result is a squeeze on profit margins and a fall in business profitability. The experiences of 1974–75 and 1982–83 in Australia have shown that when a squeeze on business profitability occurs, the consequence is a fall in business investment, a fall in economic growth, and a resulting rise in unemployment (see Stegman 1985, 1990).

On the other hand, it is not necessarily the case that a fall in real wages and a consequent increase in business profitability will reduce unemployment. Reduced real wages may mean reduced aggregate consumption expenditure, which may deter business from increasing employment levels or investment expenditure. The Australian experience of the late 1970s and mid-1980s demonstrates that increased business profitability does not necessarily lead to investment in appropriate employment-generating areas.

With regard to the relationship between relative wage levels and unemployment, most interest in Australian economic debate has centred on youth–adult and male–female relativities. We have seen that youth unemployment rates in Australia are around three times the rate for adults. Whether a fall in the wages of youth relative to adults would do much to reduce the natural disadvantage youth has in the labour market is open to question. Additionally, such a change in wage relativities may only provide a substitution of youth for adults in employment without increasing total employment.

With regard to male–female relativities, the years following the equal pay legislation of the mid-1970s have seen an increase in average female earnings relative to average male earnings (although average female earnings are still only around 80 per cent of average male earnings). Contrary to what simple economic theory would predict, female employment has grown more strongly than male employment over this period (although much of the growth has been in part-time female employment).

Whatever the contribution of inappropriate relative wage levels to the relative unemployment rates of different labour market groups, one thing is clear. If the economy does not grow sufficiently to generate adequate growth in aggregate employment, changes in relative wages can do no more than shuffle around the incidence of unemployment. While an equitable sharing of the incidence of unemployment is a valid policy aim, reductions in the aggregate level of unemployment require policies that lift the constraints on economic growth.

Labour market flows

Some useful insights into the dynamics of changes in unemployment can be gained by modelling the aggregate labour market in terms of labour market flows. If we define the three possible labour market states: 'Not in the labour force'(N), 'employed'(E), and 'unemployed'(U); then, as individuals change their status, we can then define the six labour market flows: NE (from 'not in the labour force' to 'employed'), EN (from 'employed' to 'not in the labour force'), and (similarly) UE, EU, UN, and NU. Figure 4.2 represents the flows diagrammatically.

The change in the number of individuals unemployed can be expressed as the difference between the flows into and out of U. That is:

$$\Delta U = EU + NU - UE - UN.$$

Because a significant proportion of the sample each month is retained in the following month, the ABS monthly labour force survey provides estimates of the aggregate changes in labour market status, that is, estimates of the aggregate labour market flows. The numbers in brackets in Figure 4.2 are the estimates for the changes in labour market status between January 1989 and February 1989. This period is selected as an example because it illustrates a

Figure 4.2 Labour market flows

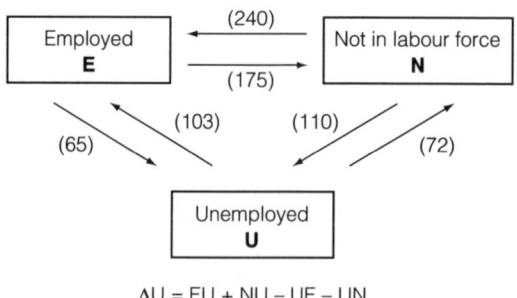

$$\Delta U = EU + NU - UE - UN$$

Note: Figures in brackets are for Jan.–Feb. 1989 and denote thousands of persons.

significant characteristic of the Australian labour market: its dynamism. For although there was no change in the total number of people unemployed between the two surveys, 765 000 individuals experienced a change in their labour market status—the net flows into and out of unemployment were offsetting.

The picture of the Australian labour market that emerges from these and other data on employment experience collected by the ABS is one where although the majority of workers are in long-tenure employment, a significant minority of the work force changes jobs frequently. Many workers have jobs with short duration or quit voluntarily and experience brief spells of unemployment before commencing their next short-tenure job. That is to say, a significant minority of workers have short-tenure, high-turnover jobs—jobs with 'secondary labour market' characteristics.

The behaviour of the various labour market flows over the business cycle provides insights into the characteristics of labour market recessions and the sources of increased unemployment. Despite the popular conception that dramatic increases in unemployment are the result of large-scale retrenchments and plant closures, these phenomena are more closely related to structural change rather than cyclical downturns in the economy. Indeed, the EU flow may actually decrease in a labour market recession where, for example, there is a fall in the number of voluntary resignations (because workers are pessimistic about finding a new job) which is greater than any increase in lay-offs and retrenchments. However, the UN flow is likely to increase in a labour market recession because of the 'discouraged worker' effects.

The main reasons for cyclical increases in unemployment are typically increases in the NU flow (as employment opportunities for new entrants disappear) and decreases in the UE flow (because of the lack of new jobs to replace completed short-tenure jobs). Rather than a brief, 'between-jobs' spell of unemployment, 'secondary market' workers have increased difficulty in finding a new job. And, as has been emphasised above, the probability of a worker experiencing a UE status change decreases with the length of unemployment.

Although the flows in previous recessions in Australia have tended to follow this cyclical pattern, the labour force survey statistics for the recession of the early 1990s suggest some atypical characteristics. Because the downturn in aggregate economic activity has coincided with a period of enormous structural change involving much labour shedding, plant closures and retrenchments appear to have played a much more significant role in the increase in unemployment than is typical of a cyclical downturn. This is evidenced by the high EU flows and the significant numbers of middle-aged, male, white-collar and long-tenure workers (i.e. 'primary labour market' workers) going into the unemployment pool.

Current policy

In December 1993 the Australian Government released a detailed discussion paper, 'Restoring Full Employment' (hereafter referred to as the Green Paper). The Green Paper provides an assessment of recent unemployment policy and recommendations for future policy.

The Green Paper sees Australian government policy as providing a two-pronged attack on the problems associated with unemployment. First, policy aims to provide the capacity for, and achievement of, high rates of growth in aggregate activity. The necessity of high GDP growth rates for reductions in unemployment has been discussed above. Second, since overall reductions in the level of unemployment will be only slowly achieved (even assuming the most optimistic growth outcomes), policy also has to be directed toward achieving an equitable sharing of the burden of unemployment. This requires social service benefits systems and labour market schemes which address the problems of the long-term unemployed and other disadvantaged groups.

With regard to the first policy objective, the aims of policy are to provide macroeconomic policy settings (fiscal, monetary and wages policies), and to instigate microeconomic reforms so as to allow a high rate of growth in aggregate economic activity. The twin constraints on the pursuit of pro-growth demand policies (expansionary fiscal and monetary policies) are the balance of payments constraint and the extent to which the supply side of the economy can respond in a non-inflationary way to increases in demand—hence the importance given to microeconomic reform by the Government in its unemployment strategy. Whereas in the 1980s policy relied on a centralised wages policy and currency devaluation to provide for non-inflationary growth within the balance of payments constraint, the emphasis is now on reforms to product and labour markets (with a decentralised approach to wage determination), in the pursuit of allocative and cost efficiencies and gains in international competitiveness. Successful microeconomic reforms will raise the potential 'speed limit' of the economy—by containing the threat of inflation and easing the balance of payments constraint.

The Green Paper is optimistic in its assessment of both the gains already achieved and the prospects for further gains from microeconomic reform in easing the twin constraints on GDP growth. It suggests that 'it should be possible to increase the annual average rate of economic growth achievable over the remainder of the decade to between 4.5 and 5 per cent' (p. 70). A less optimistic assessment might doubt whether the Australian economy is yet capable of sustaining such a growth rate without a reawakening of inflationary pressures and a deterioration of the current account on the balance of payments. Even with increased productive efficiency and lower inflation in relation to our trading partners, these gains may well be translated into a higher valued exchange rate with no consequent gain in international competitiveness. Without more significant structural changes in the composition of its exports and imports than has so far been achieved, Australia's 'affordable' growth rate remains dependent on the vagaries of the world trading environment and international commodity markets. Such restructuring may require a more pro-active industry policy with a strategy for the *composition* of Australia's investment expenditure in productive capacity (see Stegman 1990).

Policy with regard to unemployment aims to provide labour market programs targeted at retraining and the alleviation of labour market disadvantages, and seeks to ensure that the benefits system recognises current social conditions and does not penalise the taking up of employment opportunities at the margin.[5]

Since much of the microeconomic reform which has occurred has involved labour shedding and restructuring plant closures, thus exacerbating the problems of structural and long-term unemployment, the Green paper recommends substantially increased expenditure on targeted labour market programs.[6]

In May 1994 the Government presented a major policy statement on unemployment and industry policy—the White Paper entitled 'Working Nation'. The White Paper, in accordance with Green Paper recommendations, places a heavy emphasis on targeted labour market programs to improve the relative position of the long-term unemployed and other disadvantaged groups. The main elements in this regard are a 'Jobs Compact' guaranteeing an employment placement of between six and twelve months to those who have been without work for more than eighteen months, wage subsidies for the employment of the long-term unemployed, and the implementation of a National Training Wage (at 80 per cent of the relevant award) in return for the facilitation by employers of on-the-job or off-the-job accredited training.

With regard to the achievement of the economic growth rates necessary to reduce the aggregate unemployment rate (and to provide the budget revenues necessary to fund the targeted labour market programs), the White Paper echoes the optimism of the Green Paper. The Government is apparently confident that macroeconomic policy settings and the ongoing processes of microeconomic reform can provide for sustained unemployment-reducing growth rates without hitting the current account or inflation constraints. The Government has seen no need for a more pro-active industry strategy—the only concessions in the industry component of the White Paper are a commitment to end further tariff cuts after the 5 per cent target is reached in 1996, and some minor upward adjustment to investment allowances, especially for small firms.

Notes

1 The tables and figures and some of the associated analysis appeared in Stegman (1993).
2 Analysis of the links between unemployment and crime is presented in Crow et al. (1989).
3 See Whitfield (1987) for a survey of such research.
4 For analysis of the unemployment–vacancies relationship see Harper (1980) and King (1986).
5 See the Green Paper, chapter 8, for analysis of the way current benefits policy might be improved.
6 See the Green Paper, chapters 4–6, for details on labour market program recommendations.

Recommended reading

Australian Economic Review 1994, Policy forum 1st quarter 1994, pp. 6–46
Committee on Employment Opportunities 1993, *Restoring Full Employment: A Discussion Paper* (the Green Paper), AGPS, Canberra
'Symposium: options to reduce long term unemployment', *The Economic and Labour Relations Review*, Vol. 5, No. 1, 1994
Commonwealth of Australia 1994, *Working Nation: Policies and Programs* (the White Paper), AGPS, Canberra
Whitfield, K. (ed.) 1989, *Contemporary Issues in Labour Economics*, Harper & Row, Sydney; see Chapter 2

5 The balance of payments and international debt
Colm Kearney

Australia is an open economy, that is, it is open to international trade in goods and services and in financial assets. The goods and services linkage arises from the fact that some of Australia's production is exported to foreign countries, while some goods and/or services that are consumed or invested in Australia are produced overseas and imported. The financial assets linkage arises because the actions of international investors who seek the best return on their assets have fundamental effects on the determination of Australia's exchange rate, on the ability of the Reserve Bank (RB) to affect interest rates by manipulating the stance of monetary policy, and on the level of national income and employment.

The links that exist between international economic and financial developments and the pace of economic activity in Australia are very powerful. A potent example of the power of these links can be found in the origins of the recession in Australia in the early 1990s. During the late 1980s, Australia's current account balance deteriorated very sharply. It went from a deficit of $10.2 billion (3.8 per cent of GDP) in 1987/88 to a deficit of $17.6 billion (5.5 per cent of GDP) in 1988/89, and it further deteriorated to a deficit of $21.6 billion (6.0 per cent of GDP) in 1989/90. The Government became alarmed at this deterioration and responded by implementing tight fiscal and monetary policies. The Government introduced four consecutive years of fiscal surplus beginning in 1987/88, and the interest rate on 90-day bank bills rose from 13.15 per cent in 1987/88 to 18.30 per cent in 1988/89. This policy mix succeeded in reducing the current account deficit to $15.4 billion (3.8 per cent of GDP) in 1992/93.

But the cost of this was that the policy stance contributed significantly to the depth of the recession that Australia experienced in the early 1990s. The economy is still paying the price for this in terms of continued high levels and duration of unemployment.

The balance of payments accounts

The balance of payments is a record of all transactions of the residents of a country with the rest of the world. There are two main accounts in the balance of payments: the current account and the capital account.

The current account records trade in goods and services, as well as other net incomes and transfer payments. Adding these together we arrive at the current account balance. The current account is in surplus if the sum of payments into Australia exceeds the sum of payments out of Australia in the current account. It is in deficit if the opposite situation obtains. The capital account records purchases and sales of assets, such as stocks, bonds and land. There is a capital account surplus—also known as a net capital inflow—when receipts from the sale of Australian assets exceed our payments for purchases of foreign assets. There is a capital account deficit—also known as a net capital outflow—when the opposite situation occurs on the capital account. As we shall see, the usual situation in Australia is a current account deficit and a capital account surplus.

The current account

Table 5.1 presents the format of the current account of the balance of payments. The figures provided are for the year 1992/93. The current account consists of (1) the merchandise trade balance and (2) the services balance which together add up to (3) the goods and services trade balance. To this we add (4) the net income and (5) the net transfer balance to get (6) the overall current account balance.

The merchandise trade balance consists of merchandise exports (entered with a positive sign) less merchandise imports (entered with a negative sign). The word merchandise refers to physical commodities which you can see packed up at the docks to be loaded onto or unloaded from ships, or at the airports to be airfreighted into or out of the country. Services include freight and tourism as amongst the most important traded services. Adding these together gives the balance of trade in goods and services. The net income category refers to income earned by domestic residents from non-residents (credits) less the income earned by non-residents from residents (debits). In general terms, net income refers to the net returns payable

Table 5.1 The current account 1992/93

		$m
1	Merchandise trade	
	Exports of goods	60 037
	Imports of goods	59 435
	Merchandise balance	600
2	Services balance	−2 708
3	Balance on goods and services	−2 108
4	Net income	−14 078
5	Net unrequited transfers	739
6	Current account balance	−15 447

Source: ABS.

to the owners of assets and/or resources. In the current account, net income is further divided into (i) investment income, (ii) other property income and (iii) labour and other income.

In 1992/93, Australian residents exported over $60 billion worth of merchandise and imported just over $59 billion worth, leaving the merchandise trade balance in surplus by $0.6 billion. The net services balance was in deficit to the tune of $2.7 billion. Adding these together yielded a goods and services deficit of $2.1 billion. With a net income deficit of $14.1 billion and a small net transfer surplus of $0.7 billion, the overall current account deficit for the year came in at $15.4 billion (which amounted to 3.8 per cent of GDP).

The capital account

Table 5.2 presents the format of the capital account of the balance of payments. As with the current account, the figures provided are for the year 1992/93. The capital account consists of (1) official transactions and (2) non-official transactions. The official transactions are further divided into general government foreign investments and overseas borrowings, and the RB's foreign reserve assets. The non-official transactions are the capital transactions of the private sector. They comprise net direct investment and net portfolio investment. By adding (1) and (2) we get (3), the overall capital account balance. The balancing item records the sum of unidentifiable transactions, and this amount is equal to the difference between the current account and the capital account.

In 1992/93, the general government sector increased its net reliance on foreign funds by $9.1 billion, while the RB raised its foreign reserve assets by just under $4 billion. Together, this amounted to a capital account inflow of $13.1 billion in the official

Table 5.2 The capital account 1992/93

	$m
1 Official transactions	13 105
General government	9 143
RB reserve assets	3 962
2 Non-official	961
Net direct investment	2 044
Net portfolio investment	−1 083
3 Capital account balance	14 066
Balancing item	1 381

transactions component of the capital account. This was accompanied by a non-official (i.e. private sector) net capital inflow of just under $1 billion, made up by a $2.0 billion increase in net direct investment into Australia and a $1.1 billion increase in net portfolio investment abroad. Overall, therefore, Australia recorded a capital account surplus of $14.1 billion. Adding the balancing item of $1.4 billion, we see that the current account deficit in Table 5.1 is matched by the capital account surplus in Table 5.2.

Let us now focus on the relationship between the current account and the capital account. Suppose Australia runs persistent balance of trade deficits, which means that it continually imports more than it exports. The country is then living beyond its means—it is not managing to pay the rest of the world in exports for the imports which it enjoys. Suppose in addition that the country runs a persistent capital account surplus of equal magnitude to the balance of trade deficit. This means that overseas residents are accumulating Australian assets at a greater rate than domestic residents are accumulating foreign assets. In other words, foreigners are financing Australia's current trade deficit by acquiring domestic assets such as bonds, stocks, businesses and land. These foreign investors will require a return on their investments in the form of interest, dividends, profits, rent and possibly capital gains. The return which they are paid on these assets appears in the balance of payments accounts as a negative entry in the net income component of the current account. This acts to worsen the current account balance given the trade performance and imposes a greater need to attract foreign investment.

Australia's foreign indebtedness

The process just outlined determines the country's external debt position. Persistent current account deficits require persistent capital

Table 5.3 Australia's historical balance of payments ($A millions, annual averages)

	1959/60–1968/69	1969/70–1978/79	1979/80–1989/90	1992/93
Goods and services balance	61.5	1003.7	−1370.4	6388
Current account	−620.4	−1508.2	−10 819.3	−15 446
Capital account	525.7	1260.4	8972.3	14 066

Source: Reserve Bank of Australia.

account surpluses to finance them. Unless these capital account surpluses are generated by foreigners buying Australian land (i.e. Australia continually 'sells off part of the farm' to finance its deficits), then the country's level of international indebtedness will continually rise.

Table 5.3 presents a summary of Australia's balance of payments performance over the past 30 years. In the 1960s and 1970s, Australia's trade balance on goods and services was in surplus, but the current account was in deficit. In the 1980s the goods and services trade balance deteriorated into deficit and the current account deficit worsened. This was financed by increasing capital account surpluses. This means that foreign residents have financed Australia's current account deficits by purchasing more Australian assets than domestic residents have acquired foreign assets.

Can this situation continue indefinitely? The answer is yes—as long as foreigners are willing to continue to lend to Australia under similar arrangements, that is, as long as they retain confidence in the working of our economy and in our ability to pay the return on their investments. If for some reason foreign investors lose confidence in the Australian economy, our exchange rate will collapse or we will have to dramatically raise our interest rates. Neither of these scenarios is conducive to achieving strong output and employment growth.

Tables 5.4 and 5.5 present developments in Australia's international indebtedness and debt servicing ratios since the beginning of the 1980s. The presentation in Table 5.4 is useful in so far as it allows us to see the extent to which the economy's total net external debt is due mostly to the Government or the private sector. As we shall see, this is an important policy question. The usefulness of Table 5.5 lies in its information about the size of the servicing burden which the overall debt position imposes on the economy.

Look at Table 5.4 first. It shows official, non-official and total gross external debt, external assets and net external debt in billions of dollars. Row 3 of the table shows that official net external debt rose from −$0.9 billion in 1980/81 to $35 billion in 1991/92, while

Table 5.4 Australia's foreign indebtedness ($ billions)

	1980/ 81	1981/ 82	1982/ 83	1983/ 84	1984/ 85	1985/ 86	1986/ 87	1987/ 88	1988/ 89	1989/ 90	1990/ 91	1991/ 92
Official external debt	4.8	5.7	7.7	8.9	14.9	23.4	29.9	32.8	33.7	41.0	43.9	56.0
Official external assets	5.7	6.5	10.8	12.4	13.6	13.2	18.0	20.8	21.3	24.5	22.5	21.0
Official net external debt	−0.9	−0.8	−3.1	−3.5	1.3	10.2	11.9	12.0	12.4	16.5	21.4	23.0
Non-official external debt	10.3	18.5	23.2	35.2	52.6	68.6	75.0	84.3	103.3	137.2	145.6	152.6
Non-official external assets	0.9	1.3	1.8	1.8	2.6	3.8	4.5	5.9	7.5	12.9	14.3	15.3
Non-official net external debt	9.4	17.2	26.5	33.4	49.9	64.8	70.6	78.4	95.9	124.3	131.3	137.3
Total external debt	15.2	24.2	35.9	44.1	67.4	92.0	104.9	117.0	137.0	178.2	189.4	208.6
Total external assets	6.7	7.8	12.5	14.2	16.3	17.0	22.5	26.7	28.8	37.4	36.7	36.3
Total net external debt	8.5	16.4	23.4	29.9	51.2	75.0	82.4	90.3	108.2	140.8	152.7	172.3

Source: ABS.

Table 5.5 Australia's debt interest payments and service ratios

	1980/ 81	1981/ 82	1982/ 83	1983/ 84	1984/ 85	1985/ 86	1986/ 87	1987/ 88	1988/ 89	1989/ 90	1990/ 91	1991/ 92	1992/ 93
Total net external debt as percentage of GDP	6.2	10.6	13.8	15.5	23.8	31.4	32.6	32.3	34.7	35.5	37.1	39.3	42.9
Official interest payments ($6)	0.4	0.4	0.6	0.7	1.0	1.6	2.6	3.4	3.5	3.6	3.8	3.9	3.6
Non-official interest payments ($6)	0.8	1.4	2.3	3.0	4.4	5.5	5.7	5.8	7.5	10.0	11.2	9.5	7.9
Total interest payments ($6)	1.2	1.8	2.9	3.7	5.4	7.1	8.3	9.2	11.0	13.6	15.0	13.4	11.5
Total debt service ratio (per cent)	5.4	8.0	11.5	13.2	15.4	18.3	19.4	18.3	20.4	22.0	26.3	21.1	16.9

Source: ABS.

row 6 of the table shows that non-official net external debt rose from $9.4 billion in 1980/81 to $137 billion in 1991/92. Overall, therefore, as row 9 of the table reveals, the economy's total net external debt rose by $163.8 billion over the period from 1980/81 to 1991/92. This was made up from a $35.9 billion rise in official net external debt and a $127.9 billion rise in non-official net external debt. In summary, during the period under consideration, Australia's net foreign debt rose very markedly, with the private sector's net foreign indebtedness rising at over 3.5 times the rise in official net foreign indebtedness.

Looking now at Table 5.5, we can see that row 1 reveals that the economy's total net external debt rose very markedly over the period from 6.2 per cent of total GDP in 1980/81 to 42.9 per cent of GDP in 1992/93. During this period, total net interest payments rose from $1.2 billion to $11.3 billion, with non-official net interest payments rising, as expected, to higher levels than official net interest payments. The last row of the table shows how the economy's debt service ratio has evolved over the period. The debt service ratio is measured as total net interest payments as a percentage of exports, and it is designed to show how the economy can finance its net interest payments by export earnings. Over the period from 1980/81–1992/93, Australia's debt service ratio rose from 5.4 per cent to 16.9 per cent. In summary, during the period under consideration, Australia's debt to GDP ratio rose almost sevenfold while its debt service ratio trebled. The latter rose at half the rate of the former due to good export growth and lower international interest rates.

The debt debate: does the current account matter?

We have seen in the discussion thus far that Australia is traditionally a capital-importing country which runs persistent current account deficits accompanied by capital account surpluses. Over recent decades, the size of our current account deficits and accompanying capital account surpluses has risen substantially. This has led to substantial rises in the country's level of net foreign indebtedness. The question which we pose in this section is whether Australia's current account deficits, capital account surpluses and their consequent rise in foreign indebtedness are a justifiable cause of concern to economic policymakers. In other words, does the current account and foreign debt matter? There are two alternative views on this issue: the 'traditional view' and the 'new view'.

The 'traditional view' of the current account and foreign indebtedness is that they do matter. According to this view, which is shared by the Government and the majority of economists, policymakers should monitor the situation and take corrective action to prevent excessive rises if and when it is deemed necessary. Two problems associated with this 'traditional view' are first, at what stage is corrective action warranted, and second, what kind of action should be taken.

By contrast, the so-called 'new view' of the current account and international indebtedness is that they do not matter if they are caused primarily by private sector behaviour. Given the recent emergence and growing popularity of the 'new view' amongst some economists in Australia, we shall provide a summary and evaluation of the 'new view' in this section.

One of the most influential proponents of the 'new view' of the current account in Australia has been Professor John Pitchford (1989, 1990). He argues that those who claim that the current account deficit *is* a problem with which policymakers ought to concern themselves have not properly established their case. In addition, he argues that if this case could be established, its remedy would lie entirely within a set of microeconomic policy initiatives which are aimed specifically at removing distortions which impede the economy's overall performance, rather than being directed specifically at the current account deficit.

This 'new view' of the current account constitutes a powerful challenge to the traditional and still prevailing policy orthodoxy in Australia. If this view is the correct one, recent policy settings together with their economic effects constitute an error of catastrophic proportions. But the challenge goes even further than this. It strikes at the most fundamental cornerstones of economic policymaking in economies which are open to international trade in commodities, services and financial assets. Furthermore, it is clear from the writings of Professor Pitchford, and from the responses which it has thus far elicited, that the challenge has not yet been met.

It is useful to commence our evaluation of the 'new view' by writing down the basic and well-known accounting identity which describes the flow of national income in terms of the three basic sectors in the economy, namely the domestic private sector, the government and the foreign sector.

$$Y = C^p + I^p + C^g + I^g + X - M + F \qquad (1)$$

Here, Y denotes gross domestic product, C, I, X, M and F denote respectively consumption, investment, exports, imports and net income on net foreign assets, and superscripts 'p' and 'g' denote the private and government sectors respectively. This identity states that the flow of gross domestic product is the sum of consumption and investment activity carried on by the private and government sectors, net exports and net earnings on net overseas assets. By defining the three sectors' savings as,

$$S^p = Y - T - C^p$$
$$S^g = T - C^g - I^g \qquad (2)$$
$$S^f = M - X - F$$

we can rewrite the initial identity in one of two forms:

$$I^p = S^p + S^g + S^f \qquad (3)$$
$$S^f = (I^p - S^p) - S^g \qquad (3')$$

Identity (3) states the obvious fact that domestic private investment must be financed by the savings of one or more of the three sectors, while (3') states that the current account deficit (S^f) is the sum of the private sector's deficit ($I^p - S^p$) plus the government's fiscal deficit ($-S^g$).

Identity (3') has been the basis for the recently popular 'twin deficits' analysis of current account performance. The argument goes that if ($I^p - S^p$) is close to zero and/or is stable over time, then S^f will be closely related to $-S^g$ so that lower fiscal deficits will be at least necessary in order to secure improved current account performance.[1] The reason for mentioning this, however, is to point out that the so-called 'new view' of the current account adopts a different tact with respect to identity (3').

In its usual rendition, proponents of the 'new view' model a perfectly frictionless economy with no government so the term S^g drops out of (3'). In this framework, variations in the current account deficit (S^f) simply reflect the optimal savings and investment decisions ($I^p - S^p$) of rational private sector economic agents. As such, according to the 'new view', the current account ought not to be a concern of government policy. If it is, it must only be because the Government has introduced distortions which are responsible for inducing the private sector to make socially suboptimal decisions which are reflected in the current account. But this picture is partial at best. It is based upon the implicit assumption that current account performance is determined by conditions in the domestic markets for goods, services and financial assets. It neglects to take account of the fact that current account performance is also determined by conditions in foreign markets. For example, imperfect competition, barriers to entry, economies of scale and so on may well impede the ability of domestic firms to generate export revenues which could finance their imports or their investments.

Recent developments of this 'new view', which underlie Pitchford's analysis of Australia's current account performance, are based upon the inter-temporal optimising approach which has been pioneered by, inter alia, Frenkel and Razin (1986). In this framework, rational individuals who inhabit a perfectly competitive distortion-free world act in order to maximise the discounted flow of utility from their present and future income streams subject to an inter-temporal budget constraint. In Pitchford (1989), the economy consists of one good (which is produced and consumed, but not invested), one net asset and any number of identical consumers. If short-term temporary changes in income occur in this model, individuals will react in order to smooth their consumption streams. The difference between income (plus or minus interest payments on the net asset) and consumption is the current account balance. Thus, the current account deficit (and net foreign indebtedness) will rise when income is temporarily low and it will decline again when income is temporarily high.

The essential message which emerges from this analysis is that the current account deficit represents the culmination of private individuals' inter-temporal utility-maximising consumption and saving decisions. There can consequently be no justifiable role for policymakers to attempt to achieve some different outcome for the current account. Any policy initiative which aims to do otherwise will necessarily be welfare-reducing. In Pitchford's own words:

> If firms and individuals are making the best possible spending, saving, investment and borrowing plans in the circumstances they face and the result is a current account deficit or surplus, why should this be a matter for public concern and intervention? The individuals involved and the financial institutions they deal with are almost certainly in the best position to assess the implications of all this borrowing and lending. Intervention will be justified only if some form of market failure can be established. That is not to say that mistakes are not made, especially when expectations are not realised, rather that mistakes will be less under private decision making than under a scheme which attempts to regulate decisions or impose solutions (Pitchford 1990, p. 76).

The policy implications which flow from this model are clear. To the extent that the model constitutes an accurate representation of real economic conditions, governments ought not to attempt to engineer current account outcomes which differ from those already prevailing unless the latter are caused by some kind of market failure or by previous policy errors. Again, in Pitchford's own words:

> Rather than condemning current account deficits as such, economists

investigating them should aim to find whether and to what extent they are the symptoms of distortions, regulations or policy errors. If they are none of these, the presumption must be that they arise from the desirable activity of international trade in saving and investment (Pitchford 1990, p. 8).

Pitchford proceeds to argue that if such distortions, regulations and/or policy errors can be identified which have impacted negatively on a country's current account performance, the appropriate response for government policy is to remove them. More specifically, government should not risk committing further policy errors by invoking macroeconomic policy initiatives aimed at improving the current account balance in the absence of microeconomic reforms which have the objective of eliminating any identified distortions and/or regulations. Once again, in Pitchford's own words:

Current account deficits and the debt they generate are influenced by conditions ruling in the economy. For example, there may be a tax system which discourages saving so that the current account deficit will be higher than under some superior system. The remedy is to reform the tax system. Using aggregate demand management to reduce the deficit is hardly a solution as it will cause all sorts of problems elsewhere, such as slower growth and higher unemployment and once demand restraint is eased the old deficit will re-emerge. If the deficit is a symptom of something undesirable the solution is to treat the undesired cause. The focus of attention on the current account as a major target of economic policy is therefore superficial and misplaced. The really hard task is to disentangle the factors affecting the current account balance to decide where, if at all, corrective policy is needed (Pitchford 1990, p. 42).

In summary, therefore, Pitchford puts forward the appealing and strong argument that if current account outcomes represent the culmination of rational decision-making by inter-temporally optimising private sector agents, government should not attempt to achieve alternative outcomes. Rather, it should eliminate any identified distortions, regulations and previous policy errors—not because this will impact positively on the current account balance, but because such initiatives will improve the overall workings of the economy.

This policy prescription is powerful in itself as well as in the extent to which it deviates from the prevailing policy orthodoxy which has existed in Australia over the best part of the last decade. Having outlined the essential force of the 'Pitchford line' it is important to question how robust the prescriptions are in the face of changes to the model structure.

Let us begin by noting that the absence of more than one good in the model is of no consequence; introducing a tradeable and a non-tradeable good, for example, will not alter the result. The same argument applies to the absence of more than one asset in the model; introducing money and possibly other assets (along with their yields including the exchange rate) will not alter the result as long as there are no nominal rigidities in the model. The same argument also applies to the absence of investment. In summary, these features of the model are commendable in so far as they simplify the analysis at no significant cost in terms of the generality of the results.

Some economists may criticise the assumption that agents make their inter-temporal decisions on the basis of rational expectations about future events. This criticism is hard to justify because the assumption of rational expectations dominates the other expectational behavioural assumptions which have previously prevailed in economic theory. Other economists might argue that there exists a role for government to intervene in this world if it takes a sufficiently long-term view of desirable outcomes for the current account deficit. Once again, this view is questionable because it is unrealistic to expect that governments might be possessed of planning horizons of the necessary magnitude.

Other economists again point to a critical element of the 'Pitchford line' which concerns the extent to which economic shocks deliver permanent as opposed to temporary disturbances to inter-temporal income flows. If the disturbance is permanent, consumption behaviour must adjust. Dornbusch (1983) makes this point. It is, however, impossible to be sure about which of these scenarios is correct until time has elapsed to pass judgment. The dangers of failing to adjust consumption patterns in response to a permanent decline in income flows which is mistakenly perceived to be temporary are clear. The international evidence which exists indicates that the process of stabilising the external constraint of an indebted economy is more costly the longer the adjustment is delayed.

But does the concern of minimising this adjustment cost belong to government rather than to the private institutions which incur the foreign indebtedness? Is it appropriate for government to monitor the economy's foreign debt situation and to institute policy initiatives to ensure that it does not grow at an unsustainable rate? Pitchford would argue that it is not. Even if it wished, government may not have access to better information than the private sector, and even if it did, this does not imply that government would be more successful than the private sector in carrying out the task. For present purposes, we do not take issue with Pitchford on this point.

The most fundamental and far-reaching assumptions which Pitchford makes consistently throughout his analysis are twofold, namely that all production throughout the world occurs under conditions of constant returns to scale, and that all markets are perfectly competitive. These assumptions constitute the cornerstone of traditional theories of international trade which attempt to explain trade between countries as emanating from differences in technologies (as in Ricardian theory), in relative factor endowments (as in Heckscher-Ohlin theory), and in tastes.

But these traditional trade theories have recently been questioned in terms of their ability to explain modern trade patterns. As Krugman (1986) amongst others has pointed out, they cannot adequately explain two-way cross-country trade in similar products, nor can they adequately explain trade between countries with similar technologies, relative factor endowments and/or tastes. And since a very significant proportion of world trade occurs at the intra-industry level and between similar countries, the relevance and usefulness of these traditional theories is now regarded as severely limited.

Given the fundamental nature of these assumptions together with their far-reaching policy implications, and given that the central focus of Pitchford's work is on the statistical measure of trading performance, namely the current account balance, it is remarkable that nowhere in his analysis does he consider the implications of relaxing them. This fact alone renders the relevance and usefulness of the 'Pitchford line' as being questionable. In short, Pitchford bases his policy prescriptions about how government ought to respond to a country's trading performance on a model framework which is itself incapable of adequately explaining a significant proportion of modern trade patterns.

The above point can be put another way. The 'Pitchford line' is derived from a model in which government intervention to secure some target current account outcome must of necessity be welfare-reducing because the private sector is already acting to maximise its welfare. But the assumptions which Pitchford makes in order to derive this result are precisely those which cannot adequately explain modern trade patterns. More specifically, when technology is characterised by constant returns to scale, two-way trade across similar countries must itself be welfare-reducing by the amount of transportation costs. So in Pitchford's own terms, much of modern international trading patterns implies that the private sector is *not* maximising its welfare.

Economies of scale

The realisation that international trade in commodities and services may result from economies of scale rather than from (or in addition to) differences in tastes or comparative advantage (whether based on technology or factor endowment) is not new in international economics. Helpman (1984) and Krugman (1986) provide a summary of historical work. Although the early literature was cast in partial equilibrium analysis, more recent developments have employed general equilibrium analysis to show how economies of scale can result in geographical specialisation within imperfectly competitive industries which form an important basis for a significant proportion of modern international trading patterns.

It is interesting to note, however, as Krugman points out, that although the second-best world of imperfect competition removes the inevitability of the gains from free trade being necessarily obtained, it does tend to enhance rather than detract from the potential benefits of free trade. In the current context, however, the important point is that regardless of the above, a second-best world introduces the possibility of government intervention being justified on welfare grounds. This is precisely the point which is not acknowledged in the 'Pitchford line'. In Krugman's words:

> ... showing that free trade is better than no trade is not the same thing as showing that free trade is better than sophisticated government intervention. The view that free trade is the best of all possible policies is part of the general case for laissez-faire in a market economy, and rests on the proposition that markets are efficient. If increasing returns and imperfect competition are necessary parts of the explanation of international trade, however, we are living in a second-best world where government intervention can in principle improve on market outcomes (Krugman 1977, p. 34).

Although the issue of economies of scale is complex, it obviously cannot be neglected in any useful analysis of modern international trading patterns and policy prescriptions. In addition to the traditional static notion of economies of scale, economists have recently focused attention on dynamic economies of scale such as those implied by R&D activities and by the so-called experience curve. Of perhaps even greater significance, however, in terms of explaining modern trading patterns, is the extent to which economies of scale are external or internal to the firm.

If economies of scale are external to the firm, markets can still be perfectly competitive and it has long been known (see, for example, Corden (1974)) that protection may be justifiable in this case. As Krugman (1977) points out, however, such measures are second-best by definition whereas the first-best solution inevitably involves the removal of the distortion. On this point, Pitchford is entirely correct. If the economies of scale are internal to the firm, however, the implication for market structure is that the assumption of perfect competition can no longer be upheld. This opens up a whole range of possible optimal trading strategies between and amongst firms including oligopolistic pricing which deviates from marginal costs. This in itself renders the 'Pitchford line' inapplicable. It also, however, introduces the likelihood of strategic game-playing in which firms act with the explicit objective of inducing their rivals to respond in certain ways. The upshot of this is that the range of possible behaviour amongst and between firms as well as their responses to government policy initiatives is much richer than encompassed in the more naive models which assume that all markets are perfectly competitive. In this world, it is far from clear that government intervention is necessarily welfare-reducing.

This brings us to Pitchford's fall-back position, namely that even if government intervention is warranted, it is far from clear that government is possessed of the degree of knowledge necessary to ensure that the results of its actions will be better than if it refrained from acting in the first place. This is a formidable fall-back position. There are many examples of situations in which governments have not managed to improve upon market outcomes by their interventions in the workings of the economy. However, there are also many examples of situations where governments have managed to improve upon market outcomes. The problems of unemployment, inflation and inequity are areas where considerable degrees of success have been achieved. In addition, many governments have enacted successful industry and trade development strategies. In summary, therefore, the argument boils down to whether (if it can be established that the current account and foreign indebtedness ought to be of concern to policymakers) governments have the expertise and commitment to take appropriate corrective action. The debate continues.

Current Australian trade policy

Having now identified Australia's trade and foreign debt position and the economic issues at stake in formulating and designing appropriate policy actions, it is now time to describe the current policy approach to trade. It is worth observing by way of introduction that in today's world of rapid and cheap international communication and transport systems, the availability of knowledge about production, consumption and relative price patterns together with declining transport costs mean that if governments did not interfere in the trade process, the natural tendency would be for free trade to emerge. In reality, however, governments do interfere in the international trade arena for four main reasons:

- Industries which face very stiff international competition under free trade lobby their governments to impose tariffs in order to protect them. They argue that without the tariffs, cheap foreign imports would flood into the country, worsening the economy's current account performance, raising the level of foreign indebtedness and reducing employment by forcing domestic producers out of business. Examples of this are manufacturers in Australia before the 1970s and French farmers in the 1990s.
- Free trade production patterns can compromise other non-economic objectives. For example, the Japanese Government has traditionally pursued a policy of self-sufficiency in basic food as a matter of national security. This has led Japan to impose tariffs on food imports. The recent moves to allow foreign rice into Japan and Korea provide good examples of the difficulties faced by policymakers in reducing this kind of protection.
- Governments pursue strategic trade objectives in order to foster the growth of certain industries. Typically, the industries whose growth is nurtured are those with higher value added than the industries in which the country has a traditional comparative advantage. Examples here are manufactures in India and the automotive and pharmaceutical industries in Australia.
- Governments engage in trade restriction activities in retaliation to the actions of other governments. An example here is the United States wheat subsidy to domestic producers which, in the early 1990s, was aimed at hurting European farmers who were protected by the European Community.

Governments have many trade diversionary measures available to them, including tariffs, quotas, subsidies, voluntary export restraints and a host of other industry-specific and general assistance measures. By far the most commonly used measure, however, is the tariff. The tariff was used extensively by governments in Australia until the commencement of its phasing down in the 1970s. The tariff remains a most popular trade diversion tactic internationally in the 1990s.

Australia's primary industries, agriculture and mining, have always been and remain today amongst the most efficient and competitive in the world. The economy has a natural comparative advantage in primary produce. Australia's manufacturing industry has not traditionally been internationally competitive. Rather on the contrary, previous Australian governments traditionally relied heavily upon tariffs to secure a viable manufacturing sector. It is now widely acknowledged that this policy has failed—after decades of heavy tariff protection, the Australian manufacturing sector in the late 1960s seemed to be getting less rather than more competitive.

Beginning in the early 1970s, reductions began in the rate of tariff protection in Australia.

The Whitlam Government was the first in Australia to recognise the need to pursue this path. It introduced a 25 per cent reduction in tariffs from 1972/73 to 1974/75. From then until 1984/85, the rate of tariff protection trended down at an even pace. From 1984/85, the commitment of the Labor Government to further tariff reductions picked up pace. The latest major initiative occurred in Prime Minister Hawke's industry statement of March 1991—titled 'Building a Competitive Australia'. This statement committed the Government to continued phased reduction in effective protection rates, down to 5 per cent (with a few exceptions) by the end of the 1990s. In the mid-1990s, this program continues with bipartisan support in Federal Parliament.

In addition to the program of domestic tariff reform, the Australian Government also plays an active role in promoting freer trade in the international community. Table 5.6 provides a list of the important country groups and trade associations with which Australia liaises. The Government does this by fostering the growth of free trade associations such as Asia Pacific Economic Cooperation (APEC) and the Cairns Group, and by lobbying other major groups such as the European Community (EC) and the North American Free Trade Agreement (NAFTA).

For example, during the protracted negotiations of the early 1990s on the Uruguay round of the *GATT*, the Australian Government played a very influential role in harnessing the political influence of the Cairns Group. This group comprises many primary producing countries from around the world, and the Government's objective was to forge a strong lobbying group to press for tariff reductions in agriculture. A useful feature of the Cairns Group is that some of its members also belong to other groups and associations such as the Association of South-East Asian Nations (ASEAN), APEC, NAFTA, the Organisation for Economic Cooperation and Development (OECD) and the Organisation of Petroleum Exporting Countries (OPEC). This helps to generate a potent force for change. Unfortunately, however, the influence of the Cairns Group did not extend to the EC, which was a persistent stumbling block in the GATT agricultural trade talks.

In addition to fostering the development of a free trade environment internationally, the Australian Government has recently acted to enhance the consistency of its industry and trade policies and to design them appropriately for today's post-tariff GATT world. The rationale for this policy is that current account performance does matter for the overall performance of the macroeconomy; specifically,

Table 5.6 Composition of main country groups and trade associations

ASEAN Association of South-East Asian Nations
  Brunei, Indonesia, Malaysia, Philippines, Singapore, Thailand

APEC Asia Pacific Economic Cooperation
  ASEAN 6, Australia, Canada, Japan, Korea, New Zealand, USA

Cairns Group Primary Producing Countries
  Argentina, Australia, Brazil, Canada, Chile, Colombia, Fiji, Hungary, Indonesia, Malaysia, New Zealand, Philippines, Thailand, Uruguay

EC European Community
  Belgium, Britain, Denmark, France, Germany, Greece, Ireland, Italy, Luxembourg, Netherlands, Portugal, Spain

EFTA European Free Trade Association
  Austria, Finland, Iceland, Norway, Sweden, Switzerland

FIC Forum Island Countries
  Cook Islands, Fiji, Kiribati, Marshall Islands, Micronesia, Nauru, Niue, Solomon Islands, Tonga, Tuvalu, Vanuatu, Western Samoa

NAFTA North America Free Trade Agreement
  Canada, Mexico, USA

OECD Organisation for Economic Cooperation and Development
  EC, Australia, Austria, Canada, Finland, Iceland, Japan, New Zealand, Norway, Sweden, Switzerland, Turkey, USA

OPEC Organisation of Petroleum Exporting Countries
  Algeria, Ecuador, Gabon, Indonesia, Iran, Iraq, Kuwait, Libya, Nigeria, Qatar, Saudi Arabia, United Arab Emirates, Venezuela

it operates as an external constraint on the economy's growth rate and therefore on the best achievable employment growth.

The ingredients of a successful post-tariff GATT-consistent industry and trade policy are essentially twofold: non-sectoral and sectoral. The non-sectoral ingredient comprises a system of incentives which apply to firms in any industry, the purpose of which is to promote the pursuit of international competitiveness at all stages of the firm's operation. The sectoral ingredient comprises a set of sector specific incentives which are aimed at aiding the restructuring of specific industries as they adjust to the post-tariff environment.

Concerning the non-sectoral component, it is useful to picture the operations of a typical firm as is done in Table 5.7. The depicted firm could be operating in any industry—primary (agriculture or mining), manufacturing (simply or elaborately transformed) or service (aviation, shipping, tourism, health, education or financial). In any case, the operations include (i) the basic design of the product including its innovation and development, (ii) its production using various factors of production including labour and capital, and (iii) its successful marketing and sale. It is entirely appropriate and GATT-consistent for government to put in place a system of

Table 5.7 Australia's current industry and trade policy

Research and Development
- Grants for Industry Research and Development (GIRD)
- Cooperative Research Centres (CRC)
- 150% R&D tax deduction scheme (TDS)

Production
- Best Practice Program (BPP)
  - Capital
    Investment allowances
    Depreciation tax allowances
  - Labour
    Various training schemes

Marketing and Sales
- AUSTRADE
- Export market development grants (EMDG)
- Export Finance Insurance Corporation (EFIC)
- International Trade Enhancement Scheme (ITES)

incentives at each stage of the firm's operations—and most governments do this.

At the stage of product innovation and development it has amongst others: (i) the GIRD (Grants for Industry Research and Development) scheme, (ii) the CRCs (Cooperative Research Centres), and (iii) the 150 per cent TDS (Tax Deduction Scheme for R&D expenditure). At the production stage it has amongst others: (i) various investment incentives, allowances and competitive depreciation regimes, (ii) various training schemes in the labour market, and (iii) the BPP (the Best Practice Program). At the market development stage it has amongst others: (i) AUSTRADE, (ii) EFIC (the Export Finance Insurance Corporation), (iii) the ITES (International Trade Enhancement Scheme), and (iv) the EMDG (Export Market Development Grant) scheme.

Concerning the sectoral component, the Government has had in place a significant number of industry schemes which are aimed at assisting the move towards international competitiveness in a post-tariff era. These schemes include, for example, the car plan, the steel plan and ongoing industry restructuring initiatives in agriculture and other primary industry as well as in manufacturing and service trade.

What is lacking at present in the area of industry and trade policy is a clear elucidation of government policy with respect to (i) the relationship between industry and trade policies, (ii) the underlying economic rationale for the policy structure which is in place, and (iii) a coordinated treatment of the various arms of the existing structure. The purpose of this section has been to point out the essential ingredients of the answer to this problem. By recognising the need for a coordinated set of initiatives, and by clearly elucidating the rationale and operation of the policy, the Government could make further progress towards encouraging the development of an internationally competitive economy.

Summary and conclusions

The purpose of this chapter has been to outline recent developments in Australia's balance of payments and international indebtedness, to summarise the existing policy debate about the appropriateness of the Government's targeting of current account performance and to describe the Government's present trade policy. The chapter first described Australia as being a capital-importing country which tends to run current account deficits accompanied by capital account surpluses. The implication of this for international indebtedness was shown to be a tendency for the level of net foreign debt to rise.

While Australia's net international indebtedness has risen sharply in the past decade, most of this debt has been incurred by the private sector rather than by the Government. There exists controversy amongst academic economists about the extent to which the Government ought to be concerned about Australia's growing indebtedness, and about the appropriate policy response that should be adopted. Proponents of the 'traditional view' of the current account maintain that the Government should monitor the situation and take steps to prevent continual large rises in current account deficits and foreign debt. In contrast to this, proponents of the 'new view' maintain that because most of the debt has been incurred by the private sector, the Government should adopt a more hands-off approach to the problem. This chapter has argued that the models from which are derived the 'new view' policy prescriptions are as yet insufficiently developed to form the basis for reliable policy prescriptions.

Whatever view is taken, the fact is that the Australian Government together with governments throughout the world continue to formulate and implement their international economic policies along the 'traditional view' of the current account. The present Government in Australia is currently redesigning its industry and trade policies to promote international competitiveness of Australian firms in the new post-tariff GATT world of the mid-1990s. In this respect its endeavours are bearing fruit and attracting international commendation.

Note

1 The evidence on this is weak, see Kearney and Monadjemi (1990).

Recommended reading

Applegate, C. 1993, 'Sovereign interference in private sector foreign debt: examples in the 1980s', ANU Centre For Economic Policy Research, Discussion Paper No. 286

Cohen, D. 1985, 'How to evaluate the solvency of an indebted nation', *Economic Policy*, pp. 140–67

Corden, M. 1991, 'Does the current account matter: the old view and the new', *Economic Papers*, vol. 10, pp. 1–19

Pitchford, J. 1990, 'Good and bad deficits', *Growth,* vol. 38, pp. 33–56

Stewart, M. 1994, 'Should we concern ourselves with foreign debt?', *Economic Papers*, vol. 13, pp. 114–21

6 Fiscal policy in Australia
John Nevile

Fiscal policy is concerned with the effects of government expenditure and revenue on the economy at an economy-wide level. It is not concerned with effects on individual industries or on particular groups of people such as old age pensioners, but with effects on variables such as the output of the economy as a whole, employment and unemployment, the rate of inflation, the exchange rate and the balance of payments. Government expenditure adds to aggregate demand, or total demand in the economy, and taxation revenue reduces aggregate demand. Since recessions are caused by too little aggregate demand, fiscal policy can be very important in determining the health of our economy. This chapter is primarily about fiscal policy in Australia: the major issues and how well has fiscal policy performed. However, the next section first sets out the elementary theory of fiscal policy.

How fiscal policy works

We will start by examining the simplest of all possible worlds with an economy with no transactions with foreigners, no corporate sector and with investment autonomous so that it is not affected by what happens in the economy. In this world total output (Y) is equal to government expenditure (G) plus investment in the private sector (I) plus personal consumption expenditure (C). Or in symbols

$$Y = G + I + C \tag{1}$$

Since there are no transactions with foreigners all the proceeds of selling output remain within the economy and total income equals total output.

Before we can say anything about fiscal policy we have to know how government expenditure is financed. Assume, first, that all taxation is lump sum taxation like a poll tax. Income in the private sector equals total output less taxation revenue and, making the further assumption that consumption is proportional to income, we can write

$$C = c(Y - T) \qquad (2)$$

Combining equations (1) and (2) gives the following equation for income and output.

$$Y = \frac{I + G - cT}{1 - c} \qquad (3)$$

Despite the extreme simplicity of the economic structure in the world that we have assumed, the analysis has already produced a result that is of considerable importance and which carries over to the real world. Not only does an increase in government expenditure increase output and an increase in taxation revenue reduce output, but, since c is less than one, a change in government expenditure has a bigger effect on output than does an equal change in taxation revenue. Indeed, if government expenditure and taxation revenue are both increased by the same amount then output also increases by this amount. This result is known as the balanced budget multiplier theorem and is summed up in the statement that the balanced budget multiplier is equal to one (since the increase in output is equal to the increase in the size of the government sector multiplied by one). In the real world, with foreign trade, taxes varying with income and other complications, the balanced budget multiplier rarely is exactly equal to one; but it is almost always true that changing government expenditure has a proportionally bigger effect on output than changing taxation revenue. As the Americans say, with expenditure you get a bigger bang for your buck.

Now consider the case where taxation revenue varies with income, so that

$$T = tY \qquad (4)$$

Combining equations (3) and (4) gives

$$Y = \frac{I + G}{1 - (1 - t)C} \tag{5}$$

Suppose that in this world investment increases for some reason, then output will increase. So too will taxation revenue but government expenditure will remain the same. If the government budget was previously balanced with G = T, there now will be a surplus. This result is extremely important, and also holds in the real world. It shows that the size of the government deficit or surplus not only reflects the size of government expenditure and taxation rates, but also the level of economic activity. In the real world both taxation revenue and government expenditure vary as output changes. For example, when an economy moves out of a recession taxation revenue rises as income increases and some types of government expenditure, notably unemployment benefits, tend to fall. The stance of fiscal policy, that is, whether it is expansionary or exerting a downward pressure on output, depends on the levels at which the various taxation rates and government benefits are set and the size of those government expenditures which do not change with the level of output. These things certainly have a big influence on the size of the government budget deficit or surplus, but so too does the level of output. The size of the budget deficit is a very poor indicator of the stance of fiscal policy.

If one reads any newspaper in Australia the day after the budget has been introduced into the Federal Parliament, one finds great attention paid to the budget deficit. As far as the economy-wide effects of the budget are concerned, journalists seem to be interested in only one number: the size of the budget deficit. Yet the results obtained in this section suggest that this is very misleading. It is not just the size of the budget deficit that is important but also the factors that contribute to this final figure. If the deficit declines, is this because of cuts in government expenditure or increases in taxation rates? In the real world one should go even further than this question. Different types of expenditure have different effects on output. For example, the purchase in America of aircraft for the RAAF will have little effect on output in Australia. Similarly, different types of taxation have different effects on output. To get an indication of the stance of fiscal policy it is desirable to look at both the size and composition of expenditure and revenue and not just the size of the deficit or surplus.

In addition, it is very important to take into account the effect of the economy on the budget as well as the effect of the budget on the economy. In the boom year of 1989–90 Commonwealth budget outlays and revenues showed a surplus of $8 billion. In only two years this changed to a deficit of $9 billion. The change was large, equal to 4.5 per cent of gross domestic product in 1991/92. But almost half of this large change was due to the change from boom to recession.

Of the two types of errors introduced by using the budget deficit as an indicator of the stance of fiscal policy, neglecting the effect of the economy on the budget is usually the most important. Unless there are major changes, such as the proposed introduction of a GST, the composition of total taxation revenue or of government expenditure does not change greatly from year to year, and the relative size of the government sector does not usually change rapidly either. But the economy can change very quickly from boom to recession, often in only one year. To allow for the effect of such changes on the size of the deficit it is helpful to use the structural deficit as an indicator of the stance of fiscal policy. This measures the size the deficit would be if income and output were not at their actual levels but at the normal levels which are the middle-term to long-term goals of economic policy. If one has to use a single number to measure the stance of fiscal policy the structural deficit is probably the best. It is discussed more fully in a later section of this chapter where estimates of the size of the structural deficit for Australia over the last 20 years are given. However, it should be emphasised that even the structural deficit has substantial limitations as a measure of the stance of fiscal policy. For example, in Australia the relative size of the government section, as measured by the ratio of government expenditure to gross national product, dropped by 0.3 percentage points in 1987/88. After allowing for the high level of economic activity in 1987/88 compared to the previous year, the drop was 0.23 percentage points. Even if taxation revenue had fallen by a similar amount this is large enough to exert a significant downward pressure on gross domestic product through the balanced budget multiplier.

Crowding out

The simple theory in the preceding section assumes that investment in the private sector is not affected by fiscal policy. Some economists and many media commentators do not accept that this is a useful assumption and consequently believe that increasing government expenditure has little or no effect in increasing output and income. The argument is that if an increase in government expenditure is matched by increases in taxation, the increased taxation will reduce private expenditure by a similar amount; but, if the increased expenditure increases the size of the deficit, this will increase interest rates enough to reduce private investment by an amount as large or nearly as large as the increase in government expenditure.

The first case ignores the balanced budget multiplier theorem, but it is the second case that people usually have in mind when they argue that an increase in government expenditure reduces private expenditure or 'crowds out' private expenditure, as it is often put. For example, in his column in the *Sydney Morning Herald* on 17 June 1993, Max Walsh talks of the capacity of the public sector 'to undermine the private sector by confronting it with a high interest rate regime as a consequence of large structural deficits' and concludes that, despite the depressed state of the economy, expansionary fiscal policy will not be effective because 'further expansion of the public sector deficit will simply create higher hurdles for private sector investment'.

It is true that the analysis in the previous section implicitly assumed no change in monetary policy in the sense that the monetary authorities maintain a constant rate of interest. If, instead, the monetary authorities maintained a constant stock of money, an increase in government expenditure would cause some rise in interest rates, though only in extreme circumstances would interest rates rise enough to crowd out an equal amount of private expenditure. It is not clear, however, why the monetary authorities would want to reduce the effects of expansionary fiscal policy in a recession by allowing interest rates to rise. Moreover, the analysis that shows increased government expenditure leading to higher interest rates if the stock of money is held constant, also shows that any increase in private expenditure, for example, on investment or even foreign expenditure on Australian exports, will also lead to a rise in interest rates in Australia if the monetary authorities are successful in preventing changes in the stock of money. In this respect expansionary fiscal policy is no different from any sort of stimulus that might lift the economy out of recession.

In any case, the monetary authorities in Australia do not maintain a constant volume of money. Short-term interest rates, not the volume of money, is the monetary policy instrument, and changes in the volume of money are only one of many things taken into consideration when setting interest rates. Long-term, rather than short-term, interest rates may be more relevant to investment decisions in the private sector. It is perhaps possible that large budget deficits might increase the spread between short-term and long-term interest rates, so even if short-term interest rates were held constant long-term rates could rise thus crowding out private investment. However, there is no evidence of this happening in Australia. Figure 6.1 is a scatter diagram which indicates the budget deficit for all levels of government in Australia combined, as a percentage of GDP,

Figure 6.1 Budget deficits and interest rate spread

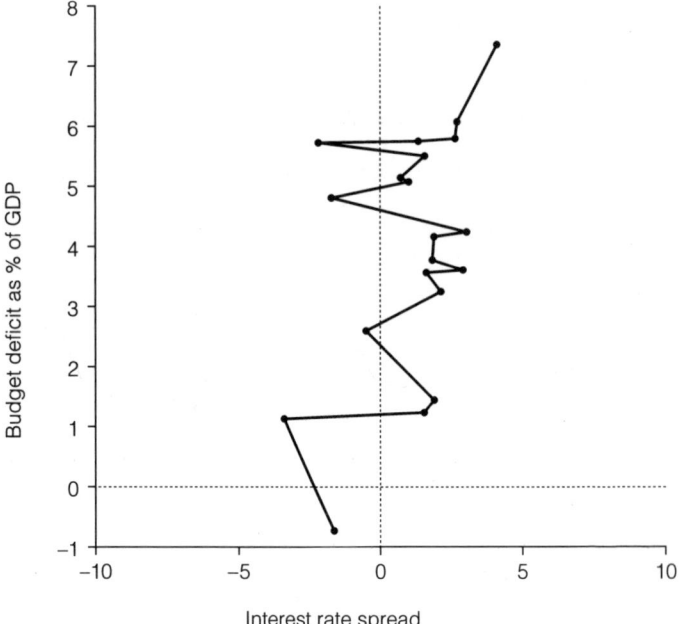

and the spread (or gap) between long-term and short-term interest rates. There is no evidence of a relationship between the size of the deficit and the interest rate spread. In theory the spread should be bigger when short-term interest rates are expected to rise in the future (because of increased inflation or because they are unusually low as a result of easy monetary policy, etc.). If larger deficits lead to expectations of greater inflation in Australia this could lead to a rise in long-term interest rates, but there is no evidence that large deficits have affected expectations in this way.

Thus, if a bigger deficit leads to higher interest rates in Australia, it must cause monetary authorities to increase short-term interest rates since it does not affect the gap between long-term and short-term interest rates. There is one plausible reason why larger deficits might induce the monetary authorities to raise short-term interest rates. A larger budget deficit will, other things being equal, provide more stimulus to the economy and hence income, and also imports will be at a higher level than if the budget deficit were smaller.

If the monetary authorities think that the higher level of imports will cause the exchange rate to fall and if they believe it important

Figure 6.2 Budget deficits and short-term interest rates

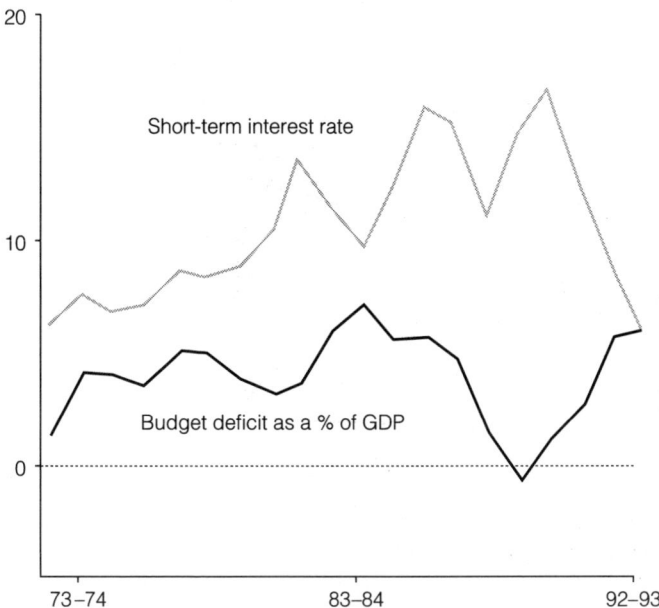

to prevent this happening, they may raise interest rates to 'protect' the existing value of the $A on the foreign exchange. This is a long chain of conditions. On some occasions something like this may have happened, but Figure 6.2 and Table 6.1 show no systematic relationship between the size of the deficit and short-term interest rates. Indeed, more often than not, when the deficit has risen sharply interest rates have fallen. (See 1975/76, 1982/83, 1983/84 and 1987/88). It is flying in the face of the facts to argue that in Australia larger deficits cause higher interest rates.

National savings and the current account deficit

In recent years a great deal of attention has been focused on the current account deficit of the balance of payments. This measures the amount we borrow from foreigners. Some academic economists argue that since this borrowing from foreigners is largely done by firms in the private sector (who presumably believe that it is profitable to do so) it is not something to be concerned about. The majority of economists, and virtually all of those responsible for policy advice to government, disagree. The basic argument for

Table 6.1 Budget deficits and interest rates in Australia, 1973/74 to 1992/93

Year	Deficit[a] $m	Money market authorised dealers interest rate %	Interest rate on 10-year bonds %
1973/74	759	6.4	8.2
1974/75	2658	7.6	9.5
1975/76	3206	7.0	10.0
1976/77	3073	7.4	10.2
1977/78	4617	8.9	9.6
1978/79	5194	8.3	9.2
1979/80	4415	8.9	10.7
1980/81	4358	10.5	12.6
1981/82	5323	13.8	15.5
1982/83	9779	11.7	14.4
1983/84	13632	9.7	13.9
1984/85	11387	12.1	13.4
1985/86	11826	15.9	13.7
1986/87	10160	15.4	13.6
1987/88	1850	11.0	12.6
1988/89	−3022	14.6	12.9
1989/90	3709	16.7	13.3
1990/91	9299	12.6	12.1
1991/92	19934	8.4	9.9
1992/93	20637	5.7	8.3

Note: a Consolidated deficit for all levels of government with asset sales and increase in provisions excluded.
Sources: Reserve Bank *Bulletin* and ABS *Government Financial Estimates, Australia.*

concern about the size of the current account deficit is simple. Australia already has a large foreign debt, and the amount we are already borrowing from abroad is a high proportion of our output (or GDP). If we continue to borrow increasing amounts from abroad (i.e. if the current account deficit increases continuously as a proportion of GDP) sooner or later foreigners will wonder if we will be able to service the debt and will cease lending to Australia. This will precipitate a massive devaluation of the Australian dollar on foreign exchange markets and hence large falls in *real* consumption and a rapid, painful structural adjustment. It is better to take now the measures necessary to improve the balance of payments and have a slower adjustment which will be less painful.

The current account deficit is equal to the difference between imports and exports (the trade gap) plus the net amount that Australians pay to foreigners in dividends, interest and gifts. It is also equal to the difference between investment and savings (the savings gap) plus again the net amount paid to foreigners in dividends, interest and gifts. This follows from the definitions of the various items in the national accounts so that when the Statistician measures what has happened in the economy the savings gap is the same as the trade gap and must be so by definition. But what if the trade gap which would result from the plans of participants in the economy does not equal the savings gap which would result from those plans? Will the trade gap change or will the savings gap adjust? The savings gap represents a net supply of foreign currencies and results in an inflow of foreign exchange on the capital account, as foreigners lend us money which helps finance our investment. On the other hand, the trade gap is an excess of imports over exports and this represents a net demand for foreign currencies to pay for the extra imports. Hence, if the planned trade gap is greater than the planned savings gap, this will increase the demand for foreign currency causing its value to rise or the Australian dollar to depreciate, which in turn will tend to make imports more expensive to Australians and our exports cheaper to foreign buyers. This can be expected to reduce the trade gap until it is equal to the savings gap. Conversely, if the planned savings gap is greater than the planned trade gap, one would expect the exchange rate to appreciate, which would tend to increase imports and discourage exports, until the trade gap increased to equal the savings gap. Thus, in a country like Australia, which has a floating exchange rate, one would expect the savings gap to be the dominant one. No doubt both gaps may change, but there is a market mechanism in existence to ensure that it is mainly the trade gap that changes to bring about the equality between the trade gap and the savings gap.

It follows that, if it is desired to reduce the current account deficit, the size of the savings gap must be reduced. This could be done by decreasing investment, but if this happens output, income and employment will also be depressed. This is why the current account deficit was reduced during the recession at the beginning of the 1990s. If there is to be a rate of economic growth large enough to reduce unemployment in Australia at a satisfactory pace, the level of investment will have to be increased, not decreased. Hence, a necessary condition of reducing the current account deficit without increasing unemployment is to increase the rate of savings in Australia.

Fiscal policy can be important in achieving this. Not only can particular taxes encourage (or discourage) savings, but savings in the public sector are determined by the size and composition of government expenditure and by the size of government revenues. It is important not to fall into the trap of equating the deficit with public sector dissavings. Savings is the difference between income and consumption, not the difference between revenue and expenditure. Public savings is the difference between public investment and the deficit. Reducing the deficit can increase public savings, but not if it

Table 6.2 Government expenditure in twelve OECD countries, 1986–88

	Defence	Education	Health	Income maintenance	Debt interest	Total [a]
	(percentages of GDP)					
Australia	2.3	5.2	5.3	7.3	4.0	36.4
Austria	1.1	4.5	4.9	20.3	3.9	52.8
Denmark	2.0	6.8	5.2	15.4	8.3	57.8
Finland	1.5	5.1	4.4	11.6	1.6	40.2
France	3.1	5.5	4.3	23.9	2.9	51.6
Germany	2.7	4.4	6.2	16.4	2.8	46.9
Japan	0.9	4.3	4.9	7.9	4.3	32.9
Netherlands	3.0	5.7	6.3	19.1	6.9	57.9
Norway	3.0	6.7	7.4	15.6	3.9	53.5
Sweden	2.6	5.7	6.9	17.2	6.5	59.3
UK	4.9	5.1	5.1	13.2	4.5	45.5
USA	6.6	4.5	0.9	7.9	5.0	36.9

Note: a Excludes expenditure by public enterprises but includes other categories than those in previous columns.
Source: Oxley et al. (1990).

is done by reducing investment expenditure. Investment is necessary in the public sector just as much as in the private sector. (While it is true that there is sometimes wasteful public investment, it is equally true that there is sometimes wasteful private investment, e.g. the city office blocks built at the end of the 1980s that are still unfilled.) Fiscal policy can increase national savings by reducing current government expenditure or by increasing taxation. It can not increase public savings by reducing public investment.

It will be difficult to reduce government current expenditure without cutting expenditure on things that the majority of Australians think important. As Table 6.2 shows, by OECD standards not only is total government expenditure low in Australia, but so too is expenditure on social security (beloved of those on the left) and defence (beloved of those on the right). Expenditure on other major items such as health and education is not high. If fiscal policy is to make a contribution to increasing savings in Australia, it should come through increasing taxation. Australia has a very low rate of taxation compared to most OECD countries. Figure 6.3 shows that government revenue as a proportion of GDP is only around 33 per cent, which is one of the lowest ratios in the OECD. It is important to increase the savings rate in Australia and fiscal policy can make a major contribution to this, but it will require an increase in taxation rates.

Figure 6.3   Government revenue as a percentage of GDP, 1992

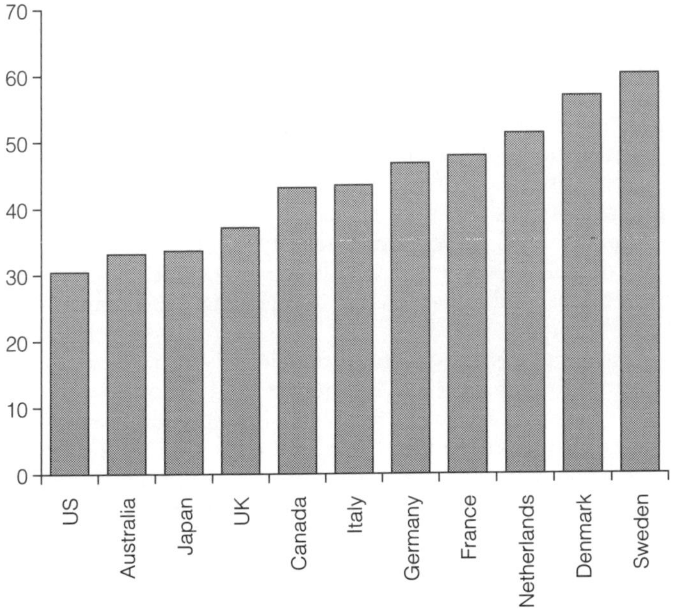

[Bar chart showing government revenue as percentage of GDP for: US (~31%), Australia (~33%), Japan (~34%), UK (~37%), Canada (~43%), Italy (~44%), Germany (~47%), France (~48%), Netherlands (~52%), Denmark (~57%), Sweden (~61%)]

Source: OECD *Economic Outlook*, June 1993.

Structural deficits

It was argued above that the structural deficit has limitations as an indicator of the stance of fiscal policy. However, many people look for a measure which sums up the stance of fiscal policy in a particular year in a single number. If they are not provided with a reasonable measure, they will use a bad one, as witnessed by the focus in the media on the actual deficit when the Commonwealth Government introduces its budget. The structural deficit is probably the best single-number indicator of the stance of fiscal policy. It gives a useful indication of any large year-to-year changes in fiscal policy and these are what are important in understanding the impact of fiscal policy on the economy. When it is used, however, no significance should be attached to small changes. No single-number indicator is accurate enough to give a useful measure of small changes in the stance of fiscal policy.

The structural deficit measures what the size of the deficit would be if the economy were at the normal or desirable level of output which it is the goal of policy to achieve. This, of course, leaves open the question of how a high level of economic activity corresponds to the normal level that is the middle-term to long-term goal of policy. The traditional method is to estimate a trend through years that are judged to be years in which economic activity is at the desirable level. The judgment about what is a desirable level of economic activity may be coloured by the relative weights one gives to the evils of unemployment and inflation. In a commodity-exporting country like Australia, where the constraint on increasing economic activity is often the balance of payments, a judgment about the appropriate level of economic activity to be selected as a longer term goal of policy, also involves a judgment about long-term trends in export prices and other factors influencing the balance of payments.

The estimates of the structural deficit for Australia made in this section assume that in 1987/88 output and income were at the normal or desirable level. If 1973/74 is considered a year in which output was also at the normal level, or even slightly above it, this implies that, since the changes to the world economy following the first oil shock the Australian economy has had the potential to grow at only 3 per cent a year. Certainly balance of payments figures in recent years suggest that it is not possible to maintain indefinitely a higher level of economic activity than that which occurred in 1987/88 until substantial structural change has taken place in the Australian economy. In 1987/88 unemployment averaged 7.6 per cent. If Australia is to reduce unemployment below this level and to reduce substantially the large number of long-term unemployed, there will have to be a trend rate of growth much greater than 3 per cent a year. There is some evidence that the structural change necessary to make this possible is already well advanced, but in a backward-looking exercise, like the one in this section, it is appropriate to stick to the 3 per cent figure.

In moving from the actual deficit to a structural deficit, adjusting for changes in the level of economic activity (the cyclical adjustment) is not all that is necessary. One also has to make an adjustment for inflation. A small but significant proportion of government expenditure in Australia is interest payments on the public debt. Inflation reduces the real value of government bonds held by the public, as it does the real value of all assets whose value is fixed in nominal terms. When the rate of inflation rises significantly, nominal interest rates also normally rise, though often with a lag. Part of the higher interest rate is a payment for the decline in the real value of the bond or debt. However, the whole of the interest payment on government debt is included in the outlay side of the government budget. The part corresponding to the decline in the real value of government debt held by the public should be excluded, as paying this leaves the government no worse off, since it is balanced by the decline in the real value of government debt. Another way of looking at this, which produces the same conclusion, is to argue that the decline in the real value of government bonds held by the public is a hidden tax caused by inflation and that this 'inflation tax' should be included in the receipts side of the budget.

This argument that the decline in the real value of government bonds held by the public should be treated as a tax when calculating the structural deficit is generally correct, but does depend on the purpose for which the structural deficit is being used. If, as is generally the case, it is being used as an indicator of the stance of fiscal policy with respect to effects on output and hence employment and other macro variables, the argument is correct as long as people realise that inflation reduces the real value of government bonds that they hold. There is econometric evidence that in times of inflation consumers regard much of their interest receipts as compensation for the effects of inflation on the value of capital lent (see, for example, Nevile 1983, p. 357). Thus, ignoring for the moment the fact that the whole of interest receipts is taxable income, that part of interest corresponding to the decline in value of government bonds is not regarded as current income and does not affect consumption. Since the value of financial capital is maintained through this part of interest payment, one does not have to consider further effects on spending of any inflation-caused decline in the real value of government bonds held by the public. In this situation the hidden inflation tax clearly should be subtracted from the deficit.

How is the situation changed by the fact that all of interest receipts are potentially taxable? It is not changed at all, except that the effective rate of tax on the remainder of income is higher, or more correctly there is a tax on financial assets with a rate equal to the product of the marginal tax rate, and the rate of inflation. For this reason disposable income is lowered by inflation, but the tax that does this is included in receipts as normally measured. In addition, the inflation tax should still be subtracted from the deficit since the real value of bonds has declined and the compensating interest payment is still included in government outlays.

If the structural deficit is being used as a measure of the size of the call, in normal times, of the government sector on private sector (or overseas) savings, the situation is a little different. Strictly speaking the inflation tax still should be treated like a tax, but it must also be subtracted from private savings when considering the total amount of savings in the economy. For simplicity and convenience many prefer to ignore the inflation tax in calculating both the government deficit and private savings: since it is included in both places it cancels out. The size of the inflation tax is also shown in

Table 6.3, which gives the structural deficit, so the reader can include it or exclude it as is felt appropriate.

The inflation tax is not just a tax on bonds. While in everyday life people do not think of currency as part of the government debt, notes and coins held by the public are actually government liabilities. Hence the size of the deficit should also be adjusted for the inflation tax on currency. However, the amount involved is not large. In 1992/93 the inflation tax on currency was of the order of $300 million or less than one-tenth of 1 per cent of GDP.

There is one final issue in calculating the structural deficit: what should be done with asset sales? The simplest procedure is to treat the net sale of second-hand, or not newly produced, assets as a deduction from expenditure on fixed capital equipment, just as one would treat the trade-in one receives on a second-hand car as a deduction from the expenditure on the new car. Some asset sales by government are just that, but the bigger ones are not. While the situation is not completely clear-cut, from an interest in the effects of fiscal policy on income and output it is generally better to exclude the purchase and sale of second-hand assets from the analysis (just as the purchase and sale of second-hand houses is excluded from the national accounts except for the services provided by real estate agents and lawyers). However, the major argument for excluding the sale of assets is that large sales of assets cannot continue indefinitely. The use of a figure for the structural deficit usually has the strong implication that, if the economy is at the 'normal' level of output and the deficit is at an appropriate level, this budget deficit can continue indefinitely without any problems. Since a large volume of asset sales cannot continue indefinitely, it may not be appropriate to include the returns from asset sales when calculating the structural deficit, if the volume of such sales is too large to continue for a long time.

If one is concerned about the deficit as a measure of the public sector call on private sector savings, whether or not the proceeds of asset sales should be included in receipts depends on to whom the assets are sold. The sale of assets to Australians does not change the call of the public sector on private sector savings. The sale of assets to foreigners does. The sale of assets is excluded from the figures for the structural deficit shown in Table 6.3.

Fiscal policy in Australia

Australia has just passed through the worst recession in 50 years and, in fact, after the Great Depression of the 1930s, the worst slump in the twentieth century. In the face of this, fiscal policy was

Table 6.3 The structural deficit and its components in Australia, 1973/74 to 1993/94

	Actual deficit	Cyclical correction	Inflation tax	Structural deficit [a]
	(percentages of GDP)			
1973/74	1.4	−0.3	4.7	−3.0
1974/75	4.1	0.4	6.8	−3.1
1975/76	4.2	0.4	5.1	−1.3
1976/77	3.6	0.5	3.7	−0.6
1977/78	5.1	1.4	3.2	0.5
1978/79	5.1	0.7	2.8	1.6
1979/80	3.8	1.0	3.6	−0.9
1980/81	3.3	1.0	3.7	−1.3
1981/82	3.6	1.2	3.4	−1.0
1982/83	6.1	3.1	3.9	−0.9
1983/84	7.4	2.0	2.6	2.9
1984/85	5.7	1.0	2.6	2.1
1985/86	5.7	0.4	3.8	1.5
1986/87	4.8	0.6	3.8	0.4
1987/88	1.3	–	3.0	−1.7
1988/89	−0.7	−0.6	2.8	−2.9
1989/90	1.1	−0.5	2.2	−0.5
1990/91	2.6	1.5	1.6	−0.4
1991/92	5.5	2.5	0.8	2.2
1992/93[b]	5.7	2.5	1.0	2.3
1993/94[c]	5.6	1.9	1.0	2.7

Notes: a Rows may not add to total due to rounding.
 b Based in part on preliminary data.
 c Based on forward estimates and estimates by the author.
Sources: Calculated from figures in various issues of the following: Reserve Bank of Australia, *Bulletin*; Reserve Bank of Australia, Occasional Paper No. 8A: Commonwealth of Australia, Budget Statements and Budget Related Paper No. 1; ABS, *Government Financial Estimates, Australia*, Cat. No. 5501.0; ABS, *Public Sector Debt, Australia*, Cat. No. 5513.0; ABS, *State and Local Government Finance, Australia*, Cat. No. 5504.0.

remarkably muted. Even more remarkable, in the middle of this slump, with unemployment around 11 per cent and showing no signs of falling, influential groups were calling for tighter, not more expansionary, fiscal policy. For example, the Business Council of Australia argued that: 'it is essential that the broad fiscal objective for the Commonwealth in 1992/93 should be to exercise prudent management and to reduce Government outlays. This would bring the Commonwealth budget deficit to about 2 per cent of GDP' (1992, p. 30).

Luckily this advice was not followed. The Commonwealth budget deficit was 2.4 per cent of GDP in 1991/92 and 3.6 per cent in 1992/93, although the consolidated structural deficit for all levels of government actually declined slightly in 1992/93. This raises two

Figure 6.4 Structural deficits as a percentage of GDP and unemployment, Australia, 1973/74 to 1992/93

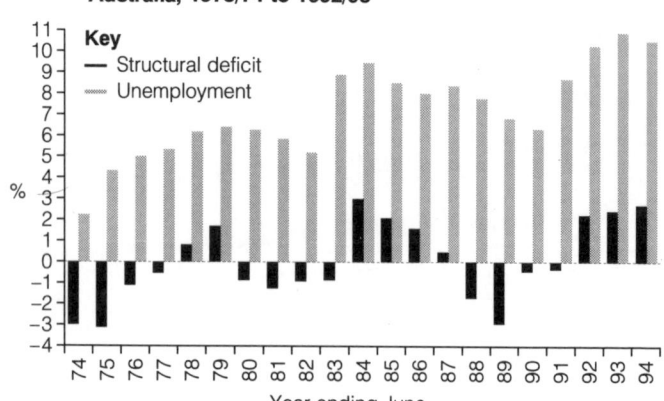

questions. First, what was the actual course of fiscal policy over the slump, and second, why did so many business organisations and media commentators call for tighter fiscal policy in the middle of the second-worst slump in the twentieth century?

Over the last 25 years as a whole, Australia has had a tight fiscal policy. In the 15 years starting with 1968/69 there was a structural surplus in all but two years. This contrasts with most OECD countries, where structural deficits were much more common. Tight fiscal policy was appropriate before 1973/74 because of the low level of unemployment, but after that date fiscal policy should have been used to reduce unemployment when it rose sharply. Did this happen?

Figure 6.4 shows the structural deficit and unemployment for the years 1973/74 to 1992/93. Before 1983 fiscal policy responded only mildly to changes in unemployment. In 1983/84, in response to the severe recession that developed in 1982/83, there was a substantial structural deficit which was gradually eliminated over the next three years. In response to the even worse slump that developed over 1990/91, there was again a structural deficit in 1991/92 but it was only 2.2 per cent of GDP compared with a 2.9 per cent structural deficit in 1983/84. Most of the increase in the structural deficit in 1991/92 was due to a cut in tax rates, although there was also a small increase in expenditure (in addition to the extra outlay on unemployment benefits made necessary by the worsening recession). In 1992/93 the structural deficit rose from 2.2 per cent of GDP to 2.3 per cent. In view of what was said above not much weight should be put on a change of this size, but there probably was a slight easing of fiscal policy. In 1993/94 there was a distinct move to more expansionary fiscal policy. Although the ratio of the structural deficit to GDP was still below that in 1983/84, it was larger than in any other year in the last 25 years. Three years after the recession started there was an adequate response in the fiscal policy area.

Why was fiscal policy virtually no more expansionary in 1992/93 than in 1991/92 and what were the reasons that some argued that it should be tighter in 1992/93 than it was in 1991/92?

Some commentators were still arguing that expansionary fiscal policy would be ineffective because it would crowd out so much private sector expenditure that there would be no net effect on output. To argue this in 1992 was to allow ideology to blind one to the facts. The arguments and supporting statistics against crowding out, which were set out above, were well known at the time. Moreover, international responses to the last major world recession, that of 1982, had shown that expansionary fiscal policy was effective. A number of countries, notably the United States and Australia, adopted expansionary fiscal policy with large budget deficits. These were precisely the countries in which employment expanded strongly and the unemployment rate fell substantially. By contrast, in countries with less expansionary fiscal policy, unemployment only fell very slowly. For example, in the United States the unemployment rate was 9.5 per cent in 1983 and 5.4 per cent in 1988, whereas in Germany the unemployment rate was 8.2 per cent in 1983 and it was still 7.6 per cent in 1988. The crowding out argument is no longer credible.

Others argued in 1992, and still argue, that one must be very cautious about any stimulus to the economy through fiscal policy in case it increases inflationary pressure. It is true that unemployment is a very powerful weapon against inflation. Anything, including expansionary fiscal policy, which reduces unemployment thereby increases, however slightly, the chance of a rise in the inflation rate. It seems odd, however, to worry about this at a time when the rate of inflation is at its lowest level for 30 years and the rate of unemployment at its highest level for 50 years. Nevertheless, it is true that there are some people who always argue that greater priority should be given to controlling inflation than to reducing unemployment. Some may be motivated by knowledge of the effects of very high inflation rates in other countries, but one can not help noting that generally people who argue thus are neither unemployed nor likely to become unemployed.

The final argument against expansionary fiscal policy flows from concern with the balance of payments and the current account deficit. Increasing taxation and/or cutting government current outlays will reduce the savings gap and reduce the current account deficit. However, this does not mean that expansionary fiscal policy is never appropriate. In a recession it is usually more important to reduce unemployment than to reduce the current account deficit which has probably already fallen as the result of the recession. If the balance of payments situation is absolutely desperate, which it was not in 1992 and 1993, some stimulus can be given to the economy by increasing both government expenditure and taxation without increasing the savings gap.

It was argued above that the appropriate way to increase public sector savings in Australia is to increase taxation. It is the Commonwealth that has the responsibility to do this, as the size of the savings gap is a national problem that must be solved nationally. The trend has been for the Commonwealth to reduce taxation, not increase it. In 1986/87 Commonwealth budget revenue was 27.8 per cent of GDP. This had declined to 25.9 by 1989/90, 23.6 in 1992/93 and is estimated to be 23.5 in 1993/94. The fall from 1989/90 to 1992/93 was desirable from the point of view of stimulating an economy in recession. However, it may have been better to reduce taxation less and to expand government capital expenditure over these three years. (In fact, public capital expenditure fell between 1989/90 and 1992/93.) In any case, once the economy is growing rapidly again the first priority of fiscal policy should be to increase taxation and public sector savings.

Recommended reading

Chand, Sheetal K. 1977, 'Summary measures of fiscal influence', *International Monetary Fund Staff Papers*, July

Commonwealth of Australia 1994, 'Statement 6, the public sector', in *Budget Statements 1994–95*, Australian Government Publishing Service, Canberra

Nevile, J.W. 1987, 'Can expansionary fiscal policy increase employment', in Philip Maxwell (ed.), *Macroeconomics: Contemporary Australian Readings*, Harper & Row, Sydney

7 Money and monetary policy
Ross Milbourne[1]

Money and credit are important to the economy because their availability and price are believed to be related to the level of economic activity. Financial markets comprise the actions of borrowers and lenders, which are coordinated by financial intermediaries. These intermediaries, which include banks as well as non-bank financial institutions such as credit unions, building societies, funds managers and insurance companies, accept deposits or loans from individuals and firms, and lend to other individuals and firms. Banks in particular accept deposits from clients which those clients wish to access for payment purposes, and this liquid form of wealth is referred to as money. Banks can then use these deposits to lend and create credit. Thus money and credit creation are linked.

Intervention in financial markets by governments, through their central banks, is undertaken in almost all countries. A key question which faces economists is whether governments should intervene in financial markets or leave the markets to themselves (a policy of *laissez-faire*). The two main arguments for intervention are that the payments system is too important to let suffer from potential failure from imprudent banking practices by institutions, and that unregulated credit expansions or contractions could lead to more severe bouts of inflation or recession, thus potentially worsening the business cycle.

In Australia, the Reserve Bank of Australia (RBA) oversees monetary policy. The RBA, in its charter, is entrusted

> to ensure that the monetary and banking policy of the Bank is

directed to the greatest advantage of the people of Australia . . . [and] best contribute to:
(a) the stability of the economy;
(b) the maintenance of full employment in Australia; and
(c) the economic prosperity and welfare of the people of Australia.
(Reserve Bank of Australia 1987, p. 8.)

The RBA attempts to meet its charter through two main types of policies: prudential regulations on banks to protect them from insolvency and to maintain confidence in the financial system; and monetary policy which is designed to influence the level of credit in the economy via its price (the rate of interest).

Prudential regulation

Banks play a special role because they are the only set of institutions whose actions can be directly influenced by Reserve Bank policy. Historically, this arrangement developed because banks play the key role in the payments clearing mechanism. A failure to honour payments by one of the banks would not only severely endanger the payments mechanism, but it may cause a bank run (a massive withdrawal of deposits from other banks) causing severe financial distress on those as well. This 'externality' or spillover effect is what most central banks attempt to avoid by prudential regulation. A loss of confidence in the banking system can cause severe real effects; the best examples of this were in Australia in 1891–93, and in the United States in 1931–33 where major bank failures were associated with severe economic depressions.

The deregulation of the financial system was mostly completed by the mid-1980s. Previously, there were three sets of regulations that the RBA used to regulate banks. First, there were interest rate restrictions on deposits and loans and restrictions on the types of deposits which could be accepted. This stifled each bank's ability to increase its deposit base. Second, the RBA often suggested quantitative lending guidelines to restrict the creation of bank credit. Third, the RBA used portfolio restrictions such as the Statutory Reserve Deposit (SRD) ratio, the minimum proportion of assets held as cash, to vary the liquidity position of banks. In addition, the RBA controlled entry to the banking market. A brief sequence of the removal of these regulations is given in Table 7.1.

Following deregulation, Australian banks dramatically expanded their lending. This increase evidently involved loans of greater risk and less collateral for which the banks did not appropriately price.[2] As a result, provisions for doubtful debts doubled as a percentage

Table 7.1 Major financial deregulations

December 1980	Interest rate ceilings on all trading bank and savings bank deposits were removed.
August 1981	Minimum term on certificates of deposit was reduced to 30 days.
March 1982	Minimum term on trading bank fixed deposits (>$50 000) reduced from 30 days to 14 and for fixed deposits (<$50 000) from 3 months to 30 days.
	Minimum term for certificates of deposit reduced to 14 days.
	The requirement of one month's notice of withdrawal on savings bank investment accounts was removed.
June 1982	The end of quantitative lending guidance.
August 1982	Savings bank asset requirements reduced to 94 per cent, and prescribed asset ratios relaxed.
December 1983	Australian dollar floated and most foreign exchange controls removed.
August 1984	All remaining controls on bank deposits removed.
	Savings banks permitted to offer chequing facilities.
February 1985	16 foreign banks invited to take up banking licences.
April 1985	Remaining ceilings on bank interest rates removed except those on owner-occupied housing loans under $100 000.
May 1985	The Prime Assets Ratio (PAR) replaced LGS convention.
September 1985	The first foreign bank began trading.
April 1986	Interest rate ceiling on new housing loans removed.
April 1987	Savings bank reserve asset ratio reduced to 13 per cent.
September 1988	SRD ratio reduced to zero (previously had been 7 per cent for trading banks), and those funds transferred to 'non-callable deposits', with those funds in excess of 1 per cent of liabilities to be gradually returned to banks.
	Free tranche for savings banks increased from 6 per cent to 40 per cent, as an interim step towards removing the distinction between savings banks and trading banks.
	PAR reduced from 12 per cent to 10 per cent. PAR to replace existing savings bank regulations.

of assets from 1984 to 1988, bank profits were severely squeezed and interest margins (the borrowing–lending differential) stopped its downward trend and rose somewhat after 1986.[3]

The perceived increased risk of the major banks and the financial system made the RBA adopt a formal position on bank supervision. The RBA now requires adequate disclosure by banks of their activities, especially their risk management strategies. In addition, the RBA has imposed capital adequacy ratios on banks. This follows trends in other OECD countries and is related to the belief that sufficient bank capital (that is equity of its shareholders) can be used in the last resort as a means to finance substantial bank losses. The capital adequacy ratio is defined on a risk-weighted basis with more risky bank assets receiving a higher weighting (that is, requiring more capital to be held). Currently, banks are required to hold a minimum level of bank capital which is 8 per cent of risk-weighted assets.[4]

Prudential regulation of the banks is not without its critics. This criticism takes two forms: those who oppose regulation and those who criticise the particular form of regulation used by the RBA. Some economists such as Hayek (1976), Fama (1980) and Sargent and Wallace (1982) have argued for a laissez-faire approach (free banking): that banks should be free to create credit and engage in intermediation to satisfy clients' needs, and that neither prudential regulation nor control of money and credit are necessary. Critics are concerned that this may lead to a loss of monetary control and thus loss of control of the price level. Hogan and Sharpe (1988) argue that prudential regulation is unnecessary, because they believe that banks have an incentive for self-regulation so as not to obtain a reputation for high-risk lending. They argue that adequate disclosure means that the market will solve the problem of poor management practices. Critics of this approach point to the poor record of all banks during the 1980s and argue that such a 'herd' mentality could always recur. It is not clear how much disclosure is adequate to maintain incentives for self-regulation.

The main criticism of capital adequacy largely centres around the fact that the weighting scheme used does not really reflect true risk. If a bank has two assets with variable returns, but the returns are negatively correlated, some combination of the assets is relatively riskless. However, the weighting scheme does not recognise this and counts the entire portfolio as risky and requires greater capital equity holding.

Despite some critics, the need for prudential supervision by the RBA is the least controversial of the RBA's roles. A much more contentious issue is the role of the RBA in macroeconomic policy, which will be discussed below.

Credit creation and monetary policy

Assets and liabilities of the banking system

Many of the issues of monetary policy stem from the role of the RBA, and the relationship between various monetary aggregates. Table 7.2 shows balance sheets of commercial banks in aggregate, and the RBA as at January 1994. The main liabilities of commercial banks are demand deposits, on which cheques can be drawn, and

Table 7.2 Balance sheets of the banks and RBA as at January 1994

Commercial Banks

	Assets		Liabilities
Cash and reserves	4 657	Demand deposits	53 529
Loans to public sector	29 987	Time deposits	170 761
Loans to private sector	261 530	Other borrowings	137 101
Other loans	92 871	Equity	33 383
Premises	5 728		
	394 773		394 773

Reserve Bank of Australia

Assets		Liabilities	
Gold and foreign exchange	19 626	Currency (private sector)	16 942
Government securities	13 369	Deposits of banks	
Other assets	626	NCDs 3089	
		Other 1568	4 657
		(Total: monetary base)	21 625
		Government deposits	1 684
		Other liabilities	10 312
	33 621		33 621

Source: Reserve Bank of Australia *Bulletin,* March 1994, tables A.1, B.1 and D.1.

other deposits, largely savings deposits and time deposits (which have fixed dates of maturity). In addition banks undertake other borrowings, mostly from overseas, and hold bank capital, or equity. On the asset side, banks hold a small fraction of their assets as reserves (a minimum of 1 per cent as non-callable deposits [NCDs] with the RBA) and hold some cash and notes for day-to-day purposes. Commercial bank lending can be generally divided into loans to governments and loans to the private sector. Other loans are mostly to overseas. Bank assets include the value of premises.

The assets of the Reserve Bank of Australia primarily consist of gold and foreign exchange holdings, and holdings of government securities which it buys as part of its open market operations. It is largely by purchases and sales of the RBA's holdings of government securities that the total assets and liabilities of the Reserve Bank are affected. As liabilities, the Reserve Bank issues currency to the public and holds bank deposits (which consist of NCDs and other bank deposits plus bank holdings of notes and coins). The sum of these liabilities of the Reserve Bank of Australia is called the monetary base (MO). In addition, the RBA acts as banker for both Federal and some State governments and holds other liabilities (mostly foreign). These are not included in the definition of the monetary base.

The ability of the commercial banks to create credit comes from the fact that only a small proportion of the deposits must be held as reserves. Of an increase in initial deposits of $100 only, say, $1 might be kept as reserves and the remaining $99 lent as credit to a borrower. Typically, this borrower deposits the money in a bank, thus again raising total deposits in the banking sector by another $99. That bank can then create further credit.

Definitions of the money supply

There are a number of alternative definitions of the money stock. First, we could define the money stock as the monetary base which is directly under the control of the RBA. Another definition is total amount of funds available to be easily spent (or liquidity), in this case currency plus demand deposits. Thus $M1 = C + D$ is one standard definition of the money stock and is often referred to as narrow money. A broader definition of the money stock is $M3 = C + D + T$, that is, currency plus total bank deposits.[5]

Because non-bank financial intermediaries (NBFIs) also accept deposits from the public, a further definition of the money stock is broad money defined as M3 plus the deposit holdings by NBFIs of the non-bank private sector. (In January 1994, these NBFI deposit holdings were $48 363 million.) From this and the figures in Table 7.2, the different money stock estimates, as at January 1994, were in $ million:

Currency	16 942	Currency	16 942
+		+	
Bank reserves at RBA	4 657	Demand deposits	53 529
M0	**= 21 625**	**M1**	**= 70 471**
		+	
		Time deposits	170 761
		M3	**= 241 232**
		+	
		deposits at NBFIs	48 363
		Broad money	**289 595**

M0 is directly under the control of the RBA. Note however that M0 is only a small proportion of M3 (less than 10 per cent); the difference between M3 and M1 (roughly $220 billion) is generated through the credit-creating activities of the banks. It is this level of credit creation that the RBA attempts to influence, and they now do so via interest rates as discussed in the next section.

The operation of the monetary policy

Financial markets engage in trading of financial instruments of various maturities. These maturities vary from overnight funds, primarily borrowed by banks to clear their exchange settlement accounts as part of the cheque-clearing process, to government bonds of ten years or more. In between are such things as 90-day treasury bills, and government bonds of shorter duration, as well as loans to the private sector over various time periods.

Interest rates of different maturities tend to be related. For example, the interest rate on a two-year bond should be roughly equal to the interest rate on a one-year bond compounded by the expected interest rate of a one-year bond bought in one year's time. Generally speaking, if long-term interest rates are substantially above current short-term interest rates, then it must be that market participants are expecting short-term interest rates to rise in the future.

The RBA currently operates monetary policy by affecting very short-term interest rates through purchases and sales of their Commonwealth government securities to short-term money market dealers (authorised dealers), who comprise an important part of the market for overnight funds (or exchange settlement funds). This market comprises three major players: the RBA, the short-term money market dealers, and the commercial banks. Each day, the banks hold funds in their exchange settlement accounts to cover net withdrawals of funds from their banks as cheques clear on a daily basis. These are transferred between banks as the exchange settlement process occurs. If banks are left with excess funds in these accounts, they can lend them to the authorised dealers overnight, who typically hold a portfolio of government securities, and finance their portfolio by borrowing from the banks. The interest rate at which these funds clear this market each night is called the cash rate. If the Government wants to embark on, say, a contractionary monetary policy, that is one which raises the cash rate, they can sell Commonwealth government securities to the dealers, leaving those dealers short of funds. These dealers must then borrow money from the banks, bidding up the cash rate to do so. As a response to this, banks must increase their liquidity from other sources, and thus must restrict their lending (that is keep more in reserves) or borrow from other sources, in either case raising other interest rates.

Since January 1990 the RBA has announced a target cash rate, and operates its portfolio of government securities to try and achieve this cash rate. Thus, not only are they affecting the overnight interest rate, but they are sending a signal to the market so that the market would then fully expect other short-term interest rates to fall into line with this cash rate. As a consequence longer term interest rates change in so far as they are determined by current short-term rates and the future expectation of short-term rates.

The theory of monetary policy

Recent monetary policy in Australia and other countries has focused on broader monetary aggregates (generally M3) and thus essentially on the creation of credit in the economy. However, early monetary theories largely concentrated on the role of money as a medium of exchange. The medium of exchange function is one of three functions of money, the other two being a store of value, and a unit of account. Early theories argued that any asset was a store of value, and that any good or asset could be a unit of account.[6] Thus, implicitly, money was defined as having a narrow definition generally thought of as currency plus demand deposits (M1), to represent those assets used for day-to-day purchases.

The Quantity Theory of Money (discussed briefly in chapter 3) symbolises this earlier view and received its clearest statement from Irving Fisher (1911). Defining M as a stock of money, P as the aggregate price level, y as the level of real income, the velocity of circulation (v) was defined as the ratio of income to money. Thus the Quantity equation (identity) could be written:

$M.v \equiv P.y$

or in percentage change terms,

$\dot{M} + \dot{v} = \dot{P} + \dot{y}$

where $\dot{M}$ is the rate of monetary growth, $\dot{v}$ is the velocity growth, $\dot{P}$ is the rate of price inflation and $\dot{y}$ is the growth of real income.

Given fixed institutions and exchange arrangements, Fisher argued for a roughly constant v. He also posited that real income was determined by production independently of the money stock. With v and y fixed, variations in the money stock imply variations in the price level. Thus, except perhaps for short periods of adjustment, the rate of growth of the money stock determined the rate of inflation, which is, in terms of the categories outlined in chapter 3, an example of demand-pull factors in action.

This view was later restated by Friedman (1956) who argued that velocity would be a stable function of a few variables, and that in the short run changes in the money stock might affect real economic activity. However, Friedman and those who followed him in this tradition (denoted Monetarists) viewed that changes in the rate of growth of the money stock most importantly affected the rate of inflation, and therefore control of the money stock was important in order to control the rate of inflation.

Keynes (1936) took a different approach to the relationship

between money and economic activity. As part of his general theory of employment, Keynes searched for an explanation of the level of investment and felt that part of this explanation was the rate of interest. Keynes posited that the rate of interest was determined by people's holding of a portfolio of assets. He divided financial assets into money and all other assets which he lumped together and called bonds. Keynes argued that variations in the supply of money affected the interest rate on bonds because for the government to induce individuals to exchange bonds for money in their portfolios, they would have to change the interest rate on bonds. Changes in the money supply affected the interest rate and thus real activity via investment. A key ingredient to the Keynesian portfolio approach is that the interest rate on money is either zero or fixed; otherwise the system has too many interest rates to determine.

A crisis for monetary theory was brought about by the emergence of assets which behaved in similar ways to money, termed 'near-money' (typically deposits) which paid interest and on which cheques could be written. With interest rates on all assets free to be determined, only currency returned a zero interest rate. The critical question for the standard approach to monetary theory was whether these deposits followed market interest rates (such as those on bonds) or whether they remained constant (and thus tied to the interest rate on currency). In other words, did they behave like money or like bonds? It was the distinction between interest and non-interest-earning assets which was fundamental to the portfolio theory approach to the determination of interest rates. If interest rates on deposits fluctuated, the existing dichotomy between 'money' and 'bonds' now made no sense.

As a result, having no theoretical link between theory and measurement, many economists regarded the definition of money as an empirical matter, and in the 1960s and 1970s attention focused on which definition of money was related to economic activity in the most stable and predictable manner; that is, which demand for money function was the most stable. As discussed more fully below, none of the definitions worked well in this regard.

The transmission mechanism of monetary policy

Table 7.3, first used in Milbourne (1990), gives a schematic view of the general transmission mechanism of monetary policy (that is, the way in which Reserve Bank policy affects the economy) inherent in most theories. The cash rate and announcements about the RBA's intentions are used to influence other market interest rates. These affect aggregate demand, and thus output, employment and prices.

Table 7.3 The transmission mechanism of monetary policy

		→ aggregate demand	→ output, labour market	→ prices
cash rate	→ other interest rates	→ exchange rate	→	output, prices
		→ intermediaries' balance sheets	→	monetary aggregates

A second effect is felt to work through the exchange rate. At the same time, interest rates affect the borrowing and lending of the balance sheets of financial intermediaries.

There is much controversy among economists as to the exact manner by which aggregate demand is affected by monetary policy, as well as questions relating to the timing, and the degree of certainty of the process. This controversy between different schools of economic thought plays an important part in their different policy prescriptions, and needs to be examined. The order of discussion below largely reflects the historical development of these theories.

Classical

The quantity theory is at the heart of the classical theory. In this theory, an increase in the money stock is seen as an increase in wealth. As a result, consumers increase spending, but with a fixed output (determined by factor supplies) prices increase.

Keynesian

The Keynesian model assumes that in the short run nominal wages remain constant for some periods of time, and/or producers leave prices unchanged for periods of time, even in the face of increased or reduced demand.[7]

In this framework, an increase in the money supply was accomplished by an open market purchase of bonds from the public. This was effected by a reduction in interest rates, which was viewed as an important determinant of investment. As a result, investment would increase, and thus increase aggregate demand. Firms would respond to this change in demand by increasing their production, rather than prices, as long as there were unemployed resources. This increased income and employment. The heart of the Keynesian model was that this was one way of stabilising income over the course of the business cycle.

An important distinction is that between real and nominal interest rates. Investment should really depend upon the real interest rate, defined as the nominal rate of interest less the expected rate of inflation. This is more appropriate for investment decisions because the return to borrowing today comes in the form of future dollars which are worth less if the rate of inflation is positive (that is, if prices are rising). In particular, Keynesian models assume either constant prices or that in the short run the rate of inflation is exogenous, so that a change in the nominal rate also changes the real rate of interest.

Monetarist

Friedman (1956) viewed an increase in the money supply as an increase in wealth (a 'helicopter' drop of money). Consumers would wish to substitute goods for money, thus initially increasing consumption. This would feed through into increased aggregate demand and then inflation. It is a similar story to the Keynesian model (except that consumption rather than investment is the main source of increased aggregate demand) but with an important difference. Friedman argued that the lags involved were long and variable, and that monetary policy should not be used as a means of stabilising income over a business cycle. In fact, inappropriately timed monetary policy could make things worse. He argued for a constant growth rate of the money supply to tie down the rate of inflation.

New Classical

Robert Lucas argued (Lucas 1972) that if people expected an increase in the growth rate of the money supply, then they would also expect the rate of inflation to increase. If this happened, workers would ask for higher nominal wage increases, and firms would increase prices in expectation of the increase in the money supply. If people had 'rational expectations', implying that on average they were statistically correct, anticipated changes in the money supply would have no real effects (that is, no effects on real wages or the real money supply) because the price level immediately would adjust. In this theory, lags for anticipated monetary policy are extremely short (i.e., almost zero).

Lucas argued that only unanticipated changes in the money supply have real effects. Thus, governments could not systematically affect output and could not successfully use monetary policy to stabilise income.

New Keynesian

A number of recent models provide microeconomic foundations for the Keynesian model, and thus have a similar transmission mechanism to the Keynesian model.[8] However, economists such as Stiglitz and Weiss (1981) have argued for a reduced role of interest rates in the preceding transmission mechanism. They argue that banks may wish not to vary interest rates in the short run, but instead will ration the amount of credit, as higher interest rates might attract a worse class of borrower (in terms of risk). In this case, interest rates might not be related to credit and therefore the money supply. Credit might directly affect investment and other spending, which then affects aggregate demand and thus income and employment (as in the preceding story).

Open economy models

The preceding models do not allow for international trade or flows of capital. With capital mobility the transmission process is altered. If physical and financial capital can move freely between countries with no transactions or other costs, we have perfect capital mobility. In this extreme case, equilibrium requires that interest rates be equalised across countries;[9] otherwise all capital would leave Australia or pour into Australia if our rate of return was below or above the rate in the rest of the world. If so, the RBA would not have much power to influence the rate of interest (certainly on medium-term to long-term maturities, which is often the relevant time period for investment decisions). Clearly this is an extreme case. However, even if there are some capital flows corresponding to differences in interest rates, the monetary transmission mechanism also involves the exchange rate as described below.

An expansionary monetary policy involves a signalled reduction in the cash rate, which should feed through to other interest rates. This should result, other things being equal, in capital outflow, resulting in a reduction in the demand for Australian dollars on foreign exchange markets. The result of this is a depreciation of the currency; this makes imports more expensive in Australian dollars, and makes Australian exports more competitive in world markets. In addition, since much of Australia's exports are in agriculture and minerals, whose price is denominated in foreign currency (mostly US dollars), the income of those exporters would increase. These factors lead to an increase of Australian spending and production and, eventually, to an increase in the price level. Classical open economy theories prescribe a quicker link between monetary policy and inflation than Keynesian open economy theories. These theories have become more important since foreign exchange markets have been deregulated. Under fixed exchange rates, capital flows were not offset by the exchange rate, and these capital flows tended to make monetary policy impotent.

Policy prescriptions

The above theories coincide with differing views on the conduct of monetary policy. The main issues are: what is the ultimate objective of monetary policy; are these best achieved via rules (independent of the current state of the economy) or via discretion (reacting to current economic circumstances); and what are the appropriate indicators and intermediate targets for monetary policy?

Classical, monetarist and new classical theories argue that the objective of monetary policy is control of the price level, to be achieved by a fixed rule of a (generally low) constant rate of growth of the money supply (monetary targeting). They view monetary growth rates as both an indicator of monetary policy and an appropriate intermediate target to meet the goal of inflation rate control. This view was prevalent in the mid-1970s to the mid-1980s when most countries experienced relatively high rates of inflation. Most central banks, including the Reserve Bank of Australia, followed some form of monetary targeting rule during this period.

Keynesian theories were born from an idea that governments should pursue active income stabilisation policies. In this way it was hoped that the volatility of output over the business cycle could be reduced. This is often referred to as activist monetary policy, or fine-tuning, with a general view that policy should be up to the discretion of the government due to the complexities of different shocks hitting the economy. Most Keynesian economists view the money supply as a poor indicator of monetary policy because they believe that the demand for money is unstable. The nominal interest rate is viewed as a more appropriate indicator of the stance of monetary policy, and the real interest rate as a more appropriate target.

The monetarist argument against an activist approach is that the lags involved in monetary policy are so long, and in Friedman's argument so variable, that such a policy might be counterproductive. Expansionary monetary policies implemented now might raise economic activity in the economy in eighteen months or two years' time, in which case the economy might have begun going into a boom and the business cycle would be made worse rather than better. In addition, many classical economists argue that even the best intentioned governments get it wrong; furthermore, classical economists assume that a certain amount of unemployment (called the natural rate) is a feature of any economy with flows into and out of the work force and that attempts to reduce unemployment below this natural rate will simply involve inflation rather than any positive effects upon economic activity. In this scenario, classical economists argue that it is more likely that monetary authorities will lead us towards excessive monetary expansion, and thus commit the economy to excessive rates of inflation.[10]

The exchange rate is another possible target of monetary policy. One advantage of stabilising the exchange rate is that there is less uncertainty facing importers and exporters if there is a relatively stable exchange rate. Currently, there are forward and futures markets operating on the exchange rate for periods of twelve months, allowing consumers and firms to purchase or sell Australian dollars at known prices in the future (at a premium) and currency options which allow the option of purchasing or selling. However, most investments require returns for longer than twelve months; financial instruments, however, are being continually developed so that even this uncertainty may be eliminated now (via the swaps market), although small business often shuns those financial 'derivatives'.

A second argument concerns the effect depreciation has on the Australian price level.[11] It raises the price of imported goods, thus adding to inflation. If the depreciation was perceived to be temporary, one policy would be to halt the depreciation by the RBA selling foreign currency. This policy would only work if the RBA was correct in its assumption that the depreciation was temporary; it could not permanently sell off its holdings of foreign currency.

The major argument against targeting the exchange rate is that Australia is heavily dependent on agriculture and mining, whose prices fluctuate considerably, thus altering the price of our exports relative to our imports (defined as the terms of trade). As is clear from Figure 7.1, since the dollar was floated in 1983 the exchange rate has offset much of the movement in the terms of trade; had the exchange rate not changed, there would have been a much bigger impact upon income.

Australian empirical evidence

Which theory should policymakers believe? One set of policies indicate that government should set a stable rate of growth of the money supply and focus solely on inflation. Another set of policies argue for active income stabilisation and for monetary policy to be expansionary or contractionary depending upon the state of the business cycle. Which theory you believe determines what policy the government should choose.

In this section we discuss the Australian evidence relating to the above theories. It is difficult to find consensus about empirical evidence because there are many different variables that one can choose to represent the theory (e.g. interest rates), there are different selections of other variables that can be considered exogenous, and

Figure 7.1 Terms of trade and the exchange rate (exchange rate is the trade weighted index)

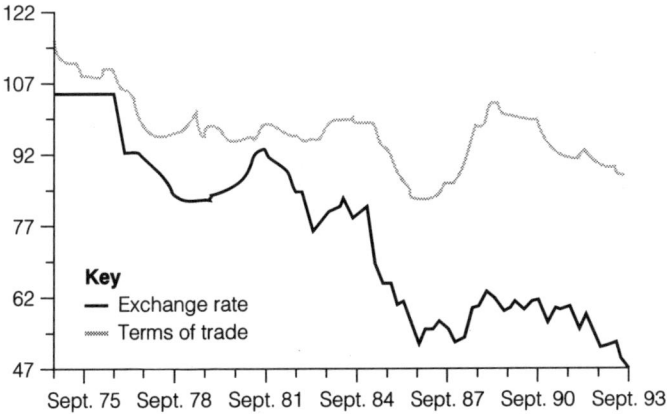

there are complex lags and structural changes that make inference from relatively short periods of sample data difficult. One area of disagreement about empirical data is the lag involved in the change in monetary policy to income and/or prices. Much of this is surveyed in Milbourne (1990). A midpoint for the estimate of this lag is roughly eighteen months (six quarters).

In addition to these problems, the question arises as to which variable should be used as an indicator of monetary policy. There are at least four: the money supply (or more specifically its growth rate), the nominal interest rate, the real interest rate, and the yield curve. The money supply had been used as a guide to policy in Australia from about 1977 until 1985. However, over the last decade, the behaviour of the growth rate of the M3 has been erratic and largely unrelated to other variables in the economy. This has been partly (but not fully) due to deregulation of financial markets and it has proven not to be a useful indicator. The nominal interest rate has been used at times as an indicator of policy. However, in periods of high inflation the nominal interest rate is not the appropriate interest rate facing investors or borrowers. For this reason, a third alternative indicator of monetary policy has been the real interest rate.

A fourth possible indicator of monetary policy is the yield curve, which for purposes of exposition can be represented as the difference between a long-term interest rate and a short-term interest rate. If the short-term nominal interest rate is greater than the long-term nominal interest rate it might be that financial market participants

Figure 7.2 Four-quarter growth in GNE and M3

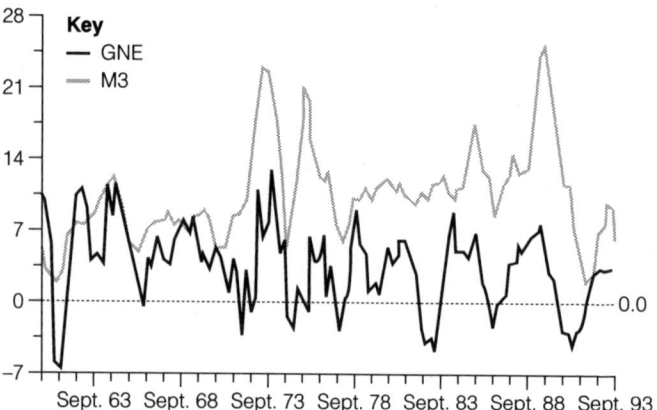

are expecting future short-term rates to be lower than the current short-term rate. Thus the current interest rate is higher than normal or expected and this might be taken as evidence of a current contractionary monetary policy. Lowe (1992) has shown that empirically the yield curve is a reasonable indicator of future output six quarters ahead.

What is the empirical evidence on the transmission mechanism? Figure 7.2 below plots the four-quarter percentage growth rate of real gross national expenditure in Australia against the four-quarter growth rate of M3. This shows the recent recession in Australia starting in 1989 and the relatively slow recovery (compared to previous recessions). We can divide the graph into three periods: prior to 1977; 1978–84; and 1984 onwards. Note that there is reasonable correlation between M3 growth and real income growth before 1977 and after 1984 but not during the intervening period of monetary targeting. Thus, precisely when the RBA hoped to use M3 growth to affect real income, the relationship broke down. This is known as Goodhart's law: when you try to exploit an empirical relationship for policy purposes, the relationship evaporates. Lucas (1976) has advanced the argument that the reason might lie in changes in expectations which accompany policy changes.

An alternative way of presenting this evidence is the velocity of M3 (Figure 7.3). Both the actual measure and the seasonally adjusted (seasonally adjusted GDP divided by seasonally adjusted M3) measure are extremely variable over the 1980s, making it difficult to argue for a constant monetary growth rate. This is the heart of the dilemma facing the RBA.

Does correlation with real income imply that M3 is useful for

Figure 7.3 Money velocity

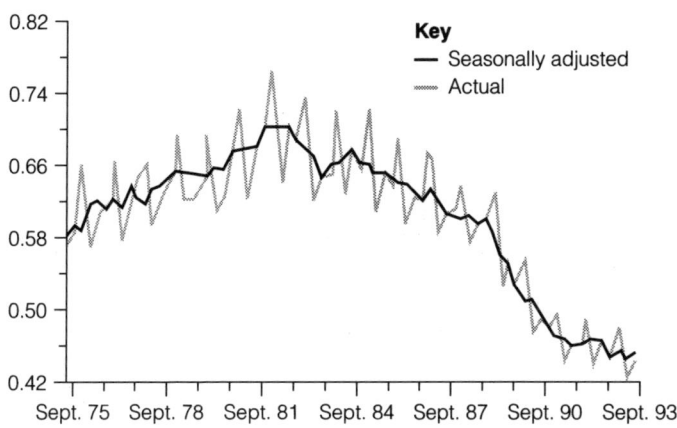

monetary policy? We have seen above that there is little correlation when M3 was targeted, and this suggests that M3 should not be a target of monetary policy. Does the correlation mean that M3 can be a useful predictor of policy effects? The answer seems to be no. To be a useful predictor, M3 has to lead real income (i.e. variations in M3 have to be closely related to subsequent variations in income). The evidence since 1983 is that income leads M3, certainly at the turning points. This is supported by statistical evidence from research conducted at the Reserve Bank.[12] This research finds that both M3 and broader monetary aggregates (which include deposits at non-bank financial intermediaries) lag both nominal and real income. Thus, changes in income seem to generate changes in money holdings and/or credit creation but not vice versa.

Since monetary aggregates have been highly erratic in the 1980s, it is still possible that monetary policy might effect economic activity via interest rates. It has also been difficult to find a stable and robust relationship between interest rates and economic activity. Figure 7.4 plots the growth rate of private investment against the real (ex-post) interest rate and this explains much of the inability of econometric evidence to establish a relationship. Of note is the very high real interest rate in 1988 and 1989 followed by a prolonged period of low rates of growth of investment (and income). Notice that real interest rates have been much less variable in the 1980s than in the 1970s and have been on an upward trend. No such trend is evident in investment growth nor do the cycles of investment and interest rates match up. Econometric evidence which allows for lags and other variables has failed to find a statistical relationship between real or nominal interest rates, and either investment or income.

Figure 7.4 Four-quarter growth in real private investment and the interest rate

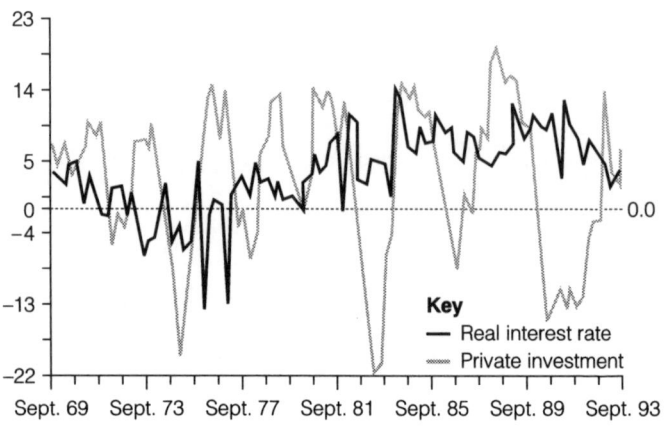

Figure 7.5 Four-quarter growth in the CPI and M3

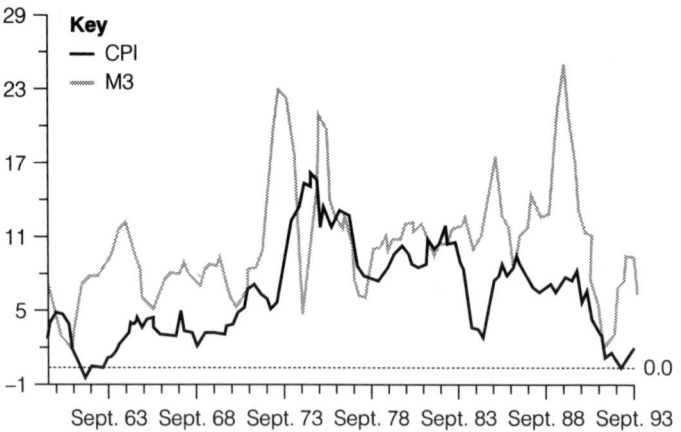

Figure 7.5 plots the rate of inflation against the growth rate of M3. There is not much connection between the two. Of course, monetary policy might affect inflation with a lag, although if so, the transmission would not appear to be through economic activity. This lack of correlation is reflected in more sophisticated statistical tests which allow for lags. Carmichael (1990) finds that other factors such as wages growth, changes in the terms of trade and other cost factors have been much more responsible for inflation than has monetary growth. This is not a definite conclusion, however, because it could

Figure 7.6 Private consumption expenditure (real) and personal credit

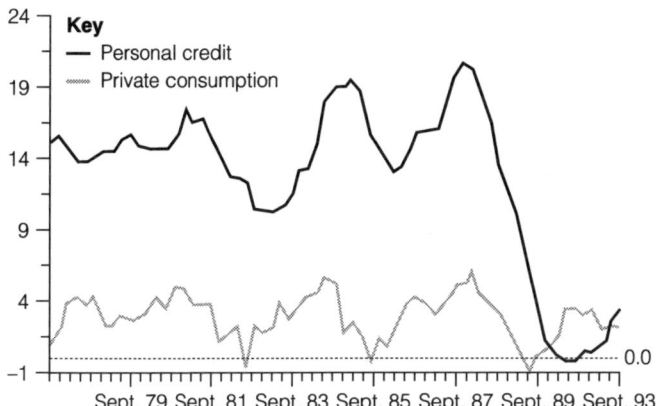

be that expectations of continuing and/or high rates of monetary growth conditioned wages growth and thus a deeper explanation of the inflation of the 1980s in Australia may go back to monetary growth. This money—wages—inflation story is somewhat harder to accept from the mid-1980s when the Accord played a role in the significant reductions in both real and nominal wage growth. On evidence presented above, it is difficult to find strong empirical support for the standard closed economy theories of the transmission mechanism in aggregate data.

What about the alternative theories suggested above? The new Keynesian theories argue that there should be a direct relationship between credit and income. Figures 7.6 and 7.7 show the relationship between credit and income. It does not display any better correlation than that between money and income. In this respect, the new Keynesian theories are no better empirically than the standard transmission mechanisms.

There have been a variety of sophisticated econometric tests of the new classical model mostly conducted in the United States. The procedures for testing these models are extremely complex. The Lucas proposition implies that anticipated monetary policy is ineffective. The empirical tests conducted on Australian data reject the new classical model. Siegloff and Groenweld (1987) show that the time series evidence is not consistent with either policy ineffectiveness or 'rational' expectations. Horne and MacDonald (1984) and Rao and Srivastava (1989) show that the lags on prices and output are too long to be consistent with the new classical model.

Figure 7.7 Growth in business investment (real) and business credit

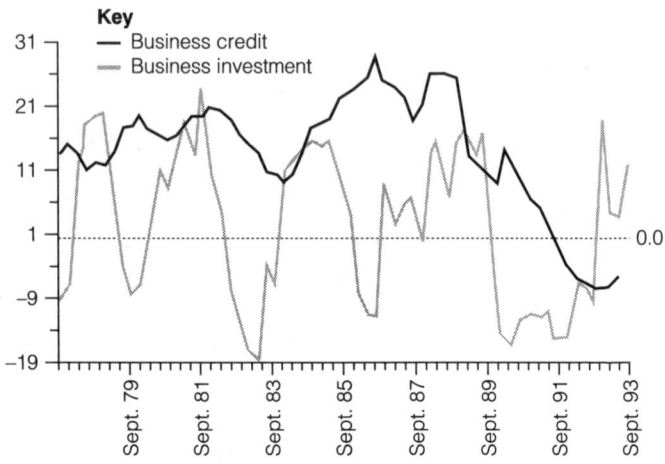

Recent Reserve Bank of Australia policy

The lack of consensus about the appropriate role of money and its effect on the economy and the lack of solid empirical support for one or other theories has meant that framing policy has been very difficult. At the risk of oversimplification, the philosophy behind the conduct of monetary policy has gone through three distinct phases since 1975 (prior to which the Reserve Bank followed a somewhat Keynesian stabilisation approach to monetary policy).

In 1977 the RBA announced that it was moving towards monetary targeting by setting upper and lower bounds for the growth rate of the money supply (M3). This approach to policy followed the new classical theory whereby announcements of the rate of monetary growth should hopefully condition expectations of inflation and allow inflation to be reduced without causing a recession. However, the actual rates of monetary growth did not stay within the target range creating a credibility problem for the RBA. It was hoped that deregulation in 1983, which would put banks on a more competitive footing with the non-bank financial intermediaries, would bring stability to bank deposits and monetary aggregates and allow for less variability in those monetary aggregates. This did not occur, and the RBA formally abolished monetary targeting in 1985.

Following the abolition of monetary targeting, the RBA announced that its philosophy was to establish a 'check list' of variables which would be used to determine the stance of monetary policy. The list of variables was never published and indeed commentators on Reserve Bank policy have argued that over various periods of time more weight has been given to some variables than others. This philosophy is a more Keynesian stabilisation approach but with variables other than income part of the objective. In the 1985/86 period the variable that the Reserve Bank was most interested in stabilising was believed to be the exchange rate; subsequent emphasis passed to the level of income, and finally to the rate of inflation. Concern with bringing down the rate of inflation and the rising level of foreign debt finally prompted the RBA to raise nominal interest rates in the period 1988/89.[13]

As discussed in chapter 4, 1989 began the great output growth decline and Australia went into a long recession. A number of factors contributed to this decline, most notably the adverse terms of trade situation in those years, but argument still remains on what role the period of high and sustained interest rates had on dampening economic activity. Until further econometric evidence is assembled on this (which may take some more time), it would be difficult to assign the relative contributions. Needless to say, many economists believe that the high sustained interest rates did contribute to the subsequent decline of output. This recession has been bad for income and employment, however it may have resurrected a belief in the importance and potency of monetary policy at a time when its role and importance was being questioned.

Since 1990 the Reserve Bank has moved to a newly defined philosophy on monetary policy and a new operating procedure. The philosophy is that the Reserve Bank is now officially concerned with the rate of inflation, and in particular with protecting the current low rate of inflation over a medium-term perspective. However, they have maintained their view that they will continue to monitor developments in the Australian economy and operate on the cash rate if they feel conditions warrant. They have also explicitly stated that the exchange rate will remain in the check list (MacFarlane 1993). An important point about this is a philosophical move more towards the classical view of the economy, and for stabilisation policy only to respond to major fluctuations in the economy rather than to fine-tuning.

Are the commitments to both low inflation and stabilisation policy necessarily compatible? Provided the RBA 'gets it right' and knows the natural level of employment or output around which they wish to stabilise those variables, then the two are not necessarily incompatible. If on average the economy deviates from one side or the other of that average or natural level, then the average rate of monetary growth can be consistent with whichever the RBA wishes to choose as compatible with its long-term rate of inflation. The danger is if the RBA does not have good information on what the appropriate level of unemployment or output is, or if market participants believe that they do not, it could prolong high inflation or high unemployment.

Notes

1 The author would like to thank Geoff Kingston, Mark Crosby and Graham Voss for comments, and Matthew Cumberworth for research assistance.
2 Collateral refers to the value of additional security which the bank may claim in the event of a payment default.
3 A discussion of these issues is contained in Milbourne and Cumberworth (1991).
4 More explicit detail and discussion is contained in the RBA *Bulletins*, September 1988 and July 1990.
5 A previous aggregate, M2, is no longer used since it relied upon the distinction between savings banks and trading banks; this distinction no longer exists.
6 For example, the price of all goods could be expressed in terms of the value of an orange.
7 Recent theories which have explained this type of behaviour as being rational include the idea that contracts between firms and workers are only agreed to at particular intervals (e.g. Fischer (1977) and Taylor (1979)), and the fact that there are costs of firms continually changing their prices (Mankiw 1985). A survey of recent theoretical models is contained in Blanchard (1988).
8 See references in last note.
9 Interest parity requires that interest rates differ by the expected percentage change in the exchange rate, since foreign investors in Australian assets care about the value of the return in their currencies when they convert the proceeds back. If the expected change in the exchange rate is equal to the difference in inflation rates, this is equivalent to equality of real interest rates.
10 A similar argument is that discretionary policy might result in excessive inflation as governments use expansionary policy to reduce unemployment in order to get re-elected, hoping that possible higher inflation will not be apparent to the electorate.
11 See chapter 3.
12 See Milbourne (1990, section 4b) and the references contained within.
13 A more complete description is contained in Milbourne (1990). There seemed to be a considerable difference between the Treasury and the RBA for the reasons for monetary contraction. The former argued that high interest rates were necessary to contain the current account deficit; the latter argued about the importance of price stability. See the quotes in Bewley and White (1990).

Recommended reading

Argy, V. 1992, *Australian Macroeconomic Policy*, Part II, Allen & Unwin, Sydney

Davis, K. 1991, 'The development of Australian monetary policy during the last decade', in C. Kearney and R. MacDonald, *Developments in Australian Monetary Economics*, Longman Cheshire, Melbourne

Milbourne, R.D. 1990, 'Money and finance', in S. Grenvile (ed.), *The Australian Economy in the 1980s*, Reserve Bank of Australia

8 Microeconomic reform
David Clark

Across the western world over the 1980s, macroeconomic policy did not live up to the claims of most of its academic advocates. As a result, the 1990s have seen much greater emphasis placed on microeconomic policy and reform.

This switch in emphasis was not the simple product of an intellectual revolution in our universities or of a conspiracy of 'economic rationalists' in Treasury, as some sociologists have wrongly claimed, but a product of the realisation that the three great faiths of modern macroeconomic policy had proven increasingly ineffective.

By the mid-1980s the first faith—the monetarists' faith in monetary targeting—was in tatters, as governments across the western world exceeded the targets they had set and financial deregulation made the main measures of money supply—M3 and broad money—increasingly transparent and thus poor guides for monetary policy setting.

The second great faith—the vulgar Keynesians' faith in fiscal fine-tuning using changes in budget deficits, expenditure and tax—also proved deficient. In the late 1980s, the biggest cut in government spending and borrowing in our history did not produce an automatic rise in unemployment. Indeed, it was accompanied by strong employment growth. Similarly, a massive loosening of fiscal policy, in the form of bigger budget deficits and greater borrowing in the early 1990s, failed to produce a significant drop in unemployment.

In addition, the Accord failed to produce the productivity growth Australia so desperately needed, merely to restrain import penetration, and depreciations of the $A failed to produce the expansion of exports and rise in import replacement academic advocates of the 'J-Curve' promised.

The third great faith—that extensive government regulation and ownership would maximise both efficiency and equity—is also in tatters, not just in western economies but in the former and remaining socialist ones. Over the 1980s a more critical attitude developed towards high budget deficits and borrowing, particularly in small, open economies like Australia's, and governments of all colours have accepted that some types of government spending can have high opportunity costs—for example, money spent on servicing government borrowing could be better spent on helping the genuine needy—and thus should be subject to closer scrutiny. Government pricing policies are also facing massive re-examination. Hence the greater interest in microeconomic reform in the 1990s.

What is microeconomic reform?

Microeconomic reform involves a panoply of measures to improve the efficiency of both our public and private sectors. Its aim is to make our products more competitive on world markets and thereby reduce our current account deficit and foreign debt and at the same time make our locally produced goods and services more able to compete against imports.

More specifically, microeconomic reform aims to increase four types of efficiency:[1]

- productive efficiency—that is, it improves the efficiency with which resources within a firm are utilised by changing managerial and employee practices;
- inter-temporal efficiency—that is, it improves the allocation of resources between current consumption and investment and encourages more investment in technology and skill enhancement;
- dynamic efficiency—that is, it improves the speed with which industries adapt to a changing environment;
- allocative efficiency—that is, it improves the allocation of resources among industries.

OECD studies suggest that the most dramatic short-term improvements are induced by measures which concentrate on raising the first three of these, particularly measures which change work practices.

The main types of microeconomic reform being undertaken by the Federal Government and the State governments are:

- reductions in restrictive work and management practices so we can achieve higher productivity growth, reduce costs and improve our international competitiveness;
- improvements in the efficiency of our transport, communications and commodity handling facilities;
- removal of unnecessary regulation of business. While some forms of regulation are necessary—for example, health and safety regulations—others can be outdated and even counterproductive;
- measures to make our public sector more efficient, including privatisation and the removal of restrictions on public sector enterprise managers to enable them to compete more effectively with private sector ones;
- tailoring of our education and training to better fit community needs and steps to make sure that those who benefit most from government expenditure in these areas pay some of the burden imposed on their fellow taxpayers. These reforms also include much greater emphasis on producing multi-skilled, rather than narrowly trained, employees and on accompanying efforts to change our industrial award structure accordingly;
- taxation reform to encourage more efficient allocation and use of our scarce productive resources;
- review of our Trade Practices legislation to ensure that it does not discourage firms from becoming more efficient and internationally competitive;
- more exposure of sheltered industry sectors to the winds of international competition, to force them to improve their productivity and marketing skills;
- the encouragement of industry restructuring, including measures to stimulate more research and development, innovation and investment;
- further efforts to reduce international trade barriers and subsidies to help improve our access to overseas markets;
- measures to increase the flexibility of our labour market and to reduce industrial disputation and demarcation disputes. This debate will be examined in more detail below, as many commentators believe changes in our industrial relations system hold out the greatest promise for productivity and competitiveness improvement.

Why microeconomic reform is unavoidable

To understand why microeconomic reform has become such a big issue in the 1990s and why it is imperative that it be accelerated further requires a little economic history.

In the 1880s Australia led the world in the productivity of its work force. According to one estimate, our labour productivity was over 50 per cent higher than that of our nearest competitors, the US and the UK. The result was the highest standard of living in the world. Since then we have fallen further and further behind in the international economic race, largely because of insufficient structural change and productivity growth below that of most other western economies.[2]

Following our most serious depression, that of the 1890s, Australia turned inwards, believing that social and political goals should be given pre-eminence. In particular we:

- adopted a 'Fortress Australia' set of industry policies, including bounties, subsidies, import quotas and tariffs, which rested on the assumption that only by protecting our industries from overseas competition would we produce a diversified and dynamic manufacturing sector;
- set up an industrial relations system, heavily borrowed from New Zealand, which gave legal recognition to trade unions, centralised dispute settlement and established the notion of a basic wage;
- introduced the widest range of government enterprises outside the Soviet Union, ranging from government joineries, mines, banks (and later insurance companies) through to even government fisheries, fish and chip shops, butcher shops and pubs;
- constructed a federal system of government which produced unnecessary duplication between State governments and the Federal Government and much misallocation of public resources, as States competed against each other.

However, such steps failed to protect the economy from the ups and downs of the international economy—in the early 1930s we experienced an unemployment rate second only to Germany's—and failed to produce a genuinely industrialised economy. Indeed, the fastest industrial development came in the 1940s—thanks largely to the diligence of German U-boat commanders in the South Atlantic which cut Australia off from its traditional sources of manufactured imports.

In the 1950s and 1960s Australia experienced another 'Golden Age', largely as a result of good prices for its now diversified range of commodity exports. This was the period when we should have rethought our circa 1890s 'Fortress Australia' policy approach but we continued to believe that the international economy would not change radically.

By the early 1970s, however, the following problems with our development model were becoming obvious:

- our failure to industrialise, despite decades of protection and government assistance. Thus we have not 'de-industrialised' over the past two decades as sociologists—and even EPAC (1993b & c)—argue.

  In fact, we failed to develop a capital goods sector and the complex input–output relationships between the major sectors of our economy which are the key hallmarks of a truly industrialised economy. This has made it much more difficult for us to expand exports and resist rising import penetration, particularly when sharp falls in the $A increase the cost of imported capital goods and other industry inputs.

  The result was a manufacturing sector which, after decades of protection and government assistance, had become more inward-looking, undynamic and dominated by multinational companies which had simply hurdled our high protection walls;
- falling pay-offs from our commodity exports, as world supply of many of our key exports grew faster than demand, and restrictions to international trade and trade blocs grew in importance;
- investment which was largely capital-widening—in other words, more roads, schools, hospitals etc.—rather than capital-deepening, more capital-intensive investment, which would have produced higher GDP per capita and productivity growth;
- a less sharply focused immigration program and education and training programs below international standards;
- a political system which was dominated by powerful economic interest groups mainly interested in defending our circa 1890s development model, with politicians on both sides of politics lacking the vision required to shift Australia onto a new path. Economic and social policy decisions were being increasingly made in response to political patronage, rather than in Australia's long-term economic interest;
- an industrial relations system and wage policy which encouraged us to naively believe that our wage levels and conditions could be set at higher levels than those of economies with much higher productivity growth, without us suffering long-term declines in our international competitiveness.

In short, Australia became a victim of its very success. Our dominant export industries—mining and agriculture—placed most emphasis on capital-intensive techniques. Maximising output came first; more efficient use of labour second. Employer–employee

MICROECONOMIC REFORM

Figure 8.1 Why productivity must rise

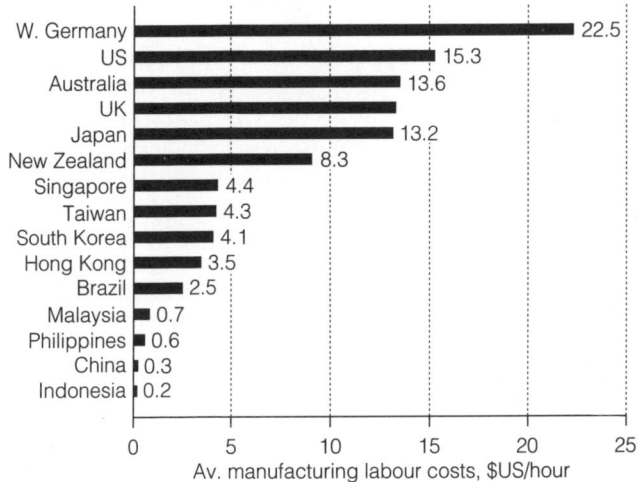

Source: DRI McGraw-Hill/Morgan Stanley.   1993 figures

negotiation and discussion were positively discouraged. A 'them-or-us' philosophy prevailed on both sides of the industrial coin. The result can be seen in Australia's high relative labour costs in Figure 8.1.

At the same time, far too little emphasis was placed on training and retraining in established industries, while the newer industries tended to display a 'bull-in-the-china-shop' approach to such matters.

The result was a slowdown in GDP per capita and productivity growth and further declines in our relative living standards.[3] Lower prices and lower growth in demand for our major exports, particularly in times of international economic downturn like the early 1980s and early 1990s, also exacerbated our problems.

Microeconomic reform aims at changing these negative features of our current industrial culture, government regulation and intervention, management practices and other obstacles which prevent Australian firms from competing more effectively against imports and Australian exporters from competing more effectively on world markets.

Microeconomic reform—an overview

As a result of such poor work practices, poor management, a naive faith in the Accord and currency depreciations, and insufficient business investment in import-replacement and export-expanding industries, over the 1980s Australian productivity growth was poor by world standards. Although international comparisons are fraught with difficulties, it is clear that while our agricultural and mining sectors were efficient by international standards, our manufacturing sector and government business enterprise productivity was well below that of comparable countries (OECD 1992a). Yet, both Federal and State governments were slow to act. For example, in 1989, the then Treasurer, Mr Keating, claimed that 'If you go into a pet shop every parrot is screeching microeconomic reform, microeconomic reform'.

However, over the past decade Australia has seen the most dramatic and wide-ranging changes in microeconomic and industry policy in its history. The most important of these policy changes have been:[4]

- the deregulation of financial markets, the floating of the $A and the abolition of exchange controls in the early 1980s;
- a more critical attitude towards our centralised and legalistic industrial relations system, resulting in a move towards more negotiation between employers and employees. Unlike New Zealand, however, we have not yet decided to dynamite our circa 1890s industrial relations model and many commentators believe that change has been far too slow. Despite much talk about enterprise bargaining since 1987, only 10 per cent of the work force is now covered by such arrangements;[5]
- reductions in business regulation, reforms in corporation law, moves towards common product standards across the states, and improvements in government purchasing and customs procedures;
- greater accountability of government business enterprises which has forced them to improve their productivity and cut staff levels. This should help restrain rises in the cost of goods and services these enterprises provide—for example, transport and electricity—in future years;
- the most dramatic privatisations in our history, ranging from partial privatisations of the Commonwealth Bank through to complete sell-offs of State insurance companies and Qantas and Australian Airlines;
- changes in the tax regime, including cuts in the company tax rate, removal of the additional tax on retained earnings of private companies, accelerated depreciation allowances, and the introduction of full dividend imputation. (The latter lowered the tax rate paid on share dividends by shareholders.) However, many argue our tax system still has too narrow an indirect tax base—collects too much of total revenue from direct taxes on

wages and not enough from indirect taxes on consumption—and provides too many disincentives to save. The absence of a capital gains tax on the family home also encourages Australians to invest in 'emoh ruo', rather than in export-expanding or import-replacing industries.
- better targeting of social security payments and new forms of cash assistance to low-income families. However, the gap for many welfare recipients between the support obtainable from governments and the income which could be earned by re-entering the work force continues to narrow;
- greater effort to reduce overlaps between the three levels of government, Federal, State and local. The most important of these have been attempts to set up a national electricity grid and initiatives in rail transport and telecommunications;
- efforts to improve government department budgeting, staffing and purchasing procedures. However, the Commonwealth Public Service still kept growing in the early 1990s, through the biggest collapse in our job market since the 1930s;
- accelerated effort by Australia to remove impediments to international trade in agricultural products, through the establishment of the Cairns Group of other rural exporters, and to set up a Asia-Pacific Economic Co-Operation group, albeit the latter will be dominated by the US and Japan;
- reductions in tariff levels and other forms of assistance. These are just starting to have an impact but should further boost manufacturing productivity.

The result, aided by the belt-tightening forced on private and government business enterprises by the recession of the early 1990s, has been an impressive increase in productivity and improvement in international competitiveness. However, with the easiest and most obvious reforms now in place, and with a pick-up in the economy, it will be much harder to maintain the pace of reform and productivity growth over the rest of the 1990s.

The industry policy revolution

Despite the hopes of the left-wing of the ALP and multinational manufacturers operating in Australia that a Labor government would increase government assistance—the Accord of 1983 between the ALP and the ACTU had a more interventionist industry policy as a key plank but this was inserted largely as a sop to the left-wing unions and parliamentarians—from the late 1980s onwards first the Hawke Government and then the Keating Government implemented the most radical shake-up of industry policies in our history. With deregulation failing to produce the increases in competition that its architects had promised, these Labor governments had little choice.

While these moves were largely driven by the need to make Australian manufacturing more outward-looking and competitive, they were also driven by an acceptance that the impact of our 'Fortress Australia' industry policy on lower income Australians had been highly regressive. While this approach helped create some jobs and protected others—in the 1960s about 70 per cent of manufacturing jobs depended on high protection levels—ordinary Australians ended up paying much higher prices for even basic manufactured goods than consumers in many other countries. For example, high protection added about $5000 to the price of the average new car and meant that low-income families paid high prices for necessities of life such as food, clothing and footwear.

The main changes in industry policy have been:

- the May 1988 Statement. It announced reductions in the maximum tariff rate on most manufactured imports to 10 or 15 per cent by July 1992. However, important exceptions to this general rule were made for motor vehicles, textiles, clothing and footwear and some agricultural equipment;
- the March 1991 Statement. It announced further reductions in the maximum rate, producing a maximum rate of 5 per cent by mid-1996. Once again, however, exceptions were made for the products mentioned, although import quotas for textiles, clothing and footwear were abolished from 1 March 1993;
- the textile, clothing and footwear (TCF) Statements (March 1991 and July 1992). The first announced the abolition of tariff quotas from 1 March 1993 and a phasing down of the maximum tariff on TCF imports from 55 to 25 per cent by the year 2000. The second, in response to the recession, provided additional support for TCF producers. A TCF imports credits scheme was also introduced from 1 July 1991. It assists TCF exports by enabling manufacturers to accrue import credits from export sales—a scheme similar to that which has operated for some years for the automotive industry.
- the 'One Nation' Statement (February 1992). Changes included: accelerated depreciation allowances for most plant and equipment with an effective life of more than five years and some buildings; a concessional tax rate for new investment companies ('pooled development funds'); a deferral of income tax payments for small companies; and the introduction of 'development allowances'. (With the last-named, projects worth $50 million plus in the traded goods sector qualify for a 10 per cent

investment allowance if they meet certain efficiency criteria and are not in receipt of substantial other assistance from the Commonwealth.) Extra funding for Austrade, the Export Access Program, for assistance to Australian exporters trying to establish new markets in developing economies, for the Australian Tourist Commission, for the Textiles, Clothing and Footwear Development Authority and for rural producers was also announced;
- 1993 Federal election promises. These included: a cut in the company tax rate from 39 cents in the dollar to 33 cents; 'One Nation development allowances' extended to automotive and communications industries and to help Mitsubishi build a new car plant; a new Department of Regional Development; measures to boost trade with Asia; an extension of the shipbuilding bounty; and new tourism programs.

As a result of these changes, the average nominal rates of assistance to industry have fallen to about 8 per cent and the average effective rate to about 14 per cent. However, even by the mid-1990s the passenger motor vehicles and textiles, clothing and footwear (TCF) industries will still be highly protected, relative to other sectors of manufacturing. Indeed, the TCF plan will be adjusted by reducing tariffs on apparel, footwear and most higher tariff fabric and footwear items by only 5 percentage points. The result will be an effective rate of protection for textiles of 58 per cent; for clothing and footwear 118 per cent; and for motor vehicles 145 per cent.

Nevertheless, these tariff reductions should lower the prices of many essential inputs for Australian industry, helping to make it more competitive on world markets, and by the end of this century little industry-specific assistance will be provided.

Contrary to widespread belief, Reserve Bank and Bureau of Industry Economics research suggests that the fall in demand—and not these changes—was the main cause of the rise in manufacturing unemployment in the early 1990s. While such cuts can—and have—certainly cost jobs in formerly highly protected industries, the shake-up in industry policy has also produced a growing number of export success stories, which in the longer term should add to job levels in manufacturing.

Indeed, the cuts in protection and assistance have already stimulated improvements in manufacturing productivity and international competitiveness (see Figure 8.2). While job-shedding forced on car manufacturers by the fall in demand for their products contributed to the rise in productivity, exposure to the ill winds of international competition have also forced change. Interestingly, Toyota has committed itself to a $700 million new factory in Australia, despite the protection cuts.

Figure 8.2 Productivity expected to rise

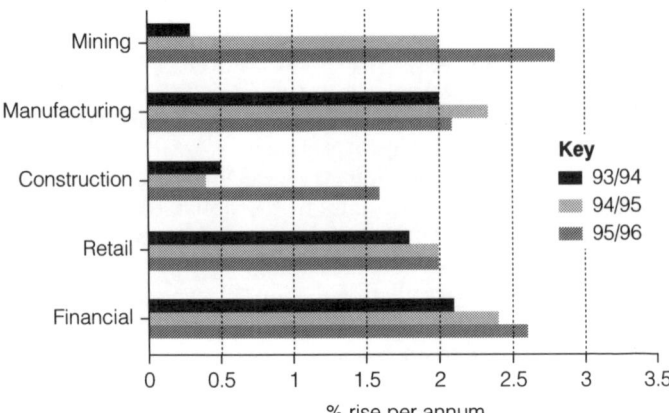

Source: NAB Survey.

The TCF sector is also starting to raise its productivity, with the result that it is now successfully selling Australian-made stockings in low wage economies like the Philippines. Many Australians do not realise that manufacturing around the world is now much more capital intensive and that our high relative labour costs are not as important as they used to be.

Other big current issues in industry policy in the 1990s include:

- should the Federal Government try and identify industries which may have better chances of competing on world markets? Supporters of such a role cite the supposed role of Japan's MITI in fostering Japan's postwar industrialisation drive. They do not mention, however, that MITI advised Honda not to go into car production and was highly doubtful about the impact the transistor would have on the electronics industry;
- an increasing realisation that to be competitive abroad we have to have more competition at home. For example, the Prices Surveillance Authority has been pressing for the establishment of a kind of monopolies commission, formed by an amalgamation of it with the Trade Practices Commission, which would also overview the activities of government business enterprises and authorities. However, business is concerned that such a move would over-centralise industry policy. (What is certain is action on the 1993 Hilmer Report (Hilmer et al. 1993) but some sections of business are likely to resist government efforts to make them more competitive.)

- export enhancement schemes. These are important in some other countries—they provide funds and/or subsidies for exporters—but through the efforts of the General Agreement on Tariffs and Trade (GATT) have declined in importance in recent years, except in the promotion of agricultural exports. Moreover, an Industry Commission review of these schemes concluded that Australia has nothing to gain from selective targeting of exports. Instead, it urged measures to lower the tax burden on exporters and to foster a greater export culture throughout the community;
- tax policy. While the defeat of the Opposition in the 1993 Federal election has put a dramatic widening of the indirect tax base through a GST or similar on the back-burner, tax policy will continue to generate much debate. Taxation of superannuation funds, tax concessions on superannuation, tax measures to stimulate personal and company saving and simplification of our incredibly complex tax laws, will all receive much attention. In late 1993, the Federal Government announced a Tax Law Improvement Project, which has begun with an examination of the *Income Tax Assessment Act*, and sales tax streamlining has also commenced;
- the costs and benefits of reducing greenhouse gas emissions. Industry Commission studies concluded that if Australia meets the 1988 Toronto emission target of a 20 per cent drop in levels by 2005 our national income will decline by about 1.5 per cent. They also argued if market-based measures such as taxes and tradeable emission permits are used to meet this target—rather than direct government regulations—the costs of meeting the target would be considerably less.

Clearly, industry policy has changed dramatically in recent years. However, the real 'proof-of-the-pudding' test of these changes will be provided if Australian manufacturing achieves significant import replacement and further inroads into world markets. If it is to do so, all commentators believe the next area of microeconomic reform is critical.

Labour market reform

A clash of two visions

A lot of academic ink has been spilt on the issue of labour market reform: defenders of the status quo tend to overexaggerate the likely negative effects of radical change; supporters of radical change the positive ones. In fact, the debate rests heavily on theoretical argument—on two quite distinct 'visions'.

The first is faith in what Adam Smith called the 'invisible hand'—in other words, market forces. The deregulators believe that if labour markets are not regulated, supply and demand will set wages, the labour market will then 'clear'—that is, there will be no continuing unemployment—and labour will move between industries most productively.

The second is a faith in intervention and regulation. Defenders of our current system argue that real world labour markets are very different from the textbook world of the deregulators. Furthermore, they say that employees are not homogeneous: they learn on the job, they are not all 'rational economic men' who make job choices on purely economic grounds, and who slide up and down the indifference curves of their economics textbooks in search of their equilibrium point.

If labour markets clear so easily, they argue, then why is some unemployment the norm rather than the exception? Besides, weaker groups of employees require protection from 'the anarchy of market forces', they argue.[6] Indeed, the mathematicians in this group, led by Professor Frank Hahn at Cambridge, have shown that the preconditions necessary for the 'invisible hand' to achieve all that is hoped for it are incredibly complex and thus unlikely to be found in any real world economy. But this takes us to the very frontiers of modern economics.

On the other hand, believers in the first vision argue that unemployment is caused by regulation, rather than unemployment being a rationale for it. They argue that the interventionists have neglected the microeconomics of unemployment in their belief that appropriate fiscal and monetary policy measures would be sufficient. They argue we should devote a lot more attention to microeconomic matters—rather than macroeconomic ones—especially given the failure of the Accord to produce a much more flexible and dynamic economy.

But to some extent the walls between these two faiths are breaking down. Most sensible interventionists are beginning to accept that we should pay more attention to microeconomic issues and that some forms of intervention can be counterproductive and may benefit one group at the expense of another.

Clearly, the final position you take on labour market deregulation will be greatly influenced by which of these two 'visions' you are most sympathetic towards—in other words, whether you believe that the individual should be given maximum freedom in labour markets, and elsewhere in the economy, or whether you believe that the state must continue to intervene and regulate. This should not be used as an excuse, however, to avoid critical examination of both sides of the debate.

Is enterprise bargaining a solution?

At the centre of the labour market deregulation debate are two key suggestions:

- that we place more emphasis on settling industrial disputes where they occur—at the workplace—rather than sending them off to industrial tribunals; or as the Business Council of Australia puts it, we need to downgrade industrial relations and upgrade employee relations;
- that employees be given greater opportunity to negotiate conditions of employment and wages with their employers, taking into account the peculiar conditions of their firm or industry, rather than having Australia-wide conditions laid down by tribunals.

Such a view has not been confined to employers.[7] Nor is it a simple element in the 'New Right' agenda. During the First World War, the radical left, anarcho-syndicalist Industrial Workers of the World, were strong opponents of our already highly centralised and legalistic industrial relations system and made criticisms of it not dissimilar to those made by the H.R. Nicholls Society in our times.

Enterprise bargaining is seen as the best approach to achieving both goals. This involves employees talking and negotiating directly with their employers, rather than relying on union officials and industrial tribunals to do the negotiating for them. More specifically, greater enterprise bargaining will require that:

- working arrangements be primarily negotiated and adjusted in workplaces and enterprises between employers and/or managers and their employees;
- methods and levels of pay reflect the performance of people, teams and enterprises;
- disputes are settled between employers and/or managers on the one hand and employees on the other, without the need for intervention by tribunals. If intervention by third parties is required, professional conciliators could be employed, as is done in the US.

The main effect of moves in this direction will be to reduce the power and influence of the existing Federal and State tribunals, trade unions and employers' associations. For this reason, there is plenty

Table 8.1 The pros and cons of greater enterprise bargaining

Supporters argue
- It would replace our existing highly centralised and cumbersome, two-tiered award system with agreements which would better reflect the capacity of companies to pay.
- Productivity will rise, as a result of greater recognition of individual differences between employees—we would pay the worker, rather than just pay the job.
- Industrial disputes would be settled more quickly, without the need for outside tribunal intervention.
- Greater cooperation and trust between employers and employees would replace the present 'them and us' philosophy.

Opponents reply
- Wage differentials will widen.
- Working conditions and terms of employment will deteriorate as the influence of unions falls.
- Employees will strongly oppose it, leading to a fall in trust and rise in bitterness towards employers.
- Employer-funded employee training will be reduced.
- Our federal system of industrial relations will prevent it.

---

of opposition to radical changes from all three groups, as is demonstrated in Table 8.1.

Enterprise bargaining does not mean that market forces will completely rule industrial relations. There is wide community support for maintaining minimum wage levels and other types of 'safety nets' for industrially weaker and less skilled groups of employees, even if our existing award system is abolished. For example, the Federal Opposition supports the retention of minimum wage rates.

Still, when one remembers that less than 30 per cent of our private sector work force is now in unions, that 15 per cent of union members have been unfinancial for more than six months, and only about 8 per cent of new entrants to the work force since the mid-1980s have joined unions, then it is clear that our heavily centralised and legalistic industrial relations system is undergoing a radical process of devolution, whether the 'Industrial Relations Club' practitioners, commentators and academics like it or not.

It is also interesting to note that what job growth has occurred in recent years has been largely confined to small employers who have remained largely untouched by union-engineered enterprise bargaining and who have more freedom from centrally imposed controls. There has also been a dramatic growth in contracting—the most decentralised form of such bargaining.

This means that our industrial relations system is becoming very much a half-way house between highly centralised systems on the one hand and highly decentralised ones on the other. This appears far from optimal, given that the countries which have had the best wage policy outcomes and GDP per capita outcomes over the past decade are those which tend to be at either end of this spectrum.

Still, instead of just talking about radical industrial relations reform, New Zealand has done it. There, industrial relations no longer rest on national, occupational and award negotiations conducted away from the workplace but on collective or individual contracts negotiated at the enterprise level. Multi-employer bargaining has virtually disappeared and there has been sharp growth in contracts reached between individual employers and employees. Between 50 and 60 per cent of employees are now covered by collective contracts and the rest by individual ones. Interestingly, over 30 per cent of workers had not seen changes in their old terms of employment, despite the abolition of awards.

Studies suggest that about 8 to 12 per cent of New Zealand employees have suffered a fall in their take-home pay, particularly the lesser skilled. However, many have gained from the changes, particularly those in more strategically placed industries and those prepared to change their work arrangements and attitudes.

While it is too early to make definitive judgments about the effect of the reforms, average nominal and real earnings are rising again after falling dramatically in the early 1990s, the unemployment rate is trending downwards, productivity of the manufacturing sector has risen sharply, unit labour cost growth has been very low and business investment is recovering more sharply than it has in Australia.[8]

Even such preliminary results suggest that Australian manufacturers will face increasing competition over the years ahead, largely as a result of these reforms—even when New Zealand companies suffer the highest transport costs in the world to get key inputs across the Tasman and their finished products to Australian markets. They will also encourage overseas firms to establish their operations in New Zealand rather than Australia, and more Australian companies to shift their manufacturing operations to New Zealand. Indeed, the Bureau of Industry Economics has estimated that if a similar package of reforms was introduced in Australia it would add about another 1 percentage point to Australia's GDP growth per year.

Results from Canadian, UK and Japanese experience with greater EB are more mixed. While the economic performance of the first economy has been similar over the past decade to that of Australia in many ways—and both economies face similar geographical problems and have similar social values and political systems—its much more decentralised, but still regulated, industrial relations system does appear to have helped Canada achieve better productivity growth than Australia.

Basically what has happened in the UK is a shift from multi-employer, or industry-wide, bargaining, to single-employer, or enterprise-based, bargaining, particularly over the past decade. Research suggests that while UK EB has encouraged 'concession bargaining', or the linking of pay changes to changes in work practices, the argument that EB enables a closer link between wage growth and productivity improvement is difficult to verify from UK experience. For example, according to one study unionised firms experienced faster productivity growth than their non-union counterparts in the early 1980s but they also experienced faster wage growth. UK experience also suggests that strong competition in product markets is essential if favourable macroeconomic outcomes are to follow under EB. Otherwise, in sectors with little competition, wage rises can be easily passed on in the form of higher prices, adding to inflationary pressures in the economy.[9]

It is even more dangerous to draw simple lessons for Australia from Japanese experience with its unique and untransportable industrial relations system. Two things stand out, however. The first is the impressive ability of the Japanese to restrain both national nominal and real wage growth at times of economic downturn and profit squeezes. The second is what happens within the average Japanese firm, which makes such restraint easier. As a noted authority has concluded:

> The single most important lesson we could extract from the Japanese experience, and one which is perhaps universally valid, is the effective development and utilisations of human capital in corporate organisations . . . which includes at least the following three elements: a) systems of skill formation through both systematic training programs and continuous on-the-job training; b) flexible allocation and reapplication of human resources through various forms of transfers across job lines; and c) securing the workers' understanding of the constraints and priorities of corporate operations through the joint problem-solving approach of management and unions (Shimada 1992, p. 248).

In short, while industrial relations systems cannot be simply uprooted and imposed on another country, the bulk of overseas evidence suggests that further industrial relations reform in Australia will be beneficial. However, this will take much more than reformed Accords and new industrial relations legislation. It will require a revolution in work culture and attitudes.

As the Secretary of Treasury put it, in the 1993 Higgins Memorial Lecture:

> Improving the operation of labour markets is essential to lifting total productivity, total returns. This is why improving their operation

MICROECONOMIC REFORM

Figure 8.3 GBE efficiency improves net rates of return on capital invested

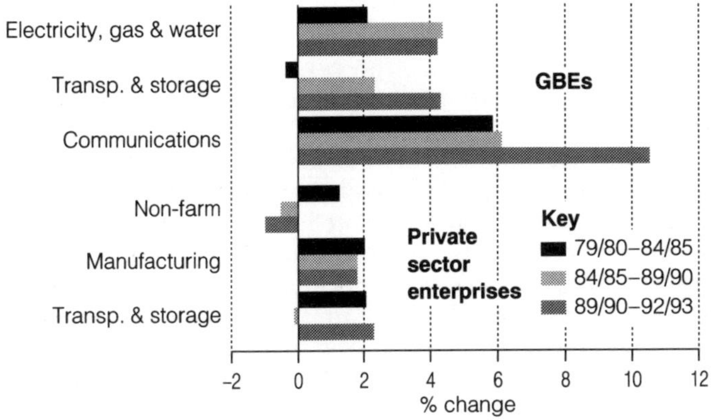

[Bar chart showing % change in net rates of return for GBEs (Electricity, gas & water; Transp. & storage; Communications) and Private sector enterprises (Non-farm; Manufacturing; Transp. & storage), across three periods: 79/80–84/85, 84/85–89/90, 89/90–92/93. X-axis ranges from -2 to 12 % change.]

Source: EPAC

must remain at the top of the structural reform agenda. Unless returns from the use of labour can be improved, the benefits from improving the use of physical capital will be lessened. If labour market rigidities or unresponsive management prevent physical capital being utilised, according to the production for which it was designed, then potential productivity gains will be lessened by one of two channels; either ex-ante by leading to decisions not to invest; or, ex-post by dissipating the gains in inappropriate work practices—or executive salaries. Preventing these results requires greater labour market flexibility in real wages and living standards. (Evans 1993).

Public sector reform

From the late 1980s onwards, and contrary to the expectations of all commentators, government business enterprises (GBEs) have experienced the biggest shake-ups in their history. The results of these are shown in Figure 8.3.

The major changes have included:

- the merger of Telecom and OTC into the Australian and Overseas Telecommunications Corporation (AOTC) in January 1992. AOTC aims to reduce the old Telecom staff levels by some 16000 over the next five years and wind back the cross subsidies which have heavily distorted its pricing structures;
- the privatisation of the satellite operator AUSSAT and its expansion into a partial competitor to Telecom, named Optus. This

duopoly will remain until 1997, when fully open competition in telecommunications is expected to commence;
- the merger of Qantas and Australian Airlines, to be followed by a 100 per cent sell-off of the new body. This conflicted with ALP policy which only allowed for a 49 per cent sell-off of Qantas. The Federal Government hopes to get a $3 billion price for the merged airline. This outcome is an interesting example of how deregulation can conflict with privatisation. Although the entry of Compass deregulated the industry, the temporary and phoney competition it provided made a mess of Australian Airlines' profit and loss accounts and the Government could not find a suitable buyer for the latter. Up until then, Qantas had even been officially forbidden from making a bid for Australian;
- sale of the Victorian GIO to the NSW GIO and a sell-off of the merged body;
- proposed sell-offs of the State banks. These have been delayed by the huge debts most accumulated in the late 1980s and the need to clean up their balance sheets before they can be put on the market.

Inter-governmental conferences also saw two vital agreements announced. The first will have the effect of allowing a product or service meeting the laws of its State of origin to satisfy the laws of any other State or Territory. This follows years of conferences about an absurd situation in which goods able to be sold in one State could not be sold in others. However, firearms and pornographic products are excluded from the agreement.

The second agreement, which also has been discussed for many years, sets up a single electricity transmission network across eastern Australia. This will break up the power generation monopolies of the States, allow free flow of power across State borders, and open the way for private sector involvement in the industry.

While some GBEs have been fully or partially privatised, and further privatisations are planned, many will remain in the public sector. However, most of these have seen their world change dramatically.

Reforms they have experienced include: more comprehensive and explicit specification of what is expected of them; adoption of corporate planning and finance targets and use of performance techniques; and a reduction in existing controls after satisfactory progress has been achieved towards meeting such targets.

Big questions remain, however. What criteria should be used in setting such targets? How does one determine 'satisfactory progress in improving performance'? What pricing and investment guidelines can be laid down for such enterprises?

For example, does a low rate of return from investment in such enterprises automatically signify that the enterprise is grossly inefficient? Or could it be a product of the fact that it is unable to use its monopoly position to maximise profits because of government restrictions on the prices it charges and on its investment policies?

In this case, privatisation without any effort to get more competition in the industry can increase the price of the service or good provided and/or lower its quality, as British privatisation experience has shown. Most people accept that GBEs should recover their costs. But should they earn profits, pay dividends, or meet a minimum rate of return on capital employed as well?

One alternative is much greater use of rate of return requirements—RRRs. These seek to relate profit—that is, the surplus after deducting aggregate costs from aggregate revenues—to an appropriate base. This base can be the resources or total assets committed to the activity or some other base such as annual sales. Such a measure—ignoring the problems of setting a RRR target for enterprises and/or industries—reminds management of GBEs that the capital they are controlling has an opportunity cost but their mere adoption, as the Victorian experience in the late 1980s showed, is no simple panacea.

What is most important is how the returns from a GBE compare with returns achieved by similar private sector enterprises. The mere setting and meeting of a particular RRR does not indicate that the GBE has optimised its performance. However, with what bodies does one compare a body like Telecom, which until very recently had a monopoly over telecommunications? How does one take into account community service obligations—such as the need to supply phones at great expense to outback communities? Indeed, should GBEs have to meet such obligations?

Unfortunately, the pricing systems used by most of our government instrumentalities rarely, if ever, meet all—or even some—of the following criteria of an efficient pricing system:

- satisfy economic efficiency criteria. In textbook language, such efficiency is achieved when the price a consumer pays for an extra unit of a good or service is related to the marginal cost of providing that service. A sensible consumer would thus decide to buy goods or services up to the point where the value which they derive from the purchase is equal to the cost of providing the last unit of that good or service;
- be easily understood by consumers;
- achieve administrative efficiency and simplicity;
- generate sufficient revenue to fund the business.

Hence the growing interest in user-pays alternatives—those which make consumers much more aware of the full costs of the goods and services governments and their instrumentalities provide.

Advocates of the user-pays principle—and these can be both Labor and Liberal–National Party supporters—argue that there is nothing 'New Right' or unethical about trying to reduce over-consumption of public goods by adopting pricing policies which discourage waste. Indeed, they argue that those who wish to retain a degree of 'mixed economy' in Australia should strongly support such a pricing policy in our government instrumentalities.

More specifically, user-pays advocates argue that such pricing policies will:

- impress on consumers that the services government instrumentalities and businesses provide not only have a cost but that they should be provided as efficiently as possible. Non-user-pays policies, they argue, greatly obscure these realities. For example, the community assumes that water or electricity authorities simply provide these key commodities, when in fact it is the tariffs and rates paid by consumers—and often additional tax revenue collected from consumers and borrowings by governments—which are the source of funds to build the power stations and dams and to distribute their products;[10]
- reduce the need for government borrowing to cover the losses of government instrumentalities and thus free funds, otherwise spent merely meeting interest payments, for more socially desirable purposes. When demand for funds is tight—as it was, for example, in the mid-1980s—less borrowing might also produce lower interest rates;
- free funds which otherwise would have been spent on building more dams and so on for much more socially useful purposes—for example, helping single-parent families and the aged poor, or building better public transport to outlying, lower income suburbs.

On the other hand, user-pays critics in government instrumentalities put four main arguments against it:

- these bodies should not operate on commercial lines, following private sector pricing policies, because their main role is to provide a community service;
- life-essential commodities like water are different to non-life essential ones and thus should be priced differently;
- there should be other measures of efficiency besides economic ones. However, these are never spelt out;

- the user-pays principle will impact more heavily on lower income groups, who are least able to afford to pay higher prices for things like water and sewerage services.

The last one is the argument with the greatest political clout. For example, in its submission to the NSW Government Pricing Tribunal inquiry into water pricing, the NSW Council of Social Services argued that efficient resource allocation should not be the sole or even primary objective of pricing policy and that a progressive pricing policy—richer consumers paying more for water than poorer ones—should be used.

The response of the tribunal to this argument was that while safety nets should be put in place to assist lower income consumers harder hit by moves towards the user-pays principle, taxation and welfare payments should be used to change income and wealth distributions, rather than the pricing policies of government instrumentalities.[11] It argued that efficient resource allocation should be the primary long-term objective of pricing policy—not a desire to improve economic equity.

Strangely, most opponents of the user-pays principle in the public sector are not opposed to making smokers pay heavier taxes on tobacco products, given that the latter are responsible in Australia for adding about $8 billion a year to health costs. Yet, they oppose making other users of taxpayers' money more responsible in their demands.

The multi-million dollar question mark hanging over the user-pays argument though is whether governments will merely use the extra revenue obtained to reduce their deficits and/or cover their fiscal profligacy, rather than use it to build better public infrastructure and/or better help the genuinely needy.

Already there has been considerable controversy in some States about bodies such as water boards being forced to pay large dividends to State treasuries, rather than use surpluses of revenue over outlays to improve and expand services or reduce environmental problems. For example, $100 million dollars of surplus accumulated by the Sydney Water Board was handled in this manner, despite strong opposition from senior management of the board.

However, there is also another serious problem with the user-pays principle based on marginal cost pricing—for example, setting the price of water equal to the cost of supplying an additional unit of water—which is never raised by its non-economist critics, probably because of their lack of understanding of the concept and its limitations. Namely, marginal cost pricing does not specifically address how embedded costs—for example, the cost of building the dams—should be assigned to specific customers or classes of customers. This problem is conveniently glossed over in most user-pays advocacy.

In short, the user-pays principle is no simple solution to the complex problems facing GBEs. Big questions also remain about the welfare 'safety nets' which are required to cushion its impact on less privileged Australians. However, as the former socialist economies also were forced to admit, the pricing of government-provided goods and services cannot be based exclusively on the desire to improve social equity and pressure group influence.

Barriers to further microeconomic reform

The relatively slow pace of microeconomic reform on our waterfront reminds us that while it is easy to call for microeconomic reform, it is much harder to achieve it. Some of the major problems hindering greater and faster microeconomic reform include:

- further resistance from all sorts of industry and interest groups, including regulatory bodies and their employees, to microeconomic reforms which threaten their privileges or powers—even though such reforms may clearly be in the national interest. Employees enjoying special perks are especially reluctant to surrender them—even if it means the closure of their enterprise, as happened with the NSW Dockyard in Newcastle. Management reform is also hampered by vested interests and resistance to change. Often takeovers of badly managed companies are the only way to bring about management shake-ups;
- the consumers of services provided by the public sector are often the last to be given a hearing in public debates about whether such services could be provided more cheaply and efficiently by the private sector. Such debates are usually dominated by the suppliers of the service, who have most to lose from any cutbacks or changes. Or to put this point more bluntly, those who scream the loudest are rarely in the most pain.
- reforms may be small and slow to have an impact—for example, changes in education systems and training—and there may be difficult trade-offs between short-term macroeconomic costs and the long-term benefits which flow from improvements in efficiency from such reform. Also, changes in taxes may reduce tax revenue and hence government spending but in the long run encourage more investment, jobs, growth and dynamism in the economy. Or cuts in protection may reduce jobs in an industry but in the long term the displaced workers may find higher paid

work in other, more dynamic and more export-orientated industries;
- limits to the degree of reform which governments, parliaments, industry, unions and society can digest over a certain period of time, particularly in a society like Australia in which the electorate usually abhors radical change. The Whitlam Government of the 1970s realised this too late but both the Hawke and Keating governments proceeded much more cautiously.

Yet, how do governments assess such limits? Opponents of financial deregulation predicted wide community kickback but little reaction eventuated. Will there be more opposition to, for example, labour market reform, or will it proceed more smoothly than many commentators suggest? In other words, will the vested interests who gain most from current arrangements and privileges 'fight to the death' or surrender peacefully? Should reform be piecemeal, step-by-step, or is a bold, boots-and-all strategy superior in overcoming resistance from vested interests? Overseas experience shows that even the sequence of reforms can be very important. For example, our approach to labour market reform—and particularly to the removal of restrictive work practices—is very much a consensus-based one. That is, unions will only agree to surrender a privilege or lurk in exchange for another. But labour market reform must be accelerated over the 1990s.

Microeconomic reform not a simple panacea for all of Australia's economic ills

According to calculations made for EPAC (EPAC 1994b) dramatic benefits will flow from further microeconomic reform. For example, it is claimed:

- achievement of world's best practice in Australian manufacturing could raise labour productivity by over 30 per cent in some industries and increase GDP by 3.5 per cent in the long run;
- further reductions in tariffs and subsidies could add another 0.8 per cent to GDP. However, the possible employment effects are difficult to calculate and would depend heavily on the general state of the economy, and of demand in particular;
- continuation of GBE reform could deliver additional GDP gains of between 1.5 and 2.5 per cent, with direct cost savings of between $2.3 and $3.7 billion in the transport sector alone;
- improving the delivery of government services by 5 to 10 per cent could raise GDP by as much as 3 per cent.

While such estimates are mere 'guesstimates', as the range of estimates shows, and because the model used to make them cannot adequately handle changes in employer and employee behaviour in response to reforms, they do suggest that further microeconomic reform will have economy-wide benefits. However, what we really need is greater effort to delineate the costs as well as the benefits.

Certainly there is no guarantee that the full benefits of microeconomic reform will be passed on to consumers. For example, a 1993 decision to reduce crewing levels on Australian-crewed coastal shipping, which produced a saving of $270 600 per ship per year, was completely negated by an increase in federal government excise in the budget the same year. Similarly, the NSW Water Board was required to pay a special dividend to the NSW Government, rather than pass on the savings from reform in the form of lower prices to consumers; Pacific Power in the same State was forced to pay much higher dividends to the Government and in Victoria the Melbourne Port Authority has also had to pay higher dividends to the State Government.

Furthermore, while further microeconomic reform is a necessary policy step for further structural change in the Australian economy and for even just a levelling-off in our foreign debt problem, it is certainly not a sufficient one. Indeed, it could even worsen the current account deficit and foreign debt problem in the short and even medium term. It is also very difficult to predict the effects of such reform.

When the Australian economy grows strongly two factors usually impact heavily on our balance of payments. The first is a growth in imports—not just of capital goods and producers' materials but also of consumer goods—resulting in a rise in import penetration ratios and a blow-out in our trade and current account deficits. Such a blow-out occurred in the strong growth era of the late 1980s.

With little investment since then—particularly in import-replacing industries and export-expanding ones—sustained strong growth is very likely to produce a rise in both the trade and current account deficits, putting downwards pressure on the $A and upwards pressure on interest rates. One should also remember that waterfront reform will make it easier and cheaper to get both exports and imports across our wharves. That this needs to be done is apparent in Figure 8.4.

The second factor is a growth in offshore borrowing, as strong growth raises Australian interest rates above rates in the major western economies. This, for example, was a major factor behind the heavy private sector borrowing abroad in the late 1980s, when even banks borrowed heavily overseas to enable them to meet heavy demand for housing finance.

Figure 8.4 Port productivity still poor

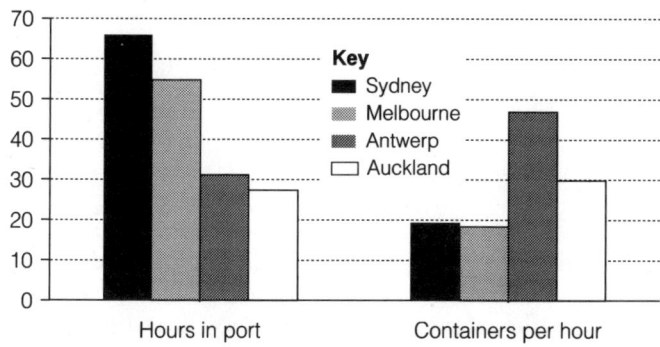

Source: Contship, 1993 figures.

Fortunately, our current account was assisted in the early 1990s by recession-induced, lower international interest rates. This kept our foreign debt servicing costs and net income deficit on the current account lower than they otherwise would have been. The importance of this can be seen in the fact that most of our current account deficit in the early 1990s was a product of foreign debt interest payments.

However, a sustained international recovery is likely to see the interest rates we pay on our foreign debt rise again, which will put upwards pressure on the net income deficit and current account once again, even if we are able to keep the trade deficit under control. Higher interest rates in Australia will also increase the relative attractiveness of borrowing offshore again, as they did in the late 1980s.

Two factors may help restrain a rise in overseas borrowing, following further substantial microeconomic reform. The first is improved private sector profitability over the rest of the 1990s and beyond. This would reduce the needs of the sector to borrow offshore. The second is a shift from capital inflow in the form of borrowings to capital inflow in equities—in other words, greater foreign investment in shares in Australian companies. Such a shift has occurred so far in the 1990s and if it continues, will provide some relief from current account pressures. Greater microeconomic reform should improve the profitability of Australian companies thus making their shares more attractive to overseas investors and thereby reducing the need to finance further expansion by overseas borrowing. A leaner and more efficient public sector—particularly GBEs—will also reduce their need to borrow both at home and abroad. This should also help restrain interest rate rises and public sector overseas borrowing.

Such short-term, and even medium-term, negative effects of microeconomic reform should not, however, be allowed to hide the long-term positive benefits, even though far too little effort has been made to draw up actual balance sheets of the effects of microeconomic reform in Australia, and even in the US there is a paucity of such studies.[12]

Indeed, with other western economies implementing similar reforms and with the countries to Australia's north in the midst of the most dramatic industrialisation in history, Australia has no choice but to accelerate the reform process, if it is to expand manufactured exports.

True, microeconomic reform certainly has produced its casualties and will continue to do so—particularly employees in GBEs and private sector employers who have been cocooned from international and domestic competition and spoon-fed taxpayers' money to make them appear competitive. But all economic policy changes produce losers as well as winners.

However, the higher labour productivity growth which should flow from most of these changes is likely to not only improve our relative standard of living but also reduce our balance of payments problems in the longer term, by increasing our export competitiveness and by decreasing the competitiveness of imports.

The recession of the early 1990s also appears to have produced more rational community attitudes towards investment, inflation and interest rates and a growing public recognition that there is no money tree—or magic pudding—in Canberra which can be used to fund unrestricted government spending.

Unfortunately, while these important policy and attitudinal changes may end Australia's long-term slide down the international standard of living ladder, there is no guarantee that they will be sufficient to produce a move up this ladder. Indeed, with the advantage of hindsight, it is clear that Australia should have moved earlier and faster with such reforms, rather than waiting for the worst recession since the 1930s to accelerate action.

One hopes, however, that more and more Australians will eventually come to realise that our future lies in matching world's best practices in all areas of human endeavour, rather than naively believing that we can continue with our traditional 'She'll be Right Mate' attitude towards our structural problems.

Only then may we escape our history.

Notes

1 See Forsyth (1992) for more detail.
2 See Boehm (1994) or Clark (forthcoming) for a more detailed overview.
3 See Figure 2.2 and 2.9 above.
4 See EPAC (1993) references and Boehm (1993) for more details.
5 See Clark (1993) and EPA (1993a) for much more detail on this debate.
6 See Thurow (1983, ch. 7) for an excellent, non-technical survey of these arguments.
7 See Easson (1992) and Costa and Duffy (1991) for union support.
8 See Clark (1993, brief 13) for an overview.
9 See EPAC (1993h).
10 See Sydney Water Board (1992 and 1993).
11 See NSW Government Pricing Tribunal (1993).
12 See Winston (1993).

Recommended reading

Clark, D. *Student Economic Briefs*, Financial Review Library, Sydney. (A new set of briefs are published each August.)
EPAC 1994, 'Economic effects of microeconomic reform' Background Paper No. 38, AGPS, Canberra
Industry Assistance Annual Reports and Research Reports of the Bureau of Industry Economics as well as *The Business Council of Australia Bulletin* are also good sources of up-to-date material.

9 The public sector: trends in Australia and other OECD countries

Peter Saunders[1]

For about the past two decades, successive Australian governments have given emphasis to the control of government expenditure, both for its own sake and as a way of reducing public sector deficits and providing scope for tax reductions. The significance attached to this objective has varied over time, both in policy discussions as well as in the actual policies implemented, but commitment to the underlying goal has not wavered. It now seems inconceivable to imagine a federal government without a 'razor gang' of senior Ministers charged with scrutinising government programs with a view to restraining, if not reducing, expenditure levels.

Against this background, this chapter explores the actual impact of government policies and other factors on the level of public expenditure in Australia and other countries which belong to the Organisation for Economic Cooperation and Development (OECD). It is instructive to consider developments internationally as well as nationally, both because this places domestic trends in a broader context and because international trends serve to highlight some of the factors influencing public expenditure which are common to all nations. The level of direct expenditure is, of course, only one dimension of public sector intervention in the economy and for this reason it is useful to discuss, again in comparative terms, what has been happening in OECD countries in other dimensions of public sector activity, and how attempts to 'roll back the state' have manifested themselves.

By 1980 the level of government spending exceeded 50 per cent of gross domestic product (GDP) in five of the nineteen OECD countries for which data are available, and was approaching that figure in four more (OECD 1993). Government revenue as a percentage of GDP—the tax burden—was generally somewhat lower but in ten countries still exceeded 40 per cent. The economic conditions in which this situation had developed throughout the 1950s, 1960s and 1970s seemed far removed from prevailing or prospective experience, yet social pressures were pushing for further expansion and the political and budgetary systems of all countries were being severely stretched. There was a widespread view that the situation at that time was simply not sustainable. The growth in public programs had fostered a climate of increasing demand for further state expansion which was out of line with what the deteriorating economic prospects could provide without placing undue strain on present and/or future taxpayers. The 'fiscal crisis of the state' predicted by O'Connor in the early 1970s (O'Connor 1973) had arrived, and even if OECD governments did not agree with O'Connor's diagnosis of what was wrong and why, most agreed that public sector reform was urgently needed.

The nature of this change in attitude towards the public sector is illustrated by the evolving views and terminology adopted by the OECD itself in its publications. As late as 1978, an OECD report on public expenditure trends commented in the following terms on the outlook for public expenditure: '... there are still plenty of demands to be met which would justify further expenditure if expansion of aggregate public expenditure rather than restriction of public sector budgets seems feasible. Many of the new initiatives envisaged could lead to significant improvements in the quality of life and better equalisation of incomes' (OECD 1978, p. 37).

It is a cautious yet optimistic assessment, one which at least acknowledges the positive impacts of state intervention on living standards and equality. In comparison, the general tenor of the following extract from the OECD report entitled *Structural Adjustment and Economic Performance*, produced less than a decade later, is both less cautious in style and far more negative in tone:

> Many of the problems of the public sector today arise from its previous growth; because the efficient management of resources is far more complicated when it is carried out at the public sector's present size and diversity, than at the scale of even only two decades ago; and because the impacts of public programmes on overall efficiency may alter as spending rises and coverage expands. But the need to reform the public sector also comes from the imperative of adapting to change; of reviewing programmes whose goals have been met or whose underlying premises are no longer valid; of adjusting overall spending and taxing to the altered trend of growth; and of

developing new forms of co-operation between the public and private sector (OECD 1987, p. 45).

Even stronger are the views expressed in 1990 in *Progress in Structural Reform*, a kind of end-of-term report in which the achievements of OECD member countries in the area of structural reform are evaluated (and any laggards appropriately admonished). There, the section on public sector reform asserts:

... in many cases government policies and programmes had been expanded too far, were not achieving their goals or achieving them at unnecessarily high cost. This, coupled with the need to restore fiscal balances, and the awareness of prospective demographic and social changes, is leading to a reassessment of major expenditure programmes and of the way in which the public sector operates (OECD 1990a, p. 14).

The contrast with the views expressed in the late 1970s could not be illustrated more starkly.

This chapter reviews the extent to which the rhetoric has been translated into practice in Australia and other OECD countries in the 1980s and beyond, and assesses some of the future implications of these changes for the relationship between state and market in industrial capitalism. Its main focus is on outlining the trends in the Australian public sector and comparing these with the more general developments occurring throughout the OECD region.

The Australian public sector in the 1980s

The Australian public sector comprises the three tiers of government—Commonwealth, State and local—as well as the public trading enterprises. Of these, the Commonwealth Government is the most important, both in relation to total spending and, more particularly, in regard to the control it exerts over the level and structure of revenue in the public sector as a whole. Within the Commonwealth sector, the Commonwealth budget sector is most important and, given the important stabilisation role of the annual budget, most well known. But it is important not to ignore the other main constituents of the public sector as a whole and the functions they serve. State governments, for example, play a major role in the provision and finance of health and education services, which not only absorb a large amount of resources, but also fulfil functions of central importance to most people. Similarly, the role of local government in planning and urban development affects the human

Figure 9.1 Longer term trends in Commonwealth budget outlays, 1953/54 to 1992/93

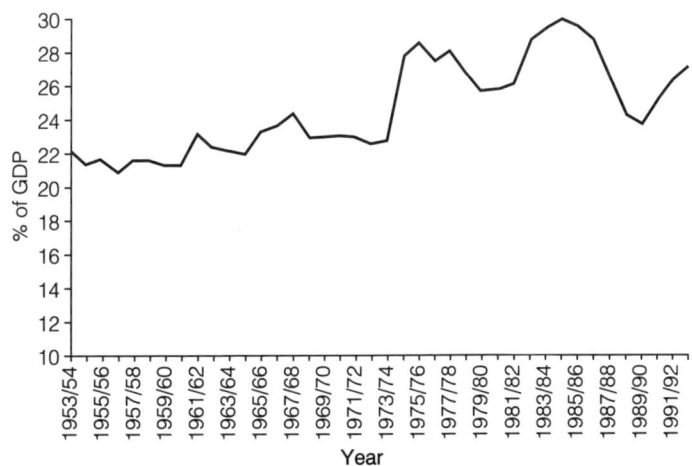

environment in ways which fundamentally influence living standards. Finally, public trading enterprises engage in activities which are important in determining the quality of people's lives, the opportunities available to them and the cost of gaining access to basic services.

In the remainder of this section, a range of data are presented and discussed which attempt to provide an overall perspective on the relative importance of these different elements in the Australian public sector. Particular attention is focused on the extent and nature of the changes experienced during the 1980s and in the early years of the 1990s. No attempt is made to discuss in detail the important definitional issues associated with the different elements of the public sector and how these relate to each other.[2]

Although debates about the size of government increased in intensity during the 1980s, it is informative to begin by analysing expenditure trends in a longer term perspective. Figure 9.1 shows movements in the ratio of Commonwealth budget outlays to GDP—referred to henceforth as the spending ratio—over the last 40 years. What is most striking about Figure 9.1 is the relative stability of the spending ratio in the period up to 1973/74 and the much greater variability since then. There is an overall upward trend in the spending ratio, but it is not dramatic and there are many periods during which it fell. As a consequence, in 1973/74 the ratio was only 0.6 percentage points higher than it was in 1953/54, while in 1992/93 the ratio was actually 0.4 percentage points lower than it was in 1974/75. Between 1973/74 and 1974/75, the ratio rose by almost 5 percentage points, largely as a consequence of the reforms and initiatives introduced by the Whitlam Government.

Since 1980 the spending ratio has been more variable than in earlier decades, rising steadily to a maximum of 29.9 per cent in 1984/85. After that, it declined considerably—by more than the Whitlam increase of 1974/75—until 1989/90, whereafter it began to rise again. There is a clear cyclical pattern to the movements shown in Figure 9.1, with the spending ratio rising during recessionary periods (e.g. in 1961–62, 1973–76, 1981–83 and 1990–93) and falling steadily in many of the intervening years of higher growth. This pattern reflects both the countercyclical nature of automatic stabilisers like unemployment assistance and health spending and the tendency for fiscal policy to become more expansionary in an attempt to assist the recovery, both of which operate in reverse in the recovery phase of the cycle.

Over the period shown in Figure 9.1, Commonwealth budget revenue rose steadily, but not dramatically, from 20.7 per cent of GDP in 1953/54 to 23.6 per cent in 1992/93. Not only was the increase in revenue below the overall increase in the spending ratio, but revenues were consistently below outlays in all but the four-year period between 1987 and 1991. This led to a rise in Commonwealth debt (relative to GDP) which further exacerbated the rise in outlays due to the increase in interest payments, and absorbed a considerable amount of the private sector savings which could otherwise have financed higher levels of private sector investment.[3] Without wishing to downplay the importance of the constraints associated with excessive levels of public sector debt, Figure 9.1 illustrates that when viewed against a longer term perspective, performance during the 1980s was generally good. Commonwealth outlays were lower in 1989/90 than they were in 1979/80 and indeed, not much higher than they were in 1969/70.

Table 9.1 extends the analysis to include the other elements of the public sector and shows how these changed between 1979/80 and 1992/93. The first point to note is that public sector outlays as a whole rose somewhat faster than Commonwealth budget outlays. In 1979/80 the former exceeded the latter by about 40 per cent, while by 1992/93 this relativity had increased to just over 50 per cent. Although the two series moved in the same direction over the period, public sector outlays tended to follow Commonwealth outlays after a short lag, and to rise faster when they were increasing, and fall more slowly when they were declining.

Table 9.1 also disaggregates total public sector outlays by level of government (columns 3 and 4) and into the general government

Table 9.1 Movements in Commonwealth budget and public sector outlays in Australia in the 1980s (percentages of GDP)

Year	Commonwealth budget outlays (CBO)	Public sector outlays (PSO)	PSO by level of government		PSO by sector	
			Commonwealth	State/local	General government transactions	Public trading enterprises
1979–80	25.8	36.0	27.0	19.6	31.9	5.5
1980–81	25.9	36.5	27.0	19.9	32.0	5.6
1981–82	26.2	38.3	27.7	20.7	32.7	6.6
1982–83	28.7	41.1	29.6	22.2	35.3	7.3
1983–84	29.4	42.0	31.1	21.7	35.8	7.7
1984–85	29.9	42.2	31.3	21.5	36.8	6.8
1985–86	29.5	42.5	31.2	21.5	36.8	7.2
1986–87	28.8	42.0	30.3	21.5	36.6	6.9
1987–88	26.6	39.1	28.0	19.9	34.3	6.1
1988–89	24.4	36.6	25.9	18.6	32.2	5.6
1989–90	23.8	38.1	26.6	19.3	32.4	6.7
1990–91	25.3	39.5	27.5	19.5	34.6	5.8
1991–92	26.5	41.4	28.2	20.7	37.3	5.7
1992–93	27.3	41.0	29.0	19.9	37.1	5.4

Source: Budget Statements 1989/90 and 1993/94, Budget Paper No. 1.

sector and public trading enterprises (columns 5 and 6). It is important to emphasise that the outlays shown here are gross outlays, not net (consolidated) outlays.[4] These figures illustrate an important feature of public sector financing transactions in Australia, the quantitative significance of transactions between the different levels of government (vertical fiscal imbalance) and between general government and public enterprises. Overall, State and local government outlays have been more stable than total Commonwealth outlays, varying within a very small range over the 1980s. Public trading enterprises, however, have been more variable, increasing their activity by over 30 per cent relative to GDP between 1979/80 and 1985/86, and experiencing a decline of similar magnitude between 1985/86 and 1992/93.

Not surprisingly, the more one disaggregates the data, the greater the variability over time they reveal. This highlights the fact that each of the components of public sector activity are subject to their own set of external forces, each of which can move independently, at least in the short term. Upward pressure on outlays in some areas (e.g. as a consequence of population ageing) are often offset by reductions elsewhere (e.g. lower defence spending in the post-Cold War era) with the result that total outlays are more stable than their constituent parts. Although governments like, for understandable reasons, to give the impression that all outlays are under direct and immediate control, the reality is far more complex. Government outlays tend to move independently of government action in the short term, in response to economic, demographic, social and political factors. That having been said, however, governments can and do exert an influence, even if it sometimes takes a little time for these to show up in the data. One of the features of Australian developments during the last two decades is how well they illustrate this, particularly at the Commonwealth level, but also throughout the public sector.

Developments in other OECD countries

In order to evaluate the changes in the Australian public sector in the 1980s, it is useful to compare these with developments in similar countries. In this section, trends in general government activity in OECD countries since 1980 are examined. Comparative data on the size and structure of the public sector are restricted to cover only the general government sector. The source for these data is the standardised System of National Accounts (SNA), convenient summaries of which are published regularly by the OECD (for example in the Reference Tables at the end of each issue of the *OECD Economic Outlook*). The SNA data form the basis of most of the OECD's analytic and policy work on issues relating to the public sector (OECD 1978; Saunders and Klau 1985; Oxley and Martin 1991). The general government sector includes the activities of central, state and local or regional governments and outlays are expressed on a consolidated basis, that is, after all transfers between the different levels of government have been netted out.[5]

With few exceptions, public enterprises are excluded entirely from these OECD statistics, mainly because national agencies have not been able to agree on a standardised way of defining precisely when an enterprise is sufficiently under government ownership and/or control to warrant being termed a public enterprise (Saunders 1987). This highlights the need to acknowledge that any attempt to distinguish between the 'state' and 'market' sectors of the economy will be somewhat arbitrary and, to some extent at least, simplistic.

Most OECD indicators of the size of the general government sector rely upon measures of total spending incurred by governments in performing the activities for which they have assumed responsibility. As noted earlier, such indicators are important because they determine the financing requirements of government, specifically the level of taxation and/or borrowing. Spending totals can, however, provide only an approximate measure of the economic impact of the government programs they represent. They do not include other government instruments such as indirect assistance in the form of tax expenditures, or public regulation of private and commercial activities. Furthermore, where reliance on these 'off-budget' instruments varies across countries, the comparability of the general government budgetary statistics is compromised.

The general government sector is thus but one—albeit the most important—element in an overall public sector which is multi-dimensional in terms of its scope and structure (Saunders 1993). Trends in general government outlays provide important information on developments in the public sector, but should not be equated with either these broader developments, or with the economic impact of government activity. There is more to government than the cost of government programs. Their value lies in highlighting the broad dimensions of the public sector, in pointing to areas where more detailed study is needed, and in providing comparative National Accounts data for a range of countries with broadly similar economic systems and political structures.

Over the two decades to 1980, the ratio of general government outlays to GDP rose substantially in all OECD countries. The smallest absolute increase (around 6 percentage points) occurred in the United States, while the largest (in excess of 31 percentage points) was experienced in Denmark and Sweden. In Australia, the ratio rose by just under 10 percentage points over this period. It would be a mistake to see these rises as occurring continuously throughout the period. In the early 1970s, the government spending ratio declined in some years in a number of countries, and it fell again in more countries after 1975. These movements reinforce the point made earlier, that government spending responds to short-term (cyclical) factors associated with fiscal policy adjustments, as well as in response to longer term demographic, economic and social pressures. The general trend in government size throughout the OECD during the 1970s was, however, upward and in no country was the spending ratio in 1980 lower than it was in 1970.

The pattern of changes in the government spending ratio between 1980 and 1992 is shown in Table 9.2. The specific years identified in the table have been selected so that they separate the period into four approximately equal length sub-periods of differing cyclical activity, covering the recession of 1981–83, the long boom between 1983 and 1989, and the severe recession between 1990 and 1992. The last two columns of Table 9.2 show, respectively, the increases in the government spending ratio between 1980 and 1989 and between 1989 and 1992.

Several interesting patterns are revealed by these statistics. Spending rose most rapidly up to 1989 in the southern European countries

Table 9.2 Trends in general government outlays, 1980 to 1992 (percentages of GDP)

Country	1980	1983	1986	1989	1992	Change in ratio 1980 to 1989	Change in ratio 1989 to 1992
Australia	31.5	35.3	37.3	32.8	38.3	+1.3	+5.5
Austria	48.1	50.4	51.6	49.0	50.2	+0.9	+1.2
Belgium	51.9	55.9	54.1	49.3	50.8	−2.6	+1.5
Canada	38.7	45.3	44.6	43.2	49.7	+4.5	+6.5
Denmark	56.2	61.6	55.7	59.6	59.5	+3.4	−0.1
Finland	35.5	39.1	40.7	36.9	51.7	+1.4	+14.8
France	46.1	51.4	51.3	49.1	52.0	+3.0	+2.9
Germany	47.9	47.8	46.4	44.8	49.4	−3.1	+4.6
Greece	33.2	41.7	47.7	49.4	48.3	+16.2	−1.1
Ireland	50.5	55.0	54.1	41.6	43.9	−8.9	+2.3
Italy	41.9	48.7	50.7	51.3	53.2	+9.4	+1.9
Japan	32.0	33.3	32.0	30.9	32.2	−1.1	+1.3
Netherlands	54.8	59.3	56.6	54.0	54.7	−0.8	+0.7
Norway	47.5	47.6	48.9	53.5	57.5	+6.0	+4.0
Portugal	25.9	47.9	44.0	41.9	46.1	+16.0	+4.2
Spain	32.0	37.9	40.7	40.9	45.1	+8.9	+4.2
Sweden	60.1	64.5	61.6	58.3	67.3	−1.4	+9.0
United Kingdom	42.9	44.7	42.5	37.6	44.1	−5.3	+6.5
United States	31.8	33.9	33.7	32.4	35.4	+1.6	+3.0
Average (unweighted)	**42.6**	**47.4**	**47.1**	**45.1**	**48.9**	**+2.6**	**+3.8**

Source: OECD Economic Outlook 53, June 1993, Table R15, p. 215.

of Greece, Spain and Portugal, reflecting a 'catch-up process' amongst these least developed OECD nations. The only other country to experience anything like the increase in these countries was Italy. There was a tendency for the spending ratio to decline, at least up to 1989, in some of the countries (Belgium, Ireland, the Netherlands and Sweden) where it was highest at the beginning of the decade. In several other countries (including Australia as well as Austria, Finland, Japan and the United States) there was hardly any change in the spending ratio over the decade as a whole, reflecting a decline after about 1985 which offset the earlier increase. This trend towards a declining ratio began in the early 1980s in a number of countries and became widespread in the mid-1980s.

What is also apparent from Table 9.2 is that the general (but not universal) tendency for the spending ratio to decline in the latter half of the 1980s stopped abruptly in 1989. Between then and 1992, the ratio rose almost everywhere—in many cases very sharply. The main reason for this reversal is, of course, the 1990–93 recession, which put upward pressure on government spending directly in some areas and elicited an expansionary policy response in others. Overall, the trends shown in Table 9.2 indicate that the government sectors of all OECD countries (including Australia) experienced broadly similar pressures over the period to 1989 and were all similarly affected by the recession. Differences existed between countries, reflecting their stage of development and particular policy positions adopted, but these were imprinted on a common overall trend characterised by spending restraint for much of the 1980s and a recession-induced expenditure upsurge in the years after 1989.

More generally, Table 9.2 presents clear evidence of a break with the historical record of continued growth in the relative size of the general government sector in the 1980s which had characterised the previous three decades. The break with past experience began about 1982 and became widespread by about 1985. Between 1986 and 1989, the government spending ratio fell in all but six of the 22 countries shown in Table 9.2 (including Australia, where the ratio fell by almost 5 percentage points). On this basis, therefore, the 'frontiers of the state' began to be rolled back during the latter years of the 1980s.

As already observed, that process ended with the onset of recession in 1990. Governments in all OECD countries could not resist the associated pressure for increased spending, nor could they take solace from what the market was able to offer in a period when aggregate market outcomes were clearly undesirable. As in previous recessions, the state was forced to step in to alleviate the problems of the failure of the market. Table 9.2 shows this to have been a particularly strong tendency in Australia, where the rise in outlays of 5.5 percentage points between 1989 and 1992 was exceeded only in Canada, Finland, Sweden and the United Kingdom. Despite this increase, by 1992 Australia remained amongst the OECD countries with the smallest general government sectors, some 10 percentage points behind the average and more than 5 percentage points behind the group of countries (Ireland, Portugal, Spain and the United Kingdom) immediately ahead of it in the OECD ranking. Government spending was below that existing in Australia in only two other countries, namely Japan and the United States.

In order to gain more insight into the aggregate trends shown in Table 9.2, Table 9.3 disaggregates total government spending into four broad types of intervention which reflect the various roles of government in contemporary industrialised capitalist nations. Unfortunately, comparative data are more difficult to assemble in this form, which explains why the estimates in Table 9.3 are somewhat more dated than those shown in Table 9.2.[6]

The first category of spending shown in Table 9.3 (the Traditional Domain) includes spending on public goods like defence and general public series; the second (the Welfare State) includes two elements, government spending on merit goods like education, health, housing and community amenities, and spending on income transfer programs for the aged, unemployed, sick, disabled, and so on; the third (the Mixed Economy) includes spending on economic services, including spending on public infrastructure and industrial subsidies; the fourth is an item (Public Debt Interest) which has come to play an increasingly important role in the public finances of all OECD countries since the mid-1970s. Gathering information together in this form is a difficult exercise, and one which involves recourse to national data in many instances.[7]

The data in Table 9.3 reveal several additional features of the structure of government in OECD nations and how those structures changed during the 1980s. To the extent that the variations displayed in Table 9.3 allow generalisations to be made, these are that the single most important factor which distinguishes countries with small government sectors from those with large government sectors is the size of the welfare state, particularly spending on income transfers. The main reason, for example, why government spending in Australia is so far out of line in Table 9.3 is its low level of spending on transfer payments, a reflection of a tightly targeted and means-tested social security system.[8]

With the notable exception of the United States, spending on merit goods shows relatively little variation across countries, the US situation reflecting the very low level of government expenditure on health care. However, although there are large differences in the structure of government spending between countries, changes in the structure of spending during the 1980s are much more similar. The change in spending on public goods has been small, generally exhibiting a slight decline relative to GDP. Spending on the mixed economy also declined relative to GDP in virtually all countries, as did spending on merit goods, although the decline in the former was generally larger, except in Sweden where both education and health spending declined considerably. The two main areas of increased spending were income transfers (though not in Australia where they remained virtually unchanged) and public debt interest—the latter exceeding the total size of the education budget in four countries by the end of the 1980s and approaching it in several others. The composition of state activity thus changed as the overall scope of the state sector declined, just as it did during the earlier period of state expansion. Developments during the 1980s have thus reinforced the longer term trends apparent in previous OECD studies of the public sector (e.g. Saunders and Klau 1985) which saw governments increase their role in income transfers while withdrawing from their role in supplying goods and services for all citizens in the form of education, health, public administration and public infrastructure.

Table 9.3 The changing structure of government in the 1980s (percentages of GDP)

	The traditional domain (public goods)	The welfare state (Merit goods)	(Income transfers)	The mixed economy (Economic services)	Public debt interest	Balancing item	Total outlays
Australia							
1979	6.5	11.8	7.5	5.8	2.1	0.0	33.7
1988	6.3	11.8	7.4	4.7	4.4	0.0	34.6
Austria							
1981	5.3	10.4	22.1	7.5	2.8	0.3	48.4
1988	5.1	10.5	23.0	6.7	3.9	0.0	49.2
Denmark							
1979	8.0	15.9	20.4	6.0	3.5	0.0	53.8
1988	8.6	14.6	22.5	5.8	7.9	0.0	59.4
Finland							
1979	4.3	9.9	12.9	8.4	0.9	0.1	36.5
1989	4.4	10.7	14.3	7.3	1.4	0.1	38.2
Germany							
1979	8.3	13.3	19.4	5.4	1.7	−0.1	48.0
1989	8.2	12.7	18.5	4.6	2.8	0.0	46.8
Japan							
1979	3.9	11.3	6.3[a]	6.6	2.6	0.4	31.1
1989	3.7	10.9	7.2[a]	5.5	4.0	0.3	31.6
Netherlands							
1979	11.1	13.4	22.1	5.7	4.2	−0.3	56.2
1989	10.0	12.3	21.1	6.3	6.7	0.1	56.5
Norway							
1980	6.2	15.7	13.8	9.9	3.4	−0.7	48.3
1989	7.6	16.2	18.8	8.4	4.0	−0.4	54.6
Sweden							
1980	8.5	17.3	24.1	7.6	4.1	0.3	61.9
1988	6.5	14.5	25.8	6.9	5.7	0.3	59.7
United Kingdom							
1979	8.4	13.6	11.9	3.7	4.4	0.8	42.8
1989	8.3	12.8	12.9	3.0	3.6	0.6	41.2
United States							
1979	7.7	6.2	10.8	4.5	2.8	0.1	32.1
1989	9.1	6.1	11.7	4.5	5.0	−0.1	36.3

Note: a Excludes administrative spending and transfers to non-profit organisations.
Source: Oxley and Martin 1991, Table 3.

A more detailed study of the trends underlying Table 9.3 highlights some of the causes and the consequences of what has happened during the 1980s (Oxley and Martin 1991; see also Table 6.2 in chapter 6). In most countries, real education and health spending per person covered by these schemes continued to rise throughout the 1980s, but at a slower rate than in the latter half of the 1970s. The growth in average transfer payments per head of each target group also rose more slowly in the 1980s than in the 1970s. A factor contributing to the first of these changes—as well as to some of the other reductions shown in Table 9.3—was the restraint exercised by governments over the wages of government employees. In all but two countries (the Netherlands and the United States) where the data could be assembled, the average wage of government employees declined relative to average private sector wages during the 1980s. Furthermore, average government wages declined in real terms in the 1980s in four countries and were held constant in two others. Offsetting this trend has been the tendency for general government employment to continue to grow in the 1980s (in absolute terms as well as relative to private sector employment) despite the fact that outlay growth has been greatest in the area of transfer payments, which have the lowest employment requirements (Oxley and Martin 1991, Table 5).

In summary, the SNA data reveal that the Australian experience was not unique, as most OECD governments managed to reduce the relative size of the general government sector during the 1980s. However, the extent of that success varied, both across countries and across different programs and types of intervention. But even where government continued to grow, the rate of expansion slowed relative to earlier periods. No doubt these efforts were assisted by the relatively good economic performance throughout the OECD between 1982 and 1989, although the trends identified here remain even after adjustment for the changing cyclical situation is allowed for (Oxley and Martin 1991, p. 175).

Other trends in the public sector

Despite the changes revealed by the general government statistics shown in Tables 9.1, 9.2 and 9.3, the figures provide only a partial account of the changing nature of the state and market sectors for two reasons. The first, discussed earlier, relates to the fact that the general government sector is only one part of the overall public sector. Second, figures on the level and structure of government spending do not reveal how reforms to government policies and programs have utilised market mechanisms in order to enhance efficiency and expand choice. Some of these issues are dealt with in this and the following section.

As has been the case in Australia, the privatisation of public enterprises was at the forefront of public policy debate in many OECD countries during the 1980s. As previously noted, the difficulties of defining what makes an enterprise public mitigates against reliable cross-national comparisons, although available evidence shows the public enterprise sector to be largest in continental European countries like Austria, France and Italy, and smallest in Pacific rim countries like Canada, Japan and the United States. A recent OECD study has assembled what data are available to analyse trends in public enterprises during the 1980s (Oxley et al. 1990). These show a general, though not universal, trend towards a reduction in the relative size of public enterprises over the decade. The biggest reductions occurred in the United Kingdom, Portugal, Germany and France. Minor reductions are evident in the United States, Italy, Belgium, the Netherlands and Spain, while the relative size of public enterprises increased in Finland and Greece (Oxley et al. 1990, Chart J). For the five countries where data on the proceeds from privatisation sales are available, these were small (well below 1 per cent of total government revenue) in Germany, France and the Netherlands. In the United Kingdom, proceeds from privatisation were about 2 per cent of total government revenue, while the figure exceeded 5 per cent in New Zealand.[9]

Despite the vigorous public and political debates over the role and effects of privatisation in Australia, the process has proceeded slowly here, although at an accelerating pace. As recently as 1990, the Office of EPAC noted that despite substantial privatisation of government business enterprises (GBEs) in several overseas countries, 'to date the coverage of GBEs in the Australian economy has been relatively stable' (EPAC 1990, p. 56). Despite this, the 1991/92 OECD report on the Australian economy reported that the fourteen major Commonwealth assets sales since 1986 (including the then recent sale of 30 per cent of the Commonwealth Bank) had produced gross proceeds of about $4.2 billion (OECD 1992a, p. 95)—equivalent to about half of total Commonwealth budget outlays on education in 1991/92. Since then, 'the pace of privatisation has picked up' (OECD 1994b, p. 73) including the privatisation of 'flagship' enterprises such as Qantas and more of the Commonwealth Bank. The OECD, however, remains cautious about the benefits from such moves, arguing that: 'Whether privatisation would further improve efficiency can depend on whether competitive market conditions are put in place prior to privatisation. Experience to date suggests that much can be done to improve productivity without privatisation, especially by clearly defining commercial objectives for

GBEs and exposing them to a competitive environment' (OECD 1994b, p. 73).

Clearly, the privatisation debate, which is as much about the ends of public policy as it is about the means, is set to continue in Australia.[10] One (probably unintended) advantage of Australia having proceeded slowly along the privatisation path so far is that it provides an opportunity to learn from the experiences of (and, hopefully, benefit from) the mistakes of other countries.

The principal rationale for government regulation of aspects of the behaviour of private enterprises and individuals has been market failure. The existence of increasing returns to scale will, for example, lead to cost inefficiencies under competitive conditions, favouring instead the establishment of a single 'natural' monopoly which can reap the full benefits of scale economies. To protect the public interest, that natural monopoly can either be owned and/or controlled by government—the traditional European (and Australian) solution—or subject to extensive regulatory control—as in North America. Although the budgetary costs of regulation in the form of entry and exit controls and price or output controls may be modest, their economic costs may be much higher. One recent study estimates the annual cost of federal regulations in the United States at about 9 per cent of GDP or over a quarter of total federal government spending (Hopkins 1991; quoted in Jacobs 1992).

The trend in the OECD during the 1980s, particularly after 1985, was for deregulation to be concentrated in five main sectors of the economy: energy; transport; posts and telecommunications; banking and financial services; and broadcasting (Lacey 1992). During the 1980s, no fewer than eighteen OECD countries launched or expanded broad programs of regulatory management and reform. The actual pace of regulatory reform has, however, been slow in most countries, a reflection of the opposition and resistance of those who have gained an economic advantage from existing regulations. Attempts at regulatory reform have also encountered more broadly based opposition to the replacement of government controls and rules by market forces. As Jacobs (1992) notes, 'Rules are often equated with rights and social equity, and changes, particularly towards reliance on market forces, is [sic] seen to weaken established entitlements' (Jacobs 1992, p. 8).

One area where deregulation has been extensively implemented is in exchange and financial markets. While many see these moves as beneficial, Harcourt (1992) has recently questioned whether the underlying nature of these two markets is such as to permit the economic benefits which the theory of markets claims will normally be associated with deregulation. Certainly, the role and impact of speculative activity in both markets implies that a good deal of instability and uncertainty will result from the easing of controls, as recent experience on the European (and Australian) currency markets illustrates. Hugh Stretton (1987) has gone further, arguing that deregulation of the financial sector has often resulted in not *less* regulation, simply *worse* regulation. Finally, in relation to the reduction in trade barriers and restrictions, the pace of change has tended to be slow, although its direction is clear. Here again, recent difficulties with the latest round of GATT negotiations highlight the role of politics in the determination of the pace—and in some cases even the direction—of reform.

Marketisation

At least as fundamental to state and market relations as privatisation and deregulation, and possibly more enduring in their impact, are changes in the way government services are organised, provided, delivered and financed. These changes do not mean that various forms of government activity are replaced by market-based alternatives, but rather that government services are actively encouraged to utilise a range of market-type instruments in order to improve efficiency in service provision and delivery and expand the range of choices facing service users. In theory, these reforms allow governments to promote the merits of market competition in terms of efficiency, effectiveness, competition and choice, while still maintaining overall control of the services in question.

The range of these reforms is great, including the introduction of market-type mechanisms such as the establishment of internal markets, the contracting-out of services, franchising, modifying property rights, and the implementation of voucher schemes and user charges (Lacasse 1992). The scope of reform is broad, ranging from the introduction of performance-related pay for public servants—an approach now adopted by virtually all OECD governments (Maguire and Wood 1992)—to the use of internal markets in inter-governmental agency transactions in property leasing, printing and publishing services, and transport (Lacasse and McGlynn 1992). However, one area where reliance on market mechanisms has become most extensive is in welfare state programs, particularly in the health and community care sectors.

This has been possible because the traditional welfare states of most OECD countries in fact comprise two separate welfare states, as Le Grand (1992) has emphasised: the state which pays for or finances welfare provision and the state which directly provides welfare services to clients.[11] Within the more conventional OECD welfare state, there has been a shift away from government finance and provision of services towards government finance of services (and, in some cases, cash benefits) provided and/or delivered by independent or semi-independent agencies operating in what Le Grand (1990; 1991) refers to as internal or quasi-markets:

> They are 'markets' because they replace monolithic state providers with competitive independent ones. They are 'quasi' because they differ from conventional markets in a number of key ways. The differences are on both the supply and the demand sides. On the supply side, as with conventional markets, there is competition between productive enterprises or service suppliers . . . However, in contrast to conventional markets, these organisations are not necessarily out to maximise their profits; nor are they necessarily privately owned. Precisely what such enterprises maximise, or could be expected to maximise, is unclear, as is their ownership structure . . . On the demand side, consumer purchasing power is not expressed in money terms. Instead it takes the form of an earmarked budget or 'voucher' confined to the purchase of a specific service. Also on the demand side, in some of the areas concerned such as health and social services, the immediate consumer is not the one who exercises the choices concerning purchasing decisions; instead those choices are delegated to a third party (a case manager, a GP, or a health authority) (Le Grand 1990, p. 5).

Quasi-market reforms are thus designed to introduce competition into both the demand for and supply of welfare services, while at the same time keeping overall responsibility for service finance, access and output quality within the public sector.

These developments are currently most advanced in countries such as the United Kingdom and New Zealand, although quasi-market reforms are being introduced in the health care systems of a number of European countries (Hurst 1991). The pace of reform in the United Kingdom has accelerated since 1989 and the purchaser–provider split now permeates the entire apparatus of welfare state provision. Much of the provision of health care is undertaken by independent trusts or managed units operating within each health authority, which compete for contracts issued by the purchasing authorities, including certain GP fund-holders who are given a voucher for the purchase of services on behalf of their patients (Le Grand 1992).

Similar changes have taken place in community care with the appointment of a care manager for each client with responsibility

> . . . to construct a package of care for the client concerned, based on a pre-determined budget. In making up the package of care, the care manager would consider bids from competing organisations, including public, voluntary and private sector agencies . . . the

system can be viewed as essentially a voucher scheme, with care managers allocating budgets on behalf of clients between competing institutions and with the allocation of resources being determined by client choice (as delegated to care managers) instead of by bureaucratic decision (Le Grand 1992, p. 5).

This kind of development in community care is now being pursued in a number of countries, including Australia under the pilot Community Options Projects, funded by the Commonwealth Government (Graham, Ross and Payne 1992; Graham 1993). Other areas where similar arrangements are being examined in a number of countries include housing, vocational training and child care. In contrast, despite the wide discussion of voucher schemes in education, these have not yet been widely implemented anywhere (Lacasse and McGlynn 1992). Finally, both New Zealand and the United Kingdom have established executive agencies with responsibility for the payment of social security benefits, once again separating service delivery from funding and policy formulation.

It is not possible here to canvass the range of issues to which these developments give rise. Much of their success will depend upon how contracts are specified, how failure to comply with contractual conditions is enforced, and how existing contract-holders can be made subject to competition from potential new entrants. It is too early to give any realistic assessment of their longer term consequences, but it does seem clear that, like privatisation, moves to introduce market mechanisms into the organisation of government services will not be easily reversed. These developments thus have the potential to fundamentally change traditional relationships between the state and the market.

Summary

This chapter has drawn on a range of material pertaining to developments in relations between the state and the market in Australia and other OECD countries since 1980. Importantly, the trends in Australia identified at the beginning of this chapter should not be seen in isolation, as similar trends were identified in most other OECD countries. The changes have been fundamental and, in many instances, irreversible. Financial pressures on governments saw a marked reduction in the relative size of government expenditure in virtually all OECD countries in the latter half of the 1980s. No less than thirteen of the nineteen countries for which data are available spent a lower percentage of GDP on general government programs in 1989 than they did in 1986. Included in this list are such traditionally 'big government' nations as Denmark, the Netherlands and Sweden. However, government spending rose again after 1989 in virtually all OECD countries as the recession exerted direct and indirect pressures on spending. Only two countries (Denmark and Greece) managed to reduce their government spending ratio between 1989 and 1992, and even here the reductions were only marginal. The average increase experienced over this period was almost 4 percentage points of GDP—larger than occurred on average in the nine years to 1989.

Moves to privatise public enterprises and deregulate economic sectors previously subject to regulation have also taken place, albeit more slowly. The pace of change has, however, tended to accelerate in recent years (including in Australia) and more recent data may reveal even more significant changes. Accompanying these changes has been the introduction of market mechanisms in a wide range of public sector activities. Managerial reforms in the public sector—though not discussed here—have also been extensive and their impacts significant.

These changes are fundamentally altering traditional relationships between the state and market sectors of all OECD economies. It is too soon in the process to assess the extent to which they will reap the economic benefits claimed for competitive markets. Economic arguments associated with choice, competition and efficiency have been used to justify many of the reforms, despite the fact that economic theory itself indicates that some of these gains will only be realised in practice if very stringent conditions prevail (Atkinson and Stiglitz 1980; Barr 1992). In practice, final outcomes will depend as much on the role and influence of politics in the reform process as on theoretical economic argument and analysis.

Despite their changing role, governments in Australia and throughout the OECD are still seen to be responsible for economic performance and the achievement of social objectives, and political pressures will no doubt continue to remind them of this. The increased reliance on market mechanisms is a fundamental change, one which makes the distinction between the state and the market itself problematic and of somewhat dubious relevance. Governments are increasingly maintaining responsibility for, and control over, their economic and social objectives while relying on market principles to assist them to achieve them. This process has been interrupted by the recession, although it is too early to say yet whether this will cause a reversal of the earlier trend towards smaller government, or a reaffirmation of the role of government in modern mixed economies.

Notes

1. An earlier version of some of the comparative material presented in this paper was originally contained in a paper presented to the Academy of Social Sciences Annual Symposium entitled 'Market and State Relations in the 1990s', held at the ANU in November 1992. I would like to thank Peter Kriesler for his comments on this version of the paper.
2. Readers wishing for more information on this aspect can consult Saunders (1987) and *Statement No. 6* which appears each year in *Budget Paper No. 1*. The latter is an invaluable source for information on the underlying statistical and measurement framework and provides a regular updated series of the outlays of each part of the public sector.
3. I leave aside issues associated with the role of public sector investment and the peculiarities of the ways in which consumption and investment are defined in the government accounts.
4. This explains why, because of double-counting, the sum of the separate elements in Table 9.1 exceeds total outlays for the public sector as a whole.
5. Some small differences with national treatment nonetheless remain, which explains the divergence between the Australian figures in Tables 9.1 and 9.2.
6. Some more recent data on social spending in OECD countries can be found in the report on social protection recently released by the OECD (OECD 1994a).
7. This explains the presence of the Balancing Item in Table 9.3, which also serves as a reminder that these data are not as reliable nor as comparable as those in Table 9.2. The data nonetheless represent the fruits of considerable effort by OECD economists and are undoubtedly the best of their kind currently available.
8. See also Table 6.2 in chapter 6.
9. Unfortunately, Australia is not included in this OECD analysis.
10. In a study of privatisation in the United Kingdom, Rowthorn and Chang (1991) rationalise the privatisation process in terms of a *political* rather than an *economic* explanation, arguing that privatisation offered the Thatcher Government an effective insurance policy against future governments reversing the changes which were taking place. They conclude that public enterprise efficiency is as much an issue of politics as of economics and that any approach which ignores this will be of limited relevance to understanding the political economy of privatisation. Furthermore, they argue that while privatisation should not be used to supplement the funds of cash-starved governments, nor to achieve purely ideological objectives, a clear implication from their analysis is that the political pressures driving privatisation are likely, if unchecked, to result in precisely these outcomes.
11. Australia is something of an exception here, having traditionally relied more heavily than many other OECD countries on a range of non-government agencies, including in some cases private profit-making concerns, for the provision of welfare services financed by government; see Saunders and Fine (1992).

Recommended reading

Gemmell, N. (ed.) 1993, *The Growth of the Public Sector: Theories and International Evidence*, Edward Elgar, Aldershot

Gruen, F. and Grattan, M. 1993, *Managing Government: Labor's Achievements and Failures*, Longman Cheshire, Melbourne

Oxley, H. and Martin, J.P. 1991, 'Controlling government spending and deficits: trends in the 1980s and prospects for the 1990s', *OECD Economic Studies*, No. 17, Autumn, pp. 145–89

Saunders, P. 1994, *Welfare and Inequality: National and International Perspectives on the Australian Welfare State*, Cambridge University Press, Melbourne

10 The environment: the role of economic instruments
Anthony Owen

Over the past two decades, environmental issues have increased in prominence worldwide, and formal consideration of the impact on the environment of new development proposals is now mandatory in Australia and many other countries. Complementing this rise in awareness of the impact of human activities on the environment has been an attempt by many governments, often forced into action by high-profile 'green' organisations, to provide significant resources for research and education to raise the community's awareness of domestic environmental concerns.[1]

The scale of the problems that must be addressed are many and varied, ranging from localised pollution of highways through anti-social dumping of refuse to the prospect of global climate change resulting from human activities augmenting the natural 'greenhouse effect'. The corresponding policy options for dealing with such problems are also very varied, as are the costs of implementing such options.

In economics the environment is viewed as a composite asset that provides a variety of life-supporting services. As with other assets, excessive depreciation will lead to a diminution of the desired services that the asset can provide. The environment provides the economy with raw materials and energy, the combination of which yields consumer goods. But ultimately these raw materials and energy return to the environment as waste products. Excessive wastes will depreciate the asset, thus reducing the services the asset provides. Essentially, the role of economics is to maximise the value of the asset in the sense that it must define the 'optimal' level of human impact on the environment. This is done by creating a balance between the preservation and use of that asset.

In order to define this balance, it is necessary to place some sort of value on the various service flows received, including the negative effects of using the environment as a receptacle for waste. Ideally, this valuation should be based on the impact of human activity on the world's ecosystem, but the process by which such values may be derived is far too complex to comprehend for the current generation. However, it is the purpose of this chapter to discuss the various options that are currently under consideration to attempt at least a partial recognition of the desired processes to be followed. This is a fundamental issue underpinning the entire discipline of environmental economics.

Environmental protection has traditionally been pursued by means of a range of regulatory approaches, but it has become clear, as will be noted later, that this 'command and control' approach is ineffective or inefficient in many applications. Ironically, the very mechanism which has encouraged excessive environmental damage in much of the world, and hence contributed significantly to its accompanying high social costs—the market place—is seen by some as one important avenue by which environmental objectives and targets could possibly be met at a lower cost than by traditional regulatory measures. However, to do so effectively, the market failures which have contributed to so much of the problem in the first place need to be corrected.

This chapter describes the logic underpinning the use of economic instruments for addressing various environmental policy objectives as compared to direct regulation, which has been the dominant method to date, and the applicability of the instruments through which the objectives of policy are to be achieved. Economic instruments may be loosely grouped into two main classes: those which create property rights to environmental resources and those which are imposed directly onto prices (i.e. taxation). While the theory underlying the economic rationale for the use of instruments in the context of environmental protection is relatively simple, in practical terms there is considerable debate as to how the full environmental costs of various human activities can be evaluated and how charges can be imposed on the polluters to compensate for the environmental 'damage' they create.

Before proceeding with a formal treatment of economic instruments in the context of environmental economics, a definition of 'polluter' as it will be used in the context of this chapter would be useful. The term 'pollution' is applied to actions which damage or degrade the environment, and an individual or institution responsible for such actions is referred to as a 'polluter'. Thus the term 'polluter' has a broader definition than is usually the case in its more common use.

THE ENVIRONMENT

Internalising externalities

In a market economy, economic agents typically only consider private (i.e. their own) costs and benefits when planning levels of production, consumption, investment and so on. The economic and social consequences of environmental degradation are not generally translated into private costs to be borne by the polluter. Indeed, in a competitive framework, economic agents would have an in-built tendency to transfer such social costs onto others or into the distant future.

Such costs (or benefits) are generally known as 'externalities' since they are borne by third parties irrespective of whether or not they wish to experience them.[2] It is not possible for an individual person or nation to purchase less of the 'good' using the conventional market mechanism. Coase (1960) argued that the problem of externalities was due to the lack of property rights. In its simplest form, the Coase theorem asserts that the most efficient solution to pollution damage situations is a bargaining process between polluter and sufferer based on a clear definition of property rights. If the polluter has the right, the sufferer can pay him not to pollute; if the sufferer has the right, the polluter can compensate him to tolerate damage. Thus the 'cost' of the final decision is shared between the two parties without external intervention. In fact Coase showed that, provided the costs of making such transactions are negligible and affected parties can negotiate freely with each other, an efficient allocation would take place irrespective of which party was allocated the right (although the distribution of costs and benefits among the affected parties would change). Not surprisingly, the cost is borne by the person not owning the right.

Consider the example of a rock band that conducts its practise sessions in the residence of one of its members, much to the discomfort of neighbouring residents. If the group has the 'right' to make noise, then the neighbours would have to negotiate a solution whereby the noise level was lowered, or practise was undertaken at a less disruptive time of the day, in return for some benefit (maybe financial) to the rock group. However, if the neighbours as a group held the 'right' in the form of absence of noise, then if the rock group wished to practise it would have to negotiate a compensation package with the neighbours. A possible inefficiency that may arise if the 'right' is assigned to the rock group is the proliferation of such rock groups established simply to receive compensation (bribes?) in return for noise moderation.

Theoretical and practical reasons have been put forward as arguments for the inability of the Coase theorem to provide a solution to the attainment of an optimal level of pollution. Briefly, these are:

- transaction costs, which Coase assumes to be zero, may be of such significance that they prohibit achievement of an optimal bargaining solution;
- Coase also assumes wealth effects to be zero. However, the person assigned the property right becomes a beneficiary of a transfer of wealth. Provided their demand responds to changes in income, this transfer would raise their level of consumption.

Where individual negotiation of property rights becomes impractical, then the injured parties can resort to 'liability rules'. These are rules which award monetary damages, after the fact, to the injured parties, with the amount of the award designed to correspond to the amount of damage inflicted. Such decisions create precedents, giving potential offenders advance knowledge of the cost of their actions. Tietenberg (1992) uses as an example the incentives that exist for an oil company to prevent oil spills. Once it has had to clean up after an oil spill and to compensate fishermen for reduced catches, it quickly becomes evident that accident prevention is cheaper than retrospectively dealing with the damage once it has occurred.

However, if transaction costs are high, if the number of parties involved in a dispute is large, and if the parties have the same interests, then the inefficiency tends to be corrected by government regulation. Historically, regulatory instruments have been the basic mechanism for enacting environmental policy throughout the industrialised world. Environmental quality is seen as a public good which the state must secure by preventing private agents from damaging it. Direct regulation involves the imposition of standards regarding emissions and discharges, product or process characteristics and so on through licensing and monitoring. Legislation usually forms the basis for this form of control, and compliance is generally mandatory with sanctions for non-compliance. The standard is set either on the basis of scientific opinion of the adverse health or ecological effects of the pollution in question, or by making a social or political judgment of the value to the public of the environmental good in question.

Over the past decade, so-called 'market-based' approaches to addressing environmental problems have become popular, although their history dates from earlier seminal works by Pigou (1920) and Dales (1968), and regulation is commonly viewed as lacking in flexibility and being sub-optimal in terms of environmental and economic efficiency. The argument may be summarised as follows:

- Regulation will only produce an economically efficient (i.e. least cost) solution to meeting a given environmental standard by accident;

- Regulation may discourage new economic and technological abatement initiatives, since polluters do not incur a financial penalty for their emissions provided they remain below the standard;
- Regulation does not fully take into account differences in abatement costs between polluters, so an economically sub-optimal distribution of abatement devices will occur.

Consider again the example of our rock group. If legislation were enacted such that noise levels were not permitted to exceed a certain standard anywhere in Sydney, then there would be no incentive for the rock group to modify its behaviour other than to ensure compliance with the new standard (of course, if the penalties for non-compliance were regarded as trivial or non-enforceable, then it may ignore the standards completely). The inefficiencies associated with this solution are very evident:

- Without a significant amount of resources being allocated to research into the effects of varying noise levels on local communities (i.e. calculation of the cost of damage caused by the noise pollution), the level of the standard can only be set arbitrarily;
- There is no incentive for behaviour modification. The rock group has no incentive to move to an area where its 'desired' noise level may be less 'costly' to local residents than its current location or to play at less disruptive times of the day.

The legislation could be amended to accommodate these problems, but by now it should be apparent that the cost of achieving a reasonable approximation to an efficient solution (and policing it) would be far from trivial.

Economics of emission control

Emissions can generally be categorised as either 'fund' or 'stock' pollutants. Stock pollutants accumulate over time as emissions enter the environment, since the latter has inadequate or no absorptive capacity to deal with them. Examples could include current global production of nuclear waste and roadside dumping of beer cans. Pollutants for which the emissions rate does not exceed the absorptive capacity of the environment are called fund pollutants. Essentially the latter are transformed into substances that are not considered harmful to people or to the ecological system. Global emissions of carbon dioxide (CO_2) should fall into this category, since they are absorbed by plant life and the oceans. Today, however, emissions are too high for the earth's absorptive capacity to prevent accumulation of CO_2 as a stock in the atmosphere.

Since pollution is a classic externality, markets will generally produce more than the efficient amount of both fund and stock pollutants. For both pollutants this will imply higher than efficient damages and lower than efficient control costs. In addition, for stock pollutants an excessive amount of pollution would accumulate in the environment, imposing a detrimental externality on future, as well as current, generations.

Unlike the case of increasing scarcity of a natural resource, the price mechanism would not automatically adjust to offset this additional 'cost' of pollution. In fact, firms that take unilateral action to control their own emissions will be placed at a cost disadvantage to those ignoring their emissions. Hence the requirement for some form of government market intervention.

The taxation approach

The theoretical foundations for the taxation approach are based on the work of Pigou (1920), who was an early proponent of the imposition of taxes as a means of equating private and social cost. More recently, the OECD has expounded the virtues of such a tax through its endorsement of the 'polluter-pays principle' and a more effective use of economic instruments in conjunction with regulation.

The taxation approach requires the regulatory authority to set a pollution tax at a level that will (it is hoped) ensure that a predetermined standard will be met (or, at least, not exceeded) through the normal operations of the marketplace. Generally, the tax is simply designed to achieve a specific standard rather than attempting to reflect the unknown value of marginal net damages to the environment. Naturally, taken to its logical conclusion, if so desired the level of taxation could be set so as to completely eliminate some or all types of environmental pollution.

However, deriving the 'optimal' level of the Pigouvian tax is an impossible task. The required comprehensive statistical compendium of externality-generating activities and their ultimate contribution to marginal net damages would be vast, while quantifying such consequences would itself be a controversial task. The problem is further complicated by the fact that the optimal level of tax on an externality-generating activity is not equal to the pre-tax marginal net damage it generates, but rather to the damage it would cause after the level of the activity had been adjusted to its 'optimal' level. For example, suppose that each additional unit of consumption of electricity causes $1.00 worth of damage, but that after installation of emission control devices and other optimal adjustments, the marginal social damage is reduced to $0.50. The correct value of the Pigouvian tax is $0.50 per unit of output, which corresponds to the 'optimal' situation. A tax of $1.00 per unit of output would reduce emissions beyond the range where the marginal benefit of decreasing emissions exceeds its marginal cost. This makes determination of the optimal level of tax even more difficult.

An alternative is to attempt to reach the optimal level of tax through an iterative procedure. An initial approximation to the tax level could be made and adjusted periodically in response to changes in damage levels. As output and damages are modified, so too could be the level of tax. Ultimately, such a procedure would perhaps converge to the optimal level. However, again information requirements are a major constraint, particularly the lack of knowledge of incremental costs and damages.

Resolution of this problem is generally achieved through a combination of standards and taxes. A regulatory authority specifies maximum desirable emission levels that are conducive to meeting certain subjective standards for an 'acceptable' environment. Taxes (or emission prices) are levied to achieve this objective. For example, enterprises emitting wastes into a river may be charged a fee (tax) in proportion to the concentration of certain substances in their effluent, thus giving such producers an incentive to cut down on their individual emissions. Variations in the tax rate should ensure that the 'acceptable' standard of pollution in the river is met. This process does not require knowledge of costs or damages, only monitoring of river pollution levels to ensure that the tax rate is set at a level which achieves the desired standard.

Although this combination of standards and prices will not, in general, lead to Pareto-optimal levels of the relevant activities, it can be shown that, under appropriate conditions, it is a lower cost method of achieving the required level of pollution abatement than standard setting without charges, even though detailed data on the costs of emission reduction are unavailable.

There is some evidence of the potential cost savings to be made from using the combination of standards and taxes as opposed to direct controls.[3]

In addition to its least cost property, taxation has the advantage of flexibility in dealing with a range of environmental externalities (as opposed to direct regulation). Further, once in place, tax rates can readily be varied to reflect changing standards, whereas changes in regulatory requirements would frequently require new legislation to be enacted. However, in practice, the use of taxation as an instrument for environmental regulation has been very limited. Some suggested reasons for this lack of popularity are:

- difficulty of determining the 'optimal' level of tax required to meet a certain standard;
- taxes would require adjustment (to meet a constant standard) when the industry grows or contracts;
- difficulty of breaking with the traditional 'command and control' framework;
- fear by industry and individuals that such taxation will be levied to maximise government revenue rather than for the more altruistic motive of limiting environmental externalities (although the latter will probably be accomplished in the process);
- inflation may erode the *real* value of a tax, thereby possibly reducing its effectiveness (i.e. adjustment would be required to meet a constant standard);
- taxation becomes a very cumbersome tool if differential rates are required to account for regional differences in the scale (i.e. consequences) of pollution.

Applications

Traditionally, although there are important exceptions, taxes have been levied to provide revenue for the operation of various aspects of government rather than for more altruistic reasons, such as correction of market imperfections arising from unfettered consumption of public goods. An important area of debate over recent years has been the topic of a carbon tax, which became an area of heated debate associated with the 1993 Commonwealth budget. Combustion of fossil fuels generates significant externalities, such as emissions of SO_2, NO_x, CO_2, and particulates, and these have become of great concern over the past couple of decades with problems such as acid rain, urban smog and, more recently, the potential for global warming through rising levels of emissions of CO_2 and its implications for the biosphere.

Since almost all economic activities involve, directly or indirectly, use of energy derived from fossil fuels, reducing emissions of CO_2 can be achieved in a relatively simple manner by taxing the carbon content of the fuels. Since a carbon tax will vary by carbon content of each fossil fuel, inter-fuel substitution between both fossil and non-fossil fuels will occur as will substitution of other (now relatively cheaper) factors of production (e.g. labour and capital) for fossil fuels.[4] This process will be enhanced if investment in energy-saving technologies, or non-carbon-emitting energy sources, is encouraged through the fiscal regime. In addition, since carbon taxes will always be present as long as carbon-based fuels are used, there is a continuing financial incentive to develop alternative energy technologies or carbon disposal technologies.

The question of setting the precise level of tax to achieve the desired environmental target or objective depends on a reasonably precise knowledge of the magnitude of the relevant energy demand elasticities. Estimates of elasticities of demand for energy (and individual fuels) in Australia vary widely, and are generally based on econometric models estimated using data which do not undergo changes of the magnitude in energy prices suggested in the context of the imposition of a carbon tax. Since a carbon tax will vary by carbon content of fuel, it is also necessary to know inter-fuel substitution elasticities as well as the standard income and price elasticities. Whether or not these objections represent a serious flaw in the entire concept of modelling the economic impact of carbon taxes is an important question. Even if such an exercise is thought to produce estimates that are believed to be reasonably reliable, it is clear that the sheer magnitude of the revenue that would be generated by such a tax requires a general (rather than partial) equilibrium approach in the econometric modelling component of any study of the ultimate impact of the tax and use of the revenue raised by it.

The fact that a carbon tax cannot yield a precise level of CO_2 emission reductions for a given rate of tax should not be viewed as an argument against its implementation, since we are dealing with a stock and not a flow of pollutant. In other words, damages are related to the atmospheric concentrations, not to the flow of emissions. Therefore, if the carbon tax does not achieve the expected reduction in emissions in one period, there will be time to adjust the tax in subsequent periods. However, therein lies another problem!

Setting an appropriate level of carbon tax (either nationally or globally) depends critically on accurate estimation of the level of world economic activity and relative real incomes. Changes in energy prices have had (in the past) a complex and asymmetric influence on the level of world economic activity. Since the precise level of tax to meet a given emissions target cannot be achieved, it is imperative that some form of partial adjustment mechanism be present to ensure that changes in the rate of the carbon tax do not generate violent fluctuations in GDP with a resulting loss of business confidence.

To illustrate this point, consider the 1990 price of gasoline in a number of developed nations, and associated taxes and duties. The carbon tax equivalent of Australia's excise duty on gasoline amounted to around $US360 per tonne carbon. Equivalent figures for some other nations were: USA, $US121; Japan, $US575; Germany, $US787; UK, $US833; France, $US1181; and Italy, $US1423.[5] Most of these figures far exceed increases implied by tax rates associated with carbon taxes;[6] yet it is interesting to note that because these taxes were introduced gradually over many years they do not appear to have caused an energy price-induced recession. By way of contrast, consider the devastating effects of the major energy price increases following the 1973 and 1979 oil crises, which were caused by the inability of developed economies to adjust to the new situation over such a short time frame.

A flurry of commissioned studies on the short-term and long-term impacts on the Australian economy of the imposition of a carbon tax (imposed either unilaterally or globally) at varying rates appeared in 1991 and 1992.[7] Many of these studies were flawed in the sense that they restricted their analysis to one or two sectors of the economy, consequently ignoring fundamental feedbacks that a general equilibrium approach would have enumerated. For instance, most of them failed to provide an estimate of the total (substantial!) amount of taxation that would be raised by the imposition of a carbon tax, and the resultant question of the redistribution of such funds. However, even a general equilibrium approach would have been of limited use in assessing the impact of, for example, likely technological developments both within the energy sector and in energy-intensive industries that would be stimulated by the substantial increase in energy costs. Yet, where projections over a time horizon of 50 to 60 years are being considered the influence of changing technologies simply cannot be ignored.

Tradeable permits

The system of marketable emission permits allows the regulatory authority to determine the total quantity of emissions, but leaves the precise allocation of the source of such emissions to market forces. This is in marked contrast to the Pigouvian tax where a fee is levied which is equivalent to the marginal social damage of the emissions. In theory both instruments produce optimal results, but in practice they may yield significantly different outcomes.

The principle behind emissions trading is extremely simple. A regulatory authority explicitly sets a target level of emissions covering all sources of emissions in an industry, a region, or even a country. For the sake of an example, assume the target is set at 100 units of emissions. Permits are then issued to each source according to its emissions at some agreed baseline date—a process referred to as 'grand fathering'. Sources are then free to trade the permits, which then command a market price. Sources with low (i.e. below the market price) abatement costs will have an incentive to sell permits and abate their emissions. Conversely, sources with unit abatement costs above the market price will have an incentive to purchase permits in the market. Assuming sources minimise their total production costs, and the market for permits is competitive, it can be shown that the overall cost of achieving the emissions target will be minimised.[8]

Notwithstanding the drawbacks and problems associated with regulation and taxation as instruments for pollution control, they are both founded on well-worked and familiar structures. Regulation and taxation are familiar tools to both industry and the general public. However, with tradeable permits a new market is being established, largely on the basis of a theoretical model, with little practical experience to date. Major questions that surround the implementation of a tradeable permits scheme are:

- How should the permits be allocated?
- Should the initial allocation be sold, leased, or given away?
- Who should be permitted to trade in permits? For example, should an environmental group be permitted to purchase permits and effectively withdraw them from the marketplace?
- To what extent must monitoring be undertaken to ensure that emissions are correctly recorded (and what should be the penalties for non-compliance)?
- What will be the cost of the administrative infrastructure required to facilitate trading and associated activities (including prevention of collusive activities in the permits market)?
- To what extent must details of permit transfers (i.e. quantity, price, ownership, etc.) be made publicly available?
- Should there be a 'grace' period at the end of each year to allow for permit transfers in order to achieve compliance (and how long should it be)?

Types of tradeable emission permits

There are three types of permit systems that have featured in the literature, with selection of the appropriate type largely dependent on the nature of the sources and receptors of emissions.[9] The ambient permit system (APS) refers to the effects of a source's emissions on levels of pollution at a particular receptor point. This implies that trade in permits will not be on a one-for-one basis, since a source whose emissions per unit are more damaging to a particular receptor than those of another source will have to purchase correspondingly more emissions entitlements. Montgomery (1972) has shown that, at least in principle, the APS can achieve a least cost outcome for meeting a specified environmental standard, independent of the initial allocation of the permits. However, transaction costs for polluters are likely to be high since, in effect, separate permit sub-markets, each with different prices, will be created—one for each receptor point.

The emissions permit system (EPS) is much simpler. The EPS issues permits on the basis of source emissions and ignores the impact of these emissions on receptor points. Within a given zone or region, there would be only one market and consequently permit trading would be on a one-for-one basis. However, this system does not discriminate on the basis of different levels of damage caused by sources at different receptor points. This has relevance for greenhouse gas emissions, since their impact is basically a global problem, rather than one relating to a specific receptor point. In theory at least, the EPS cannot achieve the least cost solution.

Because both the APS and EPS are subject to serious problems, a hybrid system has been developed: the pollution-offset (PO) system. Under this system, permits are defined in terms of emissions, trade takes place within a defined zone, but trade is not on a one-for-one basis. Trade is subjected to the restriction that the transfer does not result in a violation of the environmental quality standard at any receptor point. As with the APS, it can be shown that the PO system can lead to the least cost solution independent of the initial allocation of permits, since the value of the permits is determined by the effects of the pollutants at the receptor points.

Combined taxes and permits

It is apparent from the above analysis that, in the presence of uncertainty, taxes and permits are likely to produce sub-optimal, and probably significantly different, results. In order to combine the benefits of both schemes while at the same time offsetting their individual weaknesses, Roberts and Spence (1976) have proposed a hybrid control instrument that utilises tradeable permits supplemented by emissions taxes and a subsidy.

The key concern with tradeable permits is that the cost of meeting the fixed level of emissions (i.e. the amount for which permits have been issued) may be unreasonably greater than initially perceived. If emissions charges are introduced as an option to permits, then they will effectively place a ceiling on the price at which permits can be traded. The scheme is designed to guard against extreme misjudgment of the optimal level of emissions set as part of the process of determining the aggregate value of the issued permits.

The mechanics of the scheme are as follows: the agency issues a predetermined number of tradeable emission permits for which a market emerges and a permit price is determined (which we will assume is equivalent to a cost of P per unit of emissions). At the same time, the agency charges an emissions fee equivalent to (say) F per unit of emissions. The latter can be paid irrespective of whether or not the polluter has tradeable permits. In addition, the agency is willing to provide a subsidy of S per unit of emissions for any unused permits. It follows, that in equilibrium, we must have

$S \leq P \leq F$.

This must hold because if P were greater than F, no permits would be purchased; rather it would be cheaper to pay the emissions tax, so P would be forced to fall. Conversely, if S exceeded P, it would be prudent to purchase as many permits as were available, yielding a profit of $S - P$ per unit; although it is very unlikely that anyone would be willing to sell a permit at that price!

Note that if $S = 0$ and $F = \infty$, both subsidy and emissions taxes are effectively eliminated and the system reverts to a 'pure' permits scheme. It reduces to a 'pure' taxation system if $S = F = T$, where T is the magnitude of the tax, which is the level to which the price of a permit will be automatically driven. Thus, if either the 'pure' permit or 'pure' taxation scheme is optimal, the maximisation calculation will automatically ensure the elimination of the mixed system.

The operation of the mixed system provides an effective insurance for dealing with situations where, presumably unknown to the regulator, permits or taxes fair badly. In circumstances where permits would have performed badly, it would pay the polluter under the mixed scheme to act in a way that transformed it into a taxation regime. For example, if the regulator issues permits (to a value of q*) based on an estimated cost of pollution reduction which is too high, then q* could be far below the optimum level of pollution reduction. Conversely, if the regulator underestimates the cost of pollution, q* will be correspondingly excessive. Now, if actual marginal clean-up cost is higher than F, it will pay polluters operating under the mixed arrangement to emit more than the permits allow and to pay the tax (F) on all emissions that exceed those covered by their permit holdings. If, however, clean-up costs turn out to be lower than S, it will pay polluters to continue to reduce their emissions and hold their excess permits unused in return for the subsidy payment.[10]

Applications

US Clean Air Act

When the *Clean Air Act* was passed in the USA in 1970, its primary focus was on local emissions of sulphur dioxide (SO_2) arising from coal-fired power stations. Thus, one simple solution for reducing local SO_2 emissions was the construction of tall stacks which carried emissions aloft and, theoretically, diluted them. However, throughout the 1980s an acrimonious debate (largely brought about by Canada) concerning the damage arising from cross-border migration of SO_2 emissions leading to acid rain led to a major amendment to the act, which was signed into law on 15 November 1990.

The new law is intended to permanently stabilise total US emissions of SO_2 at 10 million tons a year by the year 2000 (and 8.95 million tons thereafter), significantly reduce NO_x emissions, and control high-risk air toxins from power plant stacks. The annual cost for coal-burning electric utilities to implement this law is estimated to be in the range $US4–9 billion.

The amendment identifies the 110 highest SO_2-emitting coal-fired generating units which will have to install scrubbers, switch to low sulphur coal, find other innovative techniques to reduce emissions, or shut down. A unique provision of the law, however, creates an allowance trading system that will permit a utility to continue to operate 'dirty' plants if it can achieve offsets from other plants it controls, or purchase credits from utilities which are in compliance with the new standards. Emission allowances are based on 1985 emission levels, and each allowance is a marketable federal permit to emit one ton of SO_2 a year. However, limits are imposed on each plant on a phased basis, so that the actual lower limit is reached by 2000.

Affected utilities receive a fixed number of allowances, with a government agency withholding 2.8 per cent of all distributed allowances to assist in creating a market (they are also intended for sale, if necessary, to new power plants since they will be without permits).

There are four core rules that form the heart of the trading program: allowance trading, permitting, continuous emission monitoring, and penalties.

- The allowance system rule establishes the rules for allocation, transfer and tracking of allowances, and is designed to create a flexible system for the trading of the allowances once they are allocated. Any person can participate in the system, not only power plant companies. Thus brokers, government entities, private citizens and corporations are all permitted to trade in allowances, which permits 'green' groups to purchase permits and effectively remove them from circulation. The Environmental Protection Agency (EPA) has established an allowance-tracking system to record initial allocations and transfers, and to ensure that at the end of the year each unit has sufficient allowances to match its emissions. Transactions need only be notified if they

are to be used for compliance, and thus commercial trading can occur without government involvement. Transactions will be posted on a year to date basis, but the price at which allowances are traded will not be available. By 30 January each year, all power plants must finalise their transactions for the previous calendar year and submit them to the EPA to cover their emissions over the same period. The 30-day period of grace was felt necessary to encourage an orderly market, as it avoids end-of-year hoarding and/or desperation purchases. Any allowance not used for compliance can be carried forward for use in future years (i.e. they can be banked).
- The permitting rule indicates how a person becomes a participant in the system and establishes rules for changing approved permits.
- The continuing emission monitoring (CEM) rule sets forth the rules for accounting for SO_2 emissions and was the most controversial rule during the establishment of the trading program. CEM is crucial to the integrity of the entire SO_2 reduction program. The CEM rule requires that each power unit that is part of the program install a CEM system. This system must operate continuously measuring the flow of SO_2 (and NO_x) concentration emitted, and the volumetric flow of SO_2. Monitors have to be connected to a computerised data-handling system to provide the required stream of data. The CEM system was required to provide hourly average data on emissions, with comprehensive alternative estimates to be provided where the monitoring system was faulty or under maintenance. Daily testing of the monitoring equipment's accuracy is also required. The CEM rule requires reporting of the emissions data to the EPA. These data will go into the power plant accounts so that the performance of each plant relative to its number of allowances will be public knowledge.
- Finally, the excess emission rule indicates the penalties for non-compliance with meeting the SO_2 emission limits.

The SO_2 reduction program is an interesting mix of market-based rules and government mandates. The mandates come in the form of the permitting and monitoring requirements since all participants must follow these rules if they wish to be part of the program. The market-based rules create a structure for compliance with the statutory limits that permit power plants to achieve compliance in an efficient, low cost manner.

Applications in local fisheries

A form of marketable permits system has been present in fisheries management for many years. In order to maintain sustainable yields of commercial fish, a total catch quota is placed on various species. Individual transferable quotas (ITQs) are then issued (or sold) to fishermen in order to ensure that the total quota is not exceeded. Such quotas are tradeable. There have been a number of applications to date, and of particular importance are ITQs in the New Zealand fisheries and in the Southern Bluefin Tuna (SBT) fishery.

A major concern associated with ITQs in the New Zealand fisheries was the question of the by-catch. Basically, most fish species can be individually targeted, but other species will be 'accidentally' caught in the process (the by-catch). If fishermen do not have quotas for the by-catch species, or if they have already been exceeded, then the temptation is to dump the (now dead) fish at sea rather than face punitive action from the regulators. To overcome this problem, a secondary market for purchasing the by-catch was established, with prices set at levels that discouraged dumping at sea but did not encourage targeting of these other species.

The problem surrounding overfishing of the SBT is completely different. The SBT adult population level required to ensure a sustainable resource is uncertain. Consequently the total catch quota set for any year is at best a stab in the dark. Although ITQs were agreed to on a voluntary basis in 1986 (by the three fishing nations: Australia, Japan and New Zealand) as a means of conserving the dwindling stock of SBT, the weight of the unexploited parental biomass (i.e. the weight of the remaining adult population in the fishery) has continued to decline. Some biologists believe that, even with a zero total catch quota, stock recovery is still not guaranteed. More recently, the high price of SBT brought about by restricted supply under the low quotas being set has encouraged farming of the SBT, with initial financial results indicating that such ventures can be very profitable.

Efficiency of economic instruments

The fact that taxes and tradeable permits are equivalent instruments in a setting of perfect certainty was noted earlier. However, under particular forms of uncertainty the two approaches to environmental management may yield very different outcomes.

On the benefits side, an error in estimating the benefits curve (in other words, if the regulator does not know its true position) will result in policies which are sub-optimal. However, it can be shown that the resulting error and the corresponding social cost will be the same under taxes and tradeable permits.[11]

The attractive property of tradeable permits is that, in the absence of cheating, a specified maximum level of pollution can be guaranteed irrespective of the cost associated with reaching this level. Similarly, pollution charges or taxes guarantee that the marginal cost of emissions control will be equivalent to the level of the tax imposed, irrespective of the size of the resulting quantity of emissions. Thus, if a government agency adopted a system of marketable permits it can be assured of meeting the stipulated level of emissions, but the associated cost could be surprisingly high. In contrast, if the agency employs an emissions tax it can be certain about the resulting marginal control cost (irrespective of the true cost function), but it may be significantly adrift from its desired level of emissions.

Social welfare aspects of economic instruments

If it is assumed that environmental quality is a 'normal' good,[12] then relatively more wealthy individuals (or countries) would be expected to 'purchase' more of it than the poor. Thus the likely outcome of collective action is a compromise in which the quality of the environment will be less than desired by the wealthy and more than that preferred by the poor. In practical terms, this would show itself in the form of upper income groups pushing for greater outlays on environmental programs in opposition to the wishes of the poor, who want more income diverted to consumption of other goods. This has been crudely summarised as 'environmental concern is not the poor man's game' (Baumol and Oates 1988, p. 236). However, ignoring the distributive impacts of environmental policy may unintentionally harm certain groups in society, or may undermine the program politically.

How victims of externalities should be treated has been a source of much confusion in the economics literature, with some arguing that victims should be compensated for damages they suffer and others that they should be taxed.[13] In general, if the number of victims is large, then the efficient treatment of victims prohibits compensation. Consider the situation of people living close to Sydney airport and suffering from noise pollution in the form of arriving and departing flights. If all affected residents were paid amounts sufficient to compensate them fully for all damages, obviously no one would have any motivation to relocate away from the area. Thus, too many people would choose to live in noisy conditions since they have effectively been offered an economic incentive to accept the adverse consequences of the noise with no offsetting benefits to anyone. The incentive to engage in appropriate defensive activities (e.g. double glazing, moving, etc.) has gone. This is clearly inefficient.

There is a substantial literature on the distributional effects of environmental policy, and the interested reader is referred to chapter 15 in Baumol and Oates (1988) and the references cited therein. Baumol and Oates emphasise '*that the primary purpose of environmental programs is allocative:* their basic rationale is the direction of resource use to achieve desired levels of environmental quality' (their italics), and concur with Freeman (1972) that environmental programs are generally not very well suited to the achievement of distributional objectives. They conclude that the aim should be 'to neutralise the more serious of the objectionable redistributive consequences of . . . environmental policies' (Baumol and Oates 1988, p. 255).

Australian experience[14]

We noted earlier that, as alternatives to direct regulation, economic instruments for addressing policy objectives could be loosely grouped into two categories: taxes and permits. However, it should be evident by now that this distinction is oversimplistic, and that in practice (sometimes quite extensive) regulatory control is still required, while a combination of taxes and permits may be preferred to either one imposed individually. James (1993) has identified eleven distinct 'main instruments' of practical application to date, and has conducted an extensive survey within Australia to identify applications of such instruments:

- emission and effluent charges;
- user charges for the treatment and/or disposal of waste;
- environment levies;[15]
- proportional non-compliance fees;
- product charges;
- deposit refunds;
- tradeable pollution rights;
- tradeable resource user rights;
- user charges for natural resources and environmental amenity;
- performance bonds;
- other economic instruments.

We now consider each of these categories (with the exception of the 'other') individually,[16] paying particular attention to applications within Australia.

Emission and effluent charges

James found that examples of emission charges are rare in Australia, with the predominant form of environmental management consisting of command and control systems based on licences issued to dischargers. For example, NSW uses a licensing system for air, water and noise, administered by the Environmental Protection Authority. Licence fees vary according to discharge and scale, and are set in regulation. Revenue in 1992 was $22 million.

The usual instrument in Australia for controlling effluence (water) was also found to be the licensing system. One of the few examples of an effluent charge, with an incentive effect, is the system of fees introduced in South Australia to support the *Marine Protection Act* which came into effect in March 1993. Emissions are measured for every point source discharge to any tidal waters of South Australia. The charge is levied according to the impact level, which in effect acts as a surrogate for environmental damage costs. However, it is too early to assess the performance of this instrument.

User charges for the treatment and/or disposal of waste

In the past, water and sewerage charges were based heavily on property values, thus providing no financial incentive for responsible use (essentially it was a free good), while cross-subsidisation among different sectors of the community (e.g. by industry to households) was also a consequence of such a system. Two-part tariffs have also been popular, where a small user-pays component is added on to a fixed fee. However, the transition to a full 'user-pays' system of pricing has been made in recent years by a handful of utilities and initial results suggest that both political and public acceptance is no longer a constraint to such a policy. In many instances, for example, the Hunter Water Corporation, the adjustment from one mode of charging to a user-pays system was almost instantaneous, whereas in others, for example, the Sydney Water Board, adjustments to the new charging schedule were spread over a longer time period.

Environment levies

Environment levies are generally imposed to finance specific projects relating to rehabilitation of areas which have suffered environmental damage in the past. In 1989 the Sydney Water Board introduced an annual levy, called the Special Environmental Levy, of $80 per household with the sole aim of cleaning up some of the city's major receptors and sources of water pollution as part of its Clean Waterways Program. The levy was introduced for a fixed period of five years, after which it was planned that it would be incorporated into the user-pays charging system.

The levy received widespread public support largely because of the deplorable, and well-publicised, state of Sydney's sewerage-swept beaches. However, public confidence in the levy was shaken by accusations that funds from the levy had been paid to the State Government as some form of dividend by the Water Board. While this was denied, there is no doubt that the potential exists for the levy to be used to fund some projects that would otherwise have received government funding, thus indirectly 'transferring' funds to consolidated revenue.

Proportional non-compliance fees

Proportional non-compliance fees consist of penalty payments that are imposed if maximum limits on emissions or effluents are exceeded. To constitute an economic instrument, such fees must be directly related to the degree by which the prescribed limit has been exceeded. James could find no examples of this type of fee in his survey.

Product charges

Product charges may be imposed on inputs to economic activities as a means of indirectly controlling adverse environmental impacts. Differential taxes have been applied in Australia on recycled paper in order to encourage recycling so as to reduce waste disposal volumes (to landfill) and litter (and their associated costs).

Deposit refunds

Deposit refunds on reusable containers were once common in Australia, but the advent of disposable containers saw their disappearance and a consequent problem of environmental degradation caused by improper disposal of the latter. In addition, it is now being realised that disposal to landfill is not a no-cost option of disposal. South Australia is the only State that has introduced specific legislation for deposit refunds, and this has created strong economic incentives for the collection and return of beverage containers. The major drawback to the scheme appears to be the additional cost pressures on the State's beverage industry, since the industry in other States is not bound by the same regulations.

Tradeable pollution rights

Tradeable pollution rights consist of quantity and/or quality permits on emissions and/or effluents. The control authority determines the total load to be borne by the environment for a particular catchment, river segment, water body or airshed (atmospheric catchment area) and issues a set of discharge rights or permits. These rights may then be traded in a market, subject to any special conditions specified by the control authority. James's survey revealed only one application of tradeable pollution rights in Australia, which is for tradeable rights in salinity in the Murray–Darling Basin. The administering agency is the Murray–Darling Basin Commission, with the only participants permitted in the scheme being the States of New South Wales, Victoria and South Australia. Trades will be permitted in terms of salt concentrations, measured in electrical conductivity units.

Tradeable resource user rights

Tradeable rights for the use of natural resources can be found in a number of applications in Australia. They include tradeable rights for water use and tradeable quotas for renewable resources such as forestry and fisheries. Individual transferable quotas (ITQs) in the Southern Bluefin Tuna fishery were discussed earlier, but in 1992 they were also introduced in the South East Trawl Fishery in an attempt to curb the interrelated problems of overfishing, inappropriate fishing methods, stock depletion, declining catches and decreasing profits in the industry.

User charges for natural resources and environmental amenity

User fees are applied by all levels of government in Australia for the use of natural environmental amenities for recreation, education, and so on. Such fees are commonplace, and examples include user fees for national parks, recreation areas and conservation areas. In principle such fees should be related to the cost of use (in the form of resource degradation, etc.), but this is rarely the case and most fees are imposed to help cover management costs.

Performance bonds

Performance bonds are being used as an economic instrument in Australia in a number of applications designed to protect the environment. They have been used predominantly with the mining industry to encourage rehabilitation of mine sites upon exhaustion of the ore body. Bonds may also be required as insurance against environmental damage. If the polluter becomes insolvent, or has no desire to repair the damage, then the bond will be forfeited to meet the costs of repair.

Notes

1. In Australia, some examples would be the Australian Bureau of Statistics publication *Australia's Environment: Issues and Facts* (1992) and various publications of the Industry Commission and the Ecologically Sustainable Development Working Groups.
2. This is a very basic definition of externalities. Baumol and Oates (1988, chapters 2–4) provide a more rigorous and extensive approach to the topic.
3. Some examples are given in Tietenberg (1992).
4. The carbon tax may introduce a distortion for power generation costs if the environmental costs of competing non-fossil-based systems such as nuclear and hydro are ignored.
5. Source: Flavin and Lenssen (1992). The fact that these duties/taxes are expressed as carbon tax equivalents should not mask the fact that other user, or abuser, taxes in addition to a carbon tax may be justified. For example, gasoline taxes may also be levied to reflect costs associated with urban congestion or motor vehicle accidents.
6. For example, in a recent paper Repetto (1993) suggested that a carbon tax of about $US30 per ton phased in over five years would stabilise US emissions of CO_2 at 1990 levels by the year 2000. Most Australian studies have considered much larger increases than this figure as being required to stabilise domestic CO_2 emissions; e.g. the Industry Commission (1991) gives an estimate of $A147 per tonne for stabilisation by 2005.
7. Perhaps the most accessible study is that undertaken by the Industry Commission (1991). A more recent paper by Jones et al. (1994) addresses the topic of reducing Australian energy sector greenhouse emissions without explicit assumptions regarding the policy instruments required to bring about the emissions reduction, although it is possible to compute an implicit value for a carbon tax to achieve the given level of reduction.
8. Montgomery (1972).
9. See Tietenberg (1985) for a more detailed review of the relative merits of the APS and the EPS.
10. See Baumol and Oates (1988, pp. 75–7) for a more extensive treatment of this mixed scheme.
11. See Baumol and Oates (1988, pp. 60–1).
12. The conditions for classification as a 'normal' good are: (i) demand increases with income; (ii) the poor are not willing to pay more than the rich (i.e. rich and poor have roughly similar preference functions); and (iii) the price of environmental quality is invariant with respect to income.
13. Baumol and Oates (1988, chapters 3, 4 and 15) cover the conflicting assertions in detail.
14. The interested reader is referred to a set of papers issued by the New South Wales Environment Protection Authority (1994) which discuss the application of economic instruments to a number of environmental problems which are of particular concern in New South Wales. However, the papers have relevance for the other States and Territories.

15 James (1993) used the expression 'environmental taxes', but this is an all-encompassing title which defeats the object of breaking down economic instruments into more specific categories. The author has made this change (without consulting James).
16 The descriptions that follow are summarised from James (1993). The interested reader is encouraged to obtain a copy of this document, as these examples are covered in far greater detail than can be given here.

Recommended reading

Common, Michael 1988, *Environmental and Resource Economics: An Introduction*, Longman, London

James, David 1993, 'Using economic instruments for meeting environmental objectives: Australia's experience', a report prepared for the Department of the Environment, Sport and Territories, Canberra

Tietenberg, T.H. 1992, *Environmental and Natural Resource Economics*, 3rd edition, Harper Collins, New York

Bibliography

Abramovitz, Moses 1986, 'Catching up, forging ahead and falling behind', *Journal of Economic History*, vol. 46, pp. 385–406

Argy, V. 1992, *Australian Macroeconomic Policy in a Changing World Environment*, Allen & Unwin, Sydney

Aschauer, D.A. 1989, 'Is public expenditure productive?', *Journal of Monetary Economics*, vol. 23, pp. 177–200

Atkinson, A.B. and Stiglitz, J.E. 1980, *Lectures on Public Economics*, McGraw-Hill, New York

Australian Bureau of Statistics 1989, *Development of Multifactor Productivity Estimates for Australia 1974–75 to 1987–88*, Catalogue No. 5229.0, April

——1992, *The Australian Consumer Price Index: 12th Series Review*, Catalogue No. 6450.0

——1993, *Australian National Accounts Multifactor Productivity, 1991–92*, Catalogue No. 5234.0, April

Ball, L. 1993, 'How costly is disinflation? The historical evidence', Federal Reserve Bank of Philadelphia *Business Review*, Nov.–Dec., pp. 17–28

Barr, N. 1992, 'Economic theory and the welfare state: a survey and interpretation', *Journal of Economic Literature*, vol. 30, June, pp. 741–803

Barro, Robert J. and Lee, Jong-wha 1993, 'Losers and winners in economic growth', NBER Working Paper No. 4341

Baumol, William and Oates, William 1988, *The Theory of Environmental Policy*, 2nd edition, Cambridge University Press, Cambridge

Bewley, R. and White, G. 1990, 'Do high interest rates improve or worsen the current account?', *Economic Papers*, pp. 19–33

Blanchard, O.J. 1990, 'Why does money affect output? A survey', in B.J.

BIBLIOGRAPHY

Friedman and F.H. Hahn (eds) *A Handbook of Monetary Economics*, Amsterdam, New York

Blundell-Wignall, A. (ed.) 1992, *Inflation, Disinflation and Monetary Policy*, Reserve Bank of Australia, Sydney

Boehm, E.A. 1993, *Twentieth Century Economic Development in Australia*, Longman Cheshire, Melbourne

Bureau of Industry Economics 1991, 'International performance indicators project', Research Reports, AGPS, Canberra

Business Council of Australia, 1992, 'Summary of submission' in EPAC *Strategy for the 1992–93 Budget: Submissions from Business and Commonwealth Organisations*, Australian Government Publishing Service, Canberra

——1993, 'Fast-tracking transport reforms, a report prepared by Access Economics for the Business Council', BCA, Melbourne

——1993, 'Working relations: a fresh start for Australian enterprises, third report of the BCA's Employee Relations Study Commission', BCA, Melbourne

Carmichael, J. 1990, 'Inflation: performance and policy', in S. Grenville *The Australian Macroeconomy in the 1980s*, Reserve Bank of Australia, Sydney

Chapman, B.J. 1990, 'The labour market', in S. Grenville *The Australian Macroeconomy in the 1980s*, Reserve Bank of Australia, Sydney

Chapman, D.R. and Junor, C.W. 1981, 'Profits, variability of profits, and the Prices Justification Tribunal', *Economic Record*, vol. 57, June, pp. 128–39

Clark, D. 1992, *Student Economics Briefs, 1992–93*, Financial Review Library, Sydney

——1993, *Student Economics Briefs, 1993–94*, Financial Review Library, Sydney

——1994, *Student Economics Briefs, 1994–95*, Financial Review Library, Sydney

——(forthcoming), 'Economic history', *The Australian Encyclopaedia*, Sydney

Committee on Employment Opportunities 1993, *Restoring Full Employment*, Commonwealth of Australia (The Green Paper), AGPS, Canberra

Commonwealth of Australia, 1994, *Working Nation: Policies and Programs* (The White Paper), AGPS, Canberra

Costa, M. and Duffy, M. 1991, *Labor, Prosperity and the 1990s*, Federation Press, Sydney

Crow, I., Richardson, P., Riddington, C. and Simon, F. 1989, *Unemployment, Crime and Offenders*, Routledge, London

Dales, J.H. 1968, *Pollution, Property and Prices*, University of Toronto Press, Toronto

De Long, J. Bradford and Summers, Lawrence H. 1992, 'Equipment investment and economic growth: how strong is the nexus?', *Brookings Papers on Economic Activity* 2, pp. 157–99

Dornbusch, R. 1983, 'Real interest rates, home goods and optimal external borrowing', *Journal of Political Economy*, vol. 91, pp. 141–53

Dowrick, Steve 1990, 'Explaining the productivity slow-down of the 1980s', *Australian Bulletin of Labour*, vol. 16, no. 3, September, pp. 174–97
——1992, 'Technological catch up and diverging incomes: patterns of economic growth 1960–88', *Economic Journal*, vol. 102, pp. 600–10
——1993, 'A review of new theories of economic growth: and their implications for Australian policy', *Economic Analysis and Policy*, vol. 23, no. 2, September
Dowrick, Steve and Quiggin, John 1993, 'Australia, Japan and the OECD: GDP rankings and revealed preference', *Australian Economic Review*, no. 101, pp. 21–34
Easson, M. (ed.) 1992, *What Should Unions Do?*, Pluto Press, Sydney
EPAC 1989, 'External debt: trends and issues', Economic Planning and Advisory Council Discussion Paper No. 89/06, AGPS, Canberra
——1990, 'The size and efficiency of the public sector', Council Paper No. 44, AGPS, Canberra
——1991, *Australia's Inflation Problem: Office of EPAC Seminar*, EPAC Background Paper No. 11, AGPS, Canberra
——1993a, 'Income tax and asset choice in Australia', Research Paper No. 3, AGPS, Canberra
——1993b, 'Financial performance of government business enterprises: an update', Background Paper No. 25, AGPS, Canberra
——1993c, 'Wage bargaining systems and productivity growth', Background Paper No. 26, AGPS, Canberra
——1993d, 'Education issues', Background Paper No. 27, AGPS, Canberra
——1993e, 'Structural change and economic growth', Background Paper No. 28, AGPS, Canberra
——1993f, 'Education and training in the 1990s', Background Paper No. 31, AGPS, Canberra
——1993g, 'Issues in competition policy', Background Paper No. 32, AGPS, Canberra
——1993h, 'Enterprise bargaining systems: international case studies', Background Paper No. 33, AGPS, Canberra
——1993i, 'Australia's growth potential in the 1990s', Background Paper No. 35, AGPS, Canberra
——1994a, 'Taxation, regulation and private saving in Australia', Background Paper No. 36, AGPS, Canberra
——1994b, 'Economic effects of microeconomic reform', Background Paper No. 38, AGPS, Canberra
Evans, T. 1993, 'Higgins Memorial Lecture', Canberra, May (available from Federal Treasury, Canberra)
Evatt Foundation 1993, *Powering the Future: Electricity Supply*, Evatt Foundation, Sydney
Fama, E. 1980, 'Banking in the theory of finance', *Journal of Monetary Economics*, vol. 6, pp. 39–57
Fischer, S. 1977, 'Long term contracts, rational expectations, and the optimal money supply rule', *Journal of Political Economy*, vol. 85, February, pp. 163–90
Fisher, I. 1911, *The Purchasing Power of Money*, Macmillan, New York

Fitzgerald, V. 1993, 'National saving, a report to the Treasurer', AGPS, Canberra

Flavin, Chris and Lenssen, Nicholas 1992, 'Policies for a solar economy', *Energy Policy*, vol. 20, pp. 245–56

Foster, W. and Gregory, R. 1983, 'A flow analysis of the labour market in Australia' in R. Blandy and O. Covick (eds) *Understanding Labour Markets*, Allen & Unwin, Sydney

Frenkel, J.A. and Razin, A. 1986, 'Fiscal policies in the world economy', *Journal of Political Economy*, vol. 94, pp. 564–94

Friedman, M. 1956, 'The quantity theory: a restatement' in *Studies in the Quality Theory of Money*, University of Chicago Press, Chicago

Graham, S. 1993, 'Alternative approaches to the provision of community services for people with disabilities' in P. Saunders and S. Graham (eds) *Beyond Economic Rationalism: Alternative Futures for Social Policy*, Reports and Proceedings No. 105, Social Policy Research Centre, University of New South Wales, pp. 107–32

Graham, S., Ross, R. and Payne, T. 1992, *The Evaluation of Community Options in New South Wales*, Reports and Proceedings No. 103, Social Policy Research Centre, University of New South Wales

Grenville, S. (ed.) 1990 *The Australian Macroeconomy in the 1980s*, Reserve Bank of Australia, Sydney

Hamilton, C. 1989, 'Does free trade produce the goods?', *Economic Papers*, vol. 8, no. 2, pp. 23–36

Hanusch, Horst (ed.) 1988, *Evolutionary Economics: Applications of Schumpeter's Ideas*, Cambridge University Press, Cambridge

Harcourt, G.C. 1992, 'Markets, madness and a middle way', *Australian Quarterly*, vol. 64, no. 1, Autumn, pp. 1–17

Harper, I. 1980, 'The relationship between unemployment and unfilled vacancies in Australia', *Economic Record*, vol. 56, no. 154, pp. 231–43

Hayek, F. 1976, *The Denationalisation of Money*, Institute for Economic Affairs, London

Helpman, E. 1984, 'Increasing returns, imperfect markets and trade theory', ch. 7 in R.W. Jones and P.B. Kenen (eds) *Handbook of International Economics*, vol. 1, Elsevier Science Publishers

Hilmer, F., Rayner, M. and Taperell, Q. 1993, ' National competition policy: towards a new order', Report by the Independent Committee of Inquiry, AGPS, Canberra

Hogan, W.P. and Sharpe, I.G. 1988, *Market Discipline, Risk and Bank Prudential Regulation and Supervision in Australia*, Centre for Applied Economics, Paper No. 26, March

Hopkins, T. 1991, *Cost of Regulation*, US Regulatory Information Service Centre, Rochester Institute of Technology, Rochester, New York

Horne, J. and MacDonald, I.M. 1984, 'Rational expectations, gradual price adjustment and monetary policy in Australia', *Australian Economic Papers*, vol. 23, no. 42, pp. 79–89

Hughes, H. 1989, *Report of the Committee for Review of Export Market Development Assistance*, AGPS, Canberra

Hurst, J. 1991, 'Reforming health care in seven European nations', *Health Affairs*, vol. 10, pp. 7–21

Industry Commission, 'Annual reports', AGPS, Canberra
—— 1991a, *Annual Report 1990–91*, Australian Government Publishing Service, Canberra
—— 1991b, *Costs and Benefits of Reducing Greenhouse Gas Emissions, Vol. 1: Report*, Australian Government Publishing Service, Canberra
Jacobs, Michael 1993, 'Economic instruments: objectives or tools', Paper presented to the Environmental Economics—Moving to Sustainability Conference, Canberra, 15–17 November
Jacobs, S.H. 1992, 'Controlling government regulation: a new self-discipline', *OECD Observer*, June/July, pp. 32–4
Johnson, M., Kriesler, P. and Owen, T. (eds) 1991, *Contemporary Issues in Australian Economics*, Macmillan, Melbourne
Johnson, M., Kriesler, P. and Owen, T. (eds), 1994, *Issues in Australian Economics*, Allen & Unwin, Sydney
Jones, B.P., Peng, Zhao-Yang and Naughten, Barry 1994, 'Reducing Australian energy sector greenhouse gas emissions', *Energy Policy*, vol. 22, pp. 270–86
Junankar, P.N. and Kapuscinski, C.A. 1992, *The Costs of Unemployment in Australia*, EPAC Background Paper No. 24, AGPS, Canberra
Kearney, C. and Monadjemi, M. 1990, 'Fiscal policy and current account performance: international evidence on the twin deficits', *Journal of Macroeconomics*, vol. 12, pp. 197–219
Kelley, A. and Schmidt, R. 1979, 'Modelling the role of government policy in post war Australian immigration', *Economic Record*, vol. 55, no. 149, pp. 127–35
Kelly, P. 1992, *The End of Certainty*, Allen & Unwin, Sydney
Keynes, J.M. 1936, *The General Theory of Employment, Interest and Money*, Macmillan, London
Kierzkowski, H. 1984, *Monopolistic Competition and International Trade*, Clarendon Press, Oxford
King, J. 1986, 'How large is the structural element in the current unemployment?', *Australian Bulletin of Labour*, vol. 12, no. 2, pp. 102–18
Krugman, P. 1986, *Strategic Trade Policy and the New International Economics*, MIT Press, Mass
—— 1988, 'Rethinking international trade', *Business Economics*, April
Kyriakopoulos, J. 1991, 'Does moderate inflation affect economic growth?' in M.R. Johnson, et al. *Contemporary Issues in Australian Economics*, Macmillan, Sydney
Lacasse, F. 1992, 'The programme of studies on market-type mechanisms: issues and strategies', *Market-Type Mechanisms Occasional Paper No. 1*, Public Management Service, OECD
Lacasse, F. and McGlynn, A. 1992, 'A market for government services?', *OECD Observer*, June/July, pp. 32–4
Lacey, E. 1992, 'The sectoral impact of deregulation', *OECD Observer*, April/May, pp. 9–12
Le Grand, J. 1990, 'Quasi-markets and social policy', *Studies in Decentralisation and Quasi-Markets, No. 1*, School for Advanced Urban Studies, University of Bristol

—— 1991, 'Quasi-markets and social policy', *Economic Journal*, vol. 101, pp. 1256–67
—— 1992, 'Paying for or providing welfare?', paper presented to the British Social Policy Association Conference, University of Nottingham, July
Lowe, P. 1992, 'The term structure of interest rates, real activity and inflation', *Reserve Bank of Australia Research Discussion Paper 9204*, May
Lucas, R.E. 1972, 'Expectations and the neutrality of money', *Journal of Economic Theory*, vol. 4, April, pp. 103–24
—— 1976, 'Econometric policy evaluation: a critique' in K. Brunner and A. Meltzer (eds) *The Phillips Curve and Labour Markets*, Carnegie-Rochester Conference Series, vol. 1, pp. 19–46
Maguire, M. and Wood, R. 1992, 'Private pay for public work?', *OECD Observer*, April/May, pp. 29–31
Mankiw, G. 1985, 'Small menu costs and large business cycles: a macroeconomic model of monopoly', *Quarterly Journal of Economics*, vol. 100, no. 2, pp. 529–39
McTaggart, D. 1992, 'The cost of inflation in Australia' in A. Blundell-Wignall, *Inflation, Disinflation and Monetary Policy*, Reserve Bank of Australia
Menon, J. 1993, 'Exchange rates, import prices, and the macroeconomy', *Economic Papers*, vol. 12, March, pp. 37–48
Milbourne, R. and Cumberworth, M.B. 1991, 'Australian banking performance in an era of deregulation', *Australian Economic Papers*, vol. 30, no. 57, pp. 171–91
Milbourne, R. 1990, 'Money and finance' in Grenville *The Australian Macroeconomy in the 1980s*, Reserve Bank of Australia, Sydney
Munnell, Alicia H. 1992, 'Policy watch: infrastructure investment and economic growth', *Journal of Economic Perspectives*, vol. 6, no. 4, pp. 189–98
Nevile, J.W. 1979, 'Inflation in Australia' in J.W. Nevile (ed.) *Policies against Stagflation*, Longman Cheshire, Melbourne
—— 1983 'Discussion on inflation and consumption ratio' in A.R. Pagan and P.K. Trivedi (eds) *The Effects of Inflation: Theoretical Issues and Australian Evidence*, Centre for Economic Policy Research, Australian National University, Canberra
Nguyen, T. 1991, 'Inflation and economic growth' in EPAC, *Australia's Inflation Problem: Office of EPAC Seminar*, EPAC Background Paper No. 11, AGPS, Canberra
NSW Environment Protection Authority 1994, *Using Economic Instruments to Control Vehicle Emissions*, Sydney
—— 1994, *Using Economic Instruments to Control Air Pollution from Stationary Sources*, Sydney
—— 1994, *Using Economic Instruments to Control Pollution in the Hawkesbury–Nepean*, Sydney
—— 1994, *Using Economic Instruments to Control Salinity in the Hunter River*, Sydney
NSW Government Pricing Tribunal 1993, *Water: An Interim Report*, vol. 1

Norton, W.E. 1992, 'Discussion' in A. Blundell-Wignall (ed.), *Inflation, Disinflation and Monetary Policy*, Reserve Bank of Australia, Sydney
O'Connor, J. 1973, *The Fiscal Crisis of the State*, St James Press, London
OECD 1978, *Public Expenditure Trends*, OECD, Paris
——1987, *Structural Adjustment and Economic Performance*, OECD, Paris
——1990a, *Progress in Structural Reform*, OECD, Paris
——1990b, *OECD Economic Surveys: Australia, 1989/90*, OECD, Paris
——1992a, *Economic Surveys, Australia 1991/1992*, OECD, Paris
——1992b, *Structural Change and Industrial Performance*, OECD, Paris
——1993, *Economic Outlook 53, June*, OECD, Paris
——1994a, *New Orientations for Social Policy*, OECD, Paris
——1994b, *OECD Economic Surveys, Australia, 1994*, OECD, Paris
Otto, Glenn and Voss, Graham M. 1994, 'Public capital and private sector productivity', *Economic Record*, vol. 70, pp. 121–33
Owen, A.D. 1991, *Tradeable Emissions as a Greenhouse Response Measure*, A Report Prepared for the Department of the Arts, Sport, the Environment, Tourism and Territories, Canberra
Oxley, H. and Martin, J.P. 1991, 'Controlling government spending and deficits: trends in the 1980s and prospects for the 1990s', *OECD Economic Studies No. 17*, Autumn, pp. 145–89
Oxley, H., Maher, M., Martin, J.P. and Nicoletti, G. 1990, 'The public sector: issues for the 1990s', Working Paper No. 90, Department of Economics and Statistics, OECD, Paris
Pearce, David, W. and Turner, R. Kerry 1990, *Economics of Natural Resources and the Environment*, Harvester Wheatsheaf, London
Pigou, Arthur 1920, *The Economics of Welfare*, Macmillan, London
Pitchford, J.D. 1989, 'Optimum borrowing and the current account when there are fluctuations in income', *Journal of International Economics*, vol. 26, pp. 345–58
——1990, *Australia's Foreign Debt: Myths and Realities*, Allen and Unwin, Sydney
Rao, B.B. and Srivastava, V.K. 1989, 'The specification and estimation of the output equation in the rational expectations model with gradual price adjustment', *Australian Economic Papers*, vol. 28, no. 53, pp. 201–8
Repetto, Robert 1993, 'Pollution and energy taxes: their environmental and economic benefits', paper presented to the 1993 Environmental Economics Conference, National Convention Centre, Canberra, 15–17 November
Reserve Bank of Australia 1987, *Functions and Operations*, 6th edition, Sydney
——1988, *Bulletin*, September, Sydney
——1990, *Bulletin*, July, Sydney
Roberts, Marc J. and Spence, Michael 1976, 'Effluent charges and licences under uncertainty', *Journal of Public Economics*, vol. 5, pp. 193–208
Romer, Paul M. 1986, 'Increasing returns and long-run growth', *Journal of Political Economy*, vol. 94, pp. 1002–37
——1990b, 'Endogenous technological change', *Journal of Political Economy*, vol. 98, no. 2, S71–S102

Rowthorn, R. and Chang H.J. 1992, 'The political economy of privatisation', *Economic and Labour Relations Review*, vol. 3, no. 2, pp. 1–17

Sachs, J.D. 1981, 'The current account and macroeconomic adjustment in the 1970s', *Brookings Papers on Economic Activity*, pp. 201–68

Saunders, P. 1987, 'Measuring the size and growth in the public sector in Australia', in M. James (ed.), *Restraining Leviathan: Small Government in Practice*, Centre for Independent Studies, Sydney, pp. 11–45

—— 1992, *Poverty, Inequality and Recession*, Centre for Applied Economic Research, Working Paper No. 5, University of New South Wales, Kensington

—— 1993, 'Recent trends in the size and growth of government in OECD countries', in N. Gemmill (ed.) *Public Sector Growth: Theories and Evidence*, Edward Elgar, Aldershot, pp. 17–33

—— 1994, *Welfare and Inequality, National and International Perspectives on the Australian Welfare State*, Cambridge University Press, Melbourne

Saunders, P. and Fine, M. 1992, 'The mixed economy of support for the aged in Australia: lessons for privatisation', *Economic and Labour Relations Review*, vol. 3, no. 2, pp. 18–42

Saunders, P. and Klau, F. 1985, *The Role of the Public Sector. Causes and Consequences of the Growth of Government*, OECD Economic Studies Special Issue No. 4, Spring

Schelde-Andersen, P. 1992, 'OECD Country Experiences with Disinflation' in Blundell-Wignall *Inflation, Disinflation and Monetary Policy*, Reserve Bank of Australia, Sydney

Sheehan, Peter J. 1992, 'Economic theory and economic strategy: the new growth models', paper delivered at the 21st Conference of Economists, University of Melbourne, July

Shimada, K. 1992, 'Japan's industrial culture and labor–management relations' in Shumpei Kumon and Henry Rosovsky (eds) *The Political Economy of Japan*, vol. 3, Stanford University Press

Siegloff, E.S. and Groenwold, N. 1987, 'Policy ineffectiveness: tests with Australian data', *Australian Economic Papers*, vol. 26, no. 49, pp. 179–87

Stegman, T. 1982, 'The estimation of an accelerator type investment function with a profitability constraint by the technique of switching regressions', *Australian Economic Papers*, pp. 379–91

—— 1990, 'The sectoral composition of capital expenditure in Australia', *Economic Papers*, vol. 9, no. 1, pp. 41–54

—— 1993, 'Unemployment' in G. Bell and B. Hession (eds) *The Economy in Reform: Readings in Australian Economic Policy*, VCTA, Melbourne

Stevens, G. 1992, 'Inflation and disinflation in Australia: 1950–91' in Blundell-Wignall *Inflation, Disinflation and Monetary Policy*, Reserve Bank of Australia, Sydney

Stiglitz, J. and Weiss, A. 1981, 'Credit rationing in markets with imperfect information', *American Economic Review*, vol. 71, no. 3, pp. 393–410

Stretton, H. 1987, *Political Essays*, Georgian House, Melbourne, pp. 15–29

Summers, Robert and Heston, Alan 1993, 'The Penn World (Mark 5): an expanded set of international comparisons, 1950–88', *Quarterly Journal of Economics*, vol. 106, no. 2, pp. 327–68 (1991), subsequently updated to Mark 5.5, available from National Bureau of Economic Research, Boston, Mass., USA

Swan Consultants 1992, 'The scope for further productivity improvement in Australian industry', study commissioned by EPAC, AGPS, Canberra

Sydney Water Board 1992, 'Submission to the Government Pricing Tribunal of NSW 1992/93 Review of Water Pricing Policies', vol. II, September

——1993, 'Submission to the Same Tribunal, 1993/94 Pricing Package', April

Taylor, J. 1979, 'Staggered price setting in a macro model', *American Economic Review*, vol. 69, no. 2, pp. 108–13

Thurow, L. 1983, *Dangerous Currents: The State of Economics*, Oxford University Press, Oxford

Tietenberg, T.H. 1985, *Emissions Trading*, Resources for the Future, Washington DC

——1990, 'Economic instruments for environmental regulation', *Oxford Review of Economic Policy*, vol. 6, no. 1, pp. 17–33

——1992, *Environmental and Natural Resource Economics*, 3rd edition, Harper Collins, New York

Victorian Commission of Audit 1993, *Report of the Victorian Commission of Audit*, May

Whitfield, K. 1987, *The Australian Labour Market*, Harper and Row, Sydney

Winston, C. 1993, 'Economic deregulation: days of reckoning for microeconomists', *Journal of Economic Literature*, vol. xxxi, no. 3, pp. 1263–89

Index

Abramovitz, M., 32, 35, 214
ABS, *see* Australian Bureau of Statistics
Accord: as a policy, 29, 78, 142; Australia, 146, 149–53; definition of, xv; influence on inflation rate, 49–52; 1983 Accord, 30
administrative efficiency: definition of, 143; public sector reform, 161
APEC, *see* Asia Pacific Economic Cooperation
Appelgate, C., 100
appreciation: Australia, 52; definition of, xv; trade gap and saving gap, 109
Argy, V., 141, 214
Aschauer, D.A., 26, 214
ASEAN, *see* Association of South-East Asian Nations
Asia Pacific Economic Cooperation: definition of, xv; government trade policy, 96, 149; member countries, 97
Asian economies: catch-up, 31–3; comparison to Australia, 31; performance, 15

Association of South-East Asian Nations, member countries, 97
Atkinson, A.B., 188, 214
Austrade, government policy, 151
Australia, average weekly earnings, 47–52; budget experience, 103–4; carbon tax, 199; current trade policy, 94–9; debt servicing ratio, 84–6; effect of bank failures, 120; environmental policy, 208–11; fiscal policy, 114–18; foreign indebtedness, 83–6, 91; government expenditure, 110; government outlays to GDP, 178–81; government revenue, 11; growth rate, 20, 31–2; individual transferable quotas, 206, 211; inflation experience, 39–43; labour force growth, 70–1; manufacturing labour costs, 147; monetary policy empirical evidence, 132–8; monetary targeting, 131; net external debt, 84–6; public investment, 26; structural change, 112; structural deficit,

223

115–16; unemployment record, 64
Australian Airlines, privatisation, 148, 160
Australian Bureau of Statistics (ABS), 214; Australia's environment, 212; capital account, 83; consumer price index, 41, 43; current account, 82; definition of, xv; monthly labour force survey, 75–6; non-market activities, 28; price indexes, 37; real values of GDP, 17; structural deficit, 115; unemployment measure, 62–4; unemployment record, 64; unfilled vacancies survey, 73
Australian dollar: experience, 48–9, 166; floating, 121, 148; forward and future markets, 132; in 'pass through' effect, 51; open economy model, 130; trade gap and saving gap, 109
Australian public sector, composition, 172
Australia's economic performance, and economic growth, 14
Austria: government expenditure, 110; government outlays to GDP, 178–81; public enterprise sector, 183
automatic stabiliser, examples, 174

baby boom: Australia, 21; in population growth, 20; output growth, 25
balance of payments (*see also* Pitchford line, capital account, current account *and* foreign debt) 80–100; as a cost of inflation, 54; Australia's experience, 84–6; balancing item, 82; capital account, 48; constraint on growth, 71–2, 77–9, 112, 166; current account, 48; definition of, 81; effect of persistent balance of trade deficits, 83–4; fiscal policy, 117–18; income

balance, 8; labour productivity, 168; macroeconomic policy, 5, 9, 77–9; problem?, 3; services component, 8
balance of trade (*see also* current account, exports, imports): Australian experience, 84; current account, 8; definition of, xvi; effect of persistent deficits, 83–4
balanced budget multiplier, 102, 104–5
Ball, L., 214
banana republic, movement toward?, 3
bank deposits, effect of inflation, 53–4
banking system: assets and liabilities, 122–4; credit creation, 123–4; deregulation, 184
bargaining, pollution damage solution, 193
Barr, N., 188, 214
Barro, N., 34, 214
Base Weight Index: deficiencies, 38; definition of, 37–8
Baumol, W., 121, 207–8, 214
Belgium: government outlays to GDP, 178–81; public enterprise sector, 183
Bell, G., 221
Bewley, R., 140, 214
Blanchard, O.J., 140, 214
Blandy, R., 217
Blundell-Wignall, A., 60, 215, 219, 220, 221
Boehm, E.A., 169, 215
boom: and business cycle, 17; effect on budget, 104
Brazil: manufacturing labour costs, 147
broad money: Australia, 133–6, 142; definition of, 124
broadcasting, deregulation, 184
Brunner, K., 219
Budget (*see also* structural deficit): Australia, 108; balanced, 103; Commonwealth

INDEX

outlays, 173; deficit, 10, 103; deficit experience, 106, 142–3; outlays and revenues, 103–4; surplus, 10
Bureau of Industry Economics, 169, 215; enterprise bargaining, 157; unemployment, 151
business: credit, 138; investment, 138; microeconomic reform, 144
Business Council of Australia, 169, 215; enterprise bargaining, 155; fiscal policy, 115
business cycle: and budgetary stance, 10; and the growth path, 17–18; economic activity, 112; Keynesian theory, 128–9, 131; labour market flows, 76; macroeconomic debate, 18; monetarist theory, 129, 131; recovery, 34

Cairns Group: definition of, xv; government trade policy, 96, 149; member countries, 97
Canada: enterprise bargaining, 157; government outlays to GDP, 178–81; government revenue, 111; public enterprise sector, 183; sulphur dioxide from the United States, 204
capital: and business cycle, 18; average labour productivity, 69–70; contribution to growth, 28, 33; foreign exchange, 109; from abroad, 4, 166; inflows, 8, 11; international flows, 9; of banks, 121–2
capital account (*see also* foreign debt): Australia, 84, 99; capital inflow, 48, 167; capital outflow, 55, 130; definition of, 81–3; in 1970s, 48–9
capital adequacy ratio, criticism, 122; definition of, 121–2
capital-deepening, 146
capital-intensive investment, 146; average labour productivity, 70

capital mobility, open economy models, 130
capital stock: and employment, 20; multi-factor productivity, 30
capital-widening, 146
carbon tax, use as environmental policy, 198–200, 212
Carmichael, J., 40, 135, 215
cash rate: definition of, 125; open economy model, 130; target, 125; to effect interest rates, 127–8, 139
catch-up, economic performance, 31–3
Centre for Applied Economic Research, 14
Chand, S.K., 118
Chang, H.J., 189, 221
Chapman, B.J., 49–50, 215
Chapman, D.R., 215
child care, 187
China: growth rate, 31–2; manufacturing labour costs, 147
Clark, D., 12, 14, 169, 215
classical theory: monetary targeting, 131, 139; quantity theory, 128
Coase theorem, 193–4
Cohen, D., 100
commercial banks: assets and liabilities, 122–3; exchange settlement fund, 125
commodity prices, in 1970s, 48
Common, M., 213
Commonwealth bank, privatisation, 148, 183
Commonwealth government: budget outlays, 173–5; budget revenue, 174–5; debt, 174
Commonwealth government securities, 125
communications: deregulation, 184; microeconomic reform, 144, 149; public provision, 27
community care: quasi-market reforms, 186; voucher scheme, 186–7
community health, and unemployment, 62

Community Options Project, Australia, 187
comparative advantage: explaining trade 92–3; of Australia, 95
constant returns: and employment growth, 20; definition of, xv
consumer price index (CPI): Australian experience, 40–3, 49, 136; cost of living index, 38; deficiencies, 39; definition of, xv, 38–9; expenditure categories, 41–2; use in indexation, 38, 41
consumption, 2; and unemployment, 74; balance of payments, 166; debt servicing, 108; domestic, 4; fiscal policy, 102–4; government accounts, 189; monetarist theory, 129; 'new view', 87–92; taxation, 149
convergence, growth rates, 31–3
Corden, M., 93, 100
core rate of inflation, see underlying rate of inflation
corporatisation: as reform, 12; in policy decisions, 3
cost-benefit analysis, reform of markets, 34
Costa, M., 169, 215
Covick, O., 217
CPI, see consumer price index
credit creation: and monetary policy, 122–5; commercial banks, 123–4; effect on money supply, 124; link to money, 119
crime rate, link to unemployment, 62
Crosby, M., 140
Crow, I., 79, 215
crowding out: and government spending, 10–11, 27, 117; definition of, xv, 104–7
culture, effect on economic progress, 34
Cumberworth, M., 140, 219
current account (see balance of trade, Pitchford line): and government spending, 10; Australia, 8, 48, 52, 78, 84, 99; constraint on the economy, 3; definition of, 81–2; deterioration, 80–2; deterioration due to inflation, 55; does deficit matter?, 86–92; fiscal policy, 117–18; microeconomic reform, 143–4, 166; national savings, 107–11; net income, 81–2; net transfer balance, 81; 'new view', 86–92, 99, 107–8; savings gap, 109; services balance, 81; tariffs, 95; 'traditional view', 86–7, 99
Current Weight Index: deficiencies, 38; definition of, 37–8

Dales, J.H., 194, 215
Davis, K., 141
debt servicing, see foreign debt
de-industrialised, Australia, 146
De Long, J., 27, 215
demand: and budget deficit, 10; and employment, 7; excess demand, 43–4; interest rates, 127–8; Keynesian theory, 128–9; monetarist theory, 129; new Keynesian, 130
demand management policy: and unemployment, 74; 'new view', 90
demographic changes: and unemployment, 7; baby boomers, 25; government outlays, 176; in labour force, 6; public sector reform, 172
Denmark: government expenditure, 110; government outlay to GDP, 177–81, 188; government spending ratio, 188; government revenue, 111
deposit refund, 210
depreciation: as a 1980s policy, 78; Australia, 142; definition of, xv; effect of inflation, 55; foreign debt, 108; open economy model, 130; role in

INDEX

imported inflation, 45; trade gap and saving gap, 109
depression, Australia, 145
deregulation: definition of, xvi; exchange rate, 4, 8, 184–5; exchange rate and inflation, 46, 50–1; financial system, 4, 8–9, 165, 184–5; labour markets, 29, 150, 154; OECD trend, 184–5; privatisation, 160; public sector, 185, 188
devaluation, see depreciation
discouraged workers: and unemployment, 21; and unemployment measures, 62–3, 68, 76; decline in participation, 25
disinflation: definition of, 44; Keynesian policy, 44
Domestic Final Demand, Australian experience, 47–52
Dornbusch, R., 91, 215
Dowrick, S., 6, 30, 32, 34, 35, 216
Duffy, M., 169, 215
duration of unemployment, 65–6
dynamic efficiency, definition of, 143

Easson, M., 169, 216
East Asian: catch up phenomenon, 15; growth rate, 31–2
economic growth, 16; and budget deficit, 10; and demand, 7; contribution of physical investment, 26; contribution of technical progress, 28; effect of wages, 74; impact of inflation, 53, 55–6; impact on living standards, 2, 15; in macroeconomic policy, 5; investment, 109; performance, 16–17
Economic Planning Advisory Council, 216, 219; microeconomic reform, 165–8; privatisation, 183
economic recession: and budget deficit, 10; and investment, 6; in 1980s, 8; monetary policy effect, 11
economic stabilisation, 10
economic theory, nature of, 6–7
Economics Society of Australia, 14
economies of scale, see increasing returns
education: Australia, 146; contribution to growth rate, 28; influence on labour force, 24; microeconomic reform, 144, 164; participation of women, 24, 34; participation rate, 21; public provision, 27, 181–2; quasi-market reforms, 187; state government, 172; taxation and subsidies, 34; welfare state, 180
efficiency: Coase theorem, 193–4; economic criteria, 161, 188; environmental regulation, 194; government regulation and ownership, 143; government services, 185; microeconomic reform, 143–4; privatisation, 183
EFTA, see European Free Trade Association
elasticity, definition of, xvi
electricity authority, user pays, 162–3
emissions, definition of, 195–6
employment: crowding out effect, 11; current account deficit, 84; economic growth impact, 2; EPAC, 165; government, 182; in macroeconomic policy, 5; interest rates, 127–8; level of, 7; new Keynesian, 130; 1983 Accord, 30; population growth, 20; savings gap, 109; tariffs, 95
employment, part-time: labour force growth, 70–1; labour market, 6; unemployment measure, 62–3
enterprise bargaining: a solution?, 155–9; advantages and disadvantages, 156; Australia,

148; definition of, 155, 156; labour market reform, 12, 29, 34
environment, 191–213; and microeconomic reform, 5, 13; economic instruments, 13, 192, 206; environmental costs, 192; impact on living standards, 2; in economics, 191; issues in, 5, 16; neglect in economics, 3
environment levies, Sydney Water Board, 209–10
environmental policy: Australia, 208–11; carbon tax, 198–200; combined taxes and permits, 202–6; distributive impacts, 207; individual transferable quotas, 206; inefficiencies and regulation, 195; market-based approach, 194; regulatory approach, 192, 194; tradeable permits, 200–2; US Clean Air Act, 202–5
environmental problems, examples of, 191
Environmental Protection Authority, 209
environmental quality: as a normal good, 207; public good, 194
environmentalists, 2
EPAC, see Economic Planning Advisory Council
equal pay legislation, male–female relativities, 74
equality, state intervention, 171
equipment, private investment, 27
equity: government regulation ownership, 143; user pays, 163
Europe: catch-up 31–3; productivity slow down, 31
European Community: European farmers, 95; government trade policy, 96; member countries, 97
European Free Trade Association, member countries, 97
Evans, T., 159, 216
Evatt Foundation, 216

exchange, 2
exchange rate: against targeting, 132; Australia, 133; current account deficit, 84; deregulation, xvi, 9, 148; deregulation and inflation, 46, 50–1, 55; determination, 9; floating, xv; monetary policy, 11, 80, 128, 132; open economy models, 130; trade gap and saving gap, 109
experience curve, trade, 93
export access program, government policy, 151
export earnings, 4
export price index, in 1970s, 48
export prices: Australia, 47, 49; balance of payments, 112
exports: and Australian dollar, 9; Australia, 80, 142, 145, 147; composition of, 4; effect of inflation, 54–5; effect on growth, 78; in terms of trade, xvii; in trade balance, xvi, 8; Industry Commission, 153; interest rates, 106–7; open economy model, 130; trade gap, 109
external debt, see foreign debt
external sector, constraint on economy, 12
externalities: carbon tax, 198–200; definition of, 193; environment and taxation, 197

factor endowments, trade theory, 92
Fama, E., 122, 216
feminists, 2; in workforce, 34
Fender, J., 60
FIC, see Forum Island Countries
financial assets, Keynesian theory, 127
financial intermediaries: composition, 119; monetary policy, 128
financial market: definition of, 119; deregulation, 120–2, 138, 148, 184; deregulation and

INDEX

broad money, 133, 142; reform, 34
Fine, M., 189, 221
Finland: government expenditure, 110; government outlays to GDP, 178–81
firm, operation of typical firm, 97–8
fiscal balances, public sector reform, 172
'fiscal crisis of the state', O'Connor, 171
fiscal policy, 101–18; and balance of payments, 9, 80; and changes in economy, 3; Australia, 5, 8, 47–52, 114–18; automatic stabiliser, 174; definition of, 10; crowding out, 104–7; cyclical fluctuations, 19; effect on demand level, 71–2; how it works, 101–4; policy for unemployment, 77, 142; public investment, 26; twin deficit argument, 88
Fischer, S., 140, 216
Fisher, I., 126, 216
fisheries, transferable quotas, 206, 211
Fitzgerald, V., 217
Flavin, C., 212, 217
foreign debt: (see 'Pitchford line'), 8, 80–100; constraint to the economy, 3, 8; debt servicing, 8, 108; does it matter?, 86–92; income payments in the 1980s, 8; microeconomic reform, 143–4, 166; net external debt, Australia, 84–6; 'new view', 91–2, 99, 107–8
Forsyth, P., 169
Fortress Australia, 145, 150
Forum Island Countries, member countries, 97
Foster, W., 14, 66, 217
France: carbon tax, 199; farmers' tariff lobby, 95; government expenditure, 110; government outlays to GDP, 178–81; government revenue, 111; public enterprise sector, 183
free banking, 122
free trade, economic objectives, 95
Frenkel, J.A., 89, 217
Friedman, B.J., 215
Friedman, M., 126, 129, 131, 217
Frisch, H., 60

GATT, *see* General Agreement on Trade and Tariffs
Gemmell, N., 190, 221
General Agreement on Trade and Tariffs (GATT), xvi; microeconomic reform, 153, 185; Uruguay round, 96
general equilibrium, international trade, 93
Germany: carbon tax, 199; government expenditure, 110; government outlays to GDP, 178–81; government revenue, 111; public enterprise sector, 183; unemployment, 117
GDP, *see* gross domestic product
Goodhart's law, 134
goods and services balance: Australia, 84; definition of, 81
government: employment, 182; expenditure, 101, 110, 117, 187; financing requirement, 176; market failure, 184; market-type instruments, 185; marketisation, 185–7; microeconomic reform, 143–4, 164; outlays trends, 177; public debt, 112; savings determined by, 109; servicing borrowing, 143; size of, 173; spending statistics, 176–7
government business enterprises, 26, 148, 176; EPAC, 165; microeconomic reform, 167; privatisation, 159–60, 183–4, 188; return on capital, 159, 161; user pays, 164
government policy: and exchange rate, 9; and foreign debt, 8; elections, 18; emphasis on, 5;

expenditure, 10; impact on inflation, 41; tobacco and alcohol, 41; trade diversionary measures, 95
Graham, S., 187, 217
Gratten, M., 190
Great Depression, 7
Greece: government outlays to GDP, 178–81; government spending ratio, 188; growth rate, 31–2; worst slump, 114
'green organisations', community awareness, 191
'Green Paper' on employment, 77–9, 215
greenhouse gases, government policy, 13
Gregory, R., 66, 217
Grenville, S., 141, 215, 217, 219
Groenwold, N., 137, 221
gross domestic product (GDP): Australia, 5, 134, 147; budget revenue, 118; current account deficit, 80, 82, 108; cyclical factors, 10; definition of, xvi; external debt, 8, 86; government spending, 170–1; growth and Green Paper, 77–9; index of real output, 17; international comparisons, 31; investment composition, 6; labour force, 69–71; measurement of, 28; public trading enterprises, 175; sacrifice ratio, 59; small economy, 4
gross national expenditure, 134
gross national product, 104
growth rate, international comparisons, 31
Gruen, F., 190
GST, *see* taxation, goods and services tax

H.R. Nicholls Society, 155
Hahn, F.H., 154, 215
Hall, R.E., 60
Hamilton, C., 217
Hanusch, H., 34, 217

Harcourt, G.C., 184, 217
hard-core unemployment, *see* long-term unemployed
Harper, I., 79, 217
Hayek, F., 122, 217
health: European reforms, 186; market mechanism, 185; New Zealand, 186; Pharmaceutical Benefit Scheme, 41; public provision, 27, 181–2; regulation, 144; spending as automatic stabiliser, 174; state government, 172; United Kingdom, 186; welfare state, 180
Heckscher-Ohlin theory, 92
helicopter money, 129
Helpman, E., 93, 217
Hession, B., 221
Heston, A., 17, 19, 20, 21, 22, 25, 32, 221
hidden unemployment, 63
Hilmer, F., 152, 217
Hogan, W.P., 122, 217
Hong Kong: growth rate, 31–2; manufacturing labour costs, 147
Hopkins, T., 184, 217
Horne, J., 137, 217
housing: market reforms, 187; monetary policy effect, 41; private investment, 27
Hughes, H., 217
Hurst, J., 186, 217
hysteresis, definition of, 59

immigration: Australia, 146; labour market experience, 66–71; population growth, 68; recession, 20
imperfect competition, international trade, 93–4
Implicit Domestic Final Demand deflator, 38; Australian experience, 40–1; definition of, 39; volatility of, 40
Implicit Gross Domestic Product deflator (IGDPD), 38; Australia, 49, 51; definition of, 39

INDEX

implicit price deflator, defined, 39
import-competing industries, and Australian dollar, 11
import price index, 48
import substitution, 12
imported inflation, 45
imports: Australia, 51, 80, 142, 147; Australian dollar, 9, 52, 132; budget deficit, 106; composition of, 4; effect of inflation, 55; effect on growth, 78, 166; open economy model, 130; tariffs, 95; terms of trade, xvii; trade balance, xvi, 8; trade gap, 109
income: new Keynesian, 130; public sector initiative, 171
income and wealth distribution, user pays, 163
income inequality, and social accounting, 16
incomes policy, 44
increasing returns: definition of, xvi; international trade, 92–4; market failure, 184
INDECS, state of play, 14
India, strategic trade, 95
indifference curves, 154
indirect taxes: Australia, 153; definition of, xvi; effect on price, 45
Indonesia: growth rate, 31–2; manufacturing labour costs, 147
industrial relations system: Australia, 146, 148; enterprise bargaining, 156; industrial disputes, 155, 156; reform, 34, 157
industrialisation, 31
industry, microeconomic policy, 5, 144
industry commission, 218; functions, xvi; GATT, 153; greenhouse emissions, 153; 1991 annual report, 15
industry policy, 148–53
inequity, government influence, 94
inflation, 36–60; anti-inflation policies, 56–9; Australia relative to world, 46–7; Australian causes since 1960, 46–52; Australian experience, 39–43; bottlenecks, 44, 71–2; causes, 6, 43–6; community attitude, 168; 'conflict' theory of inflation, 45; cost-push, 44–5, 49, 51; costs of, 2, 3, 9, 52–6; definition of, 36–7; demand-pull, 43–4, 49, 51; depreciation, 132; government bonds, 112–13; government influence, 94; hybrid inflation, 46; impact of depreciation, 132; impact of exchange rate deregulation, 50–1; impact of government budgetary policy, 41; impact on investment, 52–3; impact of Medicare and mortgage charges, 39, 41; impact of monetary policy, 41; impossibility of precise measure, 39; inertial inflation, 46; interest rates, 127–8; links to Australian dollar, 11; macroeconomic policy, 5; measurement, 37–9; monetary targeting, 131; natural rate of unemployment, 131–2; nominal interest rate, 133; open economy model, 130; 'pass through', 51; profit-push inflation, 45; quantity theory of money, 44, 126; real GDP, 17; real interest rate, 128–9; relation to economic growth, 55; Reserve Bank influence, 139–40; role of taxes, 45; unit labour cost, 74; wage-push inflation, 44–5, 136–7
inflation premium, and interest rates, 54
inflation tax, defined, 113
inflationary expectations, and nominal interest rates, 53–4
inflationary pressure: enterprise bargaining, 158; fiscal policy, 117; labour demand, 66, 78; supply bottlenecks, 71

infrastructure: effect on productivity, 26; taxation and subsidies, 34
institutions, effect on economic progress, 34
inter-temporal efficiency, definition of, 143
inter-temporal optimising approach, 'new view', 89
interest rate: Australia, 52, 108, 136; budget deficit, 105; cash rate, 125, 127–8; community attitude, 168; crowding out, 104–7; current account deficit, 84, 167; different maturities, 125; effect of inflation, 54–5, 106; influence on demand, 11; influence on exchange rate, 9, 106–7; investment, 127, 166; lack of evidence of link with investment or income, 135; monetary policy influence, 125; near money, 127; new Keynesian, 130; open economy models, 130; portfolio theory, 127; public sector, 168; restriction, 120; spread, 106
interest rate, nominal: definition of, 54; inflation, 112, 133; monetarist inflation explanation, 54; monetary policy indicator, 133; stance of monetary policy, 131
interest rate, real: defined, 128–9; investment decisions, 129; monetary policy indicator?, 133; target in Keynesian theory, 131
intermediate goods: definition of, xvi; effect on balance of payments, 71; impact on inflation, 51; impact on production costs, 45
internalising externalities, 193–5
international commodity markets, influence on growth, 78
international competitiveness: microeconomic reform, 144, 151; non-sectoral policy, 97; role of investment, 6; unit labour cost, 74
international debt, *see* foreign debt
international trade: Australian economy, 3; current policy, 94–9; intra-industry, 92; reasons for government intervention, 93–5; strategic behaviour, 93–5; theory, 92
investment: autonomous, 101; business, 74, 78, 138; capital-widening, 146; community attitude, 168; current account deficit, 84; domestic, 8; effect on exports and imports, 12; finance of, 109; from abroad, 4; government accounts, 189; government enterprises, 161; interest rate, 127–9, 135; investment horizons, 53; Japan, 33; machinery, 27; microeconomic reform, 144; monetarist theory, 129; 'new view', 88–92; productivity, 6; real rate of return, 52–4; research and equipment, 34; savings gap, 109; spillover effects, 27; structure of, 12; unemployment, 74; workforce, 28
invisible hand, labour markets, 154
Ireland, government outlays to GDP, 178–81
Italy: carbon tax, 199; government outlays to GDP, 178–81; government revenue, 111; growth rate, 31–2; public enterprise sector, 183

J-Curve: Australia, 142–3; definition of, xvi
Jacobs, M., 218
Jacobs, S.H., 184, 218
James, M., 208–12, 221
Japan: carbon tax, 199; enterprise bargaining, 157–8; government expenditure, 110;

INDEX

government outlays to GDP, 178–81; government revenue, 111; growth rate, 31–2; individual transferable quotas, 206; international trade, 149; investment and saving, 33; leisure, 35; manufacturing labour costs, 147; MITI in industry policy, 152; public enterprise sector, 183; tariffs, 95
jobs compact, *see* 'White Paper'
Johnson, M., 218
Jones, B.P., 218
Jones, R.W., 212, 217
Junankar, P., 57, 59, 218
Junor, C.W., 2, 7, 14, 36, 49, 215

Kaldor, N., 34
Kapuscinski, C.A., 57, 59, 218
Kearney, C., 8, 9, 12, 100, 141, 218
Kelley, A., 68, 218
Kelly, P., 4, 218
Kenen, P.B., 217
Keynes, J.M., 218
Keynesian economics: bonds, 127; consensus in fiscal policy, 10; demand-pull theory, 43–4; fine-tuning, 131, 142; inflation and interest rates, 54; microeconomic foundations, 129; monetary policy transmission mechanism, 128–9; money and economic activity, 126–7; natural rate hypothesis, 56–7; policy for inflation, 44; policy influence, 5, 138–9, 142; size of government, 12–13
Kierzkowski, H., 218
King, J., 79, 218
Kingston, G., 140
Klau, F., 176, 180, 221
Korea: growth rate, 31–2; tariff, 95
Kriesler, P., 189, 218
Krugman, P., 92, 93, 218
Kumon, S., 221
Kyriakopoulos, J., 55, 218

labor government: industry policy, 149–53; trade policy, 96–9
labour: Average Labour Productivity, 70; business cycle, 18; contribution to growth, 28, 33; demand composition, 72; growth of, 69–70; impact of Accord on costs, 50; labour costs, cross-country comparison, 146; overhead labour hoarding, 29; real unit labour costs, Australia, 48, 50; unit labour cost, 74; wage rate, 7
labour force: cause of growth, 6; changes in, 7; contribution to growth, 19, 25; growth in Australia, 70–1; hours of work, 22–3; population growth, 20; size determined by, 68; women, 34
labour force participation: Australian experience, 21–2; components, 25; factors influencing, 33; men, 23; role of education, 24; women, 22–3
labour market: and business cycle, 18; changes to, 6; flows, 75–7; market forces, 154; microeconomic reform, 144, 154; monetary policy, 128; nature of, 76; productivity, 158; reform of, 12, 34, 153–9, 165; role in inflation, 43–4; secondary labour market; 76–7; segmented labour market, 43–4
labour market schemes, long-term unemployed, 77
Lacasse, F., 185, 218
Lacey, E., 184, 218
laissez-faire, international trade, 93–4
Laspeyres index, *see* Base Weight Index
Lee, J., 34, 214
Le Grand, J., 185–7, 218
Lenssen, N., 212, 217

living standard, *see* standard of living
long-term unemployed: effect of growth, 112; level of, 8; microeconomic reform, 78; unemployment rates, 66; wage subsidies, 79
Lowe, P., 134, 219
Lucas, R.E., 129, 134, 137, 219

MacDonald, I.M., 137, 141, 217
McGlynn, A., 185, 218
macroeconomic policy: and business cycle, 18; definition of, 4–5; unemployment, 79; use of budget as policy, 13
McTaggart, D., 54–7, 219
Maguire, M., 185, 219
Maher, M., 220
Malaysia: growth rate, 32; manufacturing labour costs, 147
management, enterprise bargaining, 35
Mankiw, G., 140, 219
manufactured resources, and economic growth, 16
mark-up, profit-push inflation, 45
market failure: environment, 192; government intervention, 184; 'new view', 89
market for exchange settlement funds, 125
market transactions, and economic growth, 16
marginal cost pricing, user pays, 163–4
Martin, J.P., 176, 180–1, 190, 220
Maxwell, P., 118
Meltzer, A., 219
Menon, J., 51, 219
merchandise trade balance, definition of, 81
microeconomic reform, 3, 142–69; balance of payments, 9; barriers to, 164–8; costs and benefits, 166; definition of, 5, 143–4; emphasis since 1980s, 5; external sector, 12; interventionists, 154; 'new view', 87–92; overview, 147–53; policy for unemployment, 77; why it's unavoidable, 144–7
middle-aged males, labour market experience, 66–71
Milbourne, R., 11, 127, 133, 140, 141, 219
Monadjemi, M., 100, 218
monetarist: inflation and interest rates, 54; monetary policy transmission mechanism, 129; monetary targeting, 131, 142; natural rate hypothesis, 56; quantity theory of money, 44, 126
monetary base, definition of, 123
monetary policy, 3, 119–41; Australian, 8, 5, 47–52, 132–8; balance of payments, 80; channels of influence, 11; credit creation, 122–5; crowding out, 105–7; cyclical fluctuations, 19; discretionary, 131; effect on demand level, 71–2; exchange rate, 80; impact on inflation, 41, 53; monetarist theory, 129; monetary targeting, 49, 138, 142; open economy model, 130; operation of, 124–5; policy for inflation, 44; policy for unemployment, 77; policy prescription, 131–2; rules, 131; theory of, 126–7; transmission mechanism, 127–30, 134–8
money, 119–41; functions of, 126; Keynesian theory, 127; link to credit creation, 119
money stock, *see* money supply
money supply: definition of, 124; inflation affect, 54; Keynesian theory, 127, 131; monetarist theory, 44; monetary policy indicator?, 133; monetary targeting, 138, 142; narrow money, 124, 126
money wage, Australia, 48–9, 52; definition of, 74; Keynesian

INDEX

theory, 128–9; New Zealand, 157
multi-factor productivity (*see* technical progress): growth, 28; measurement of, 30; slow down, 31; wage restraint effect, 30
Munnell, A.H., 26, 219

NAFTA, *see* North American Free Trade Agreement
NAIRU, *see* non-accelerating inflation rate of unemployment
national accounts: and economic growth, 16; and income redistribution, 53; and size of economy, 2; public sector development, 177; second-hand assets, 113
national income: and GDP, xvi
national savings: deficit, 107–11; effect of inflation, 54; fiscal policy, 110; Japan, 33; 'new view', 88–92; taxation, 109, 148, 153
national training wage, 'White Paper', 79
natural environment, as non-market relation, 2, 16
natural rate hypothesis, *see* non-accelerating inflation rate of unemployment
natural rate of output, in monetarist inflation theory, 44
natural rate of unemployment, *see* non-accelerating inflation rate of unemployment
natural resources, contribution to growth rate, 28
Naughten, B., 218
near money, 127
net external debt, Australia, 84–6
Netherlands: government expenditure, 110; government outlays to GDP, 178–82, 188; government revenue, 111; public enterprise sector, 183
Nevile, J.W., 10, 13, 48, 113, 118, 219

New Classical macroeconomics (*see* 'Pitchford line'): definition of, xvi; monetary policy ineffectiveness, 129, 137; monetary targeting, 131, 138; natural rate hypothesis, 56–7; 'new view', 91; rational expectations, xvii, 129; sacrifice ratio, 58–9
new growth theory, 33–4
new Keynesian, monetary policy transmission mechanism, 129–30, 137
New Zealand: growth rate, 32; individual transferable quotas, 206; industrial relations system, 145, 148, 157; manufacturing labour costs, 147; privatisation, 183; public enterprise sector, 183; quasi-market reforms, 186–7
Nguyen, T., 55, 219
Nicoletti, G., 220
nominal values, definition of, xvi
nominal wages, *see* money wages
non-accelerating inflation rate of unemployment (NAIRU): anti-inflation policy, 59; definition of, xvi, 139; in classical, 131; in Keynesian economics, 43, 56–7; in monetarist theory, 44, 56; in new classical, 56–7
non-bank financial intermediaries, effect on money supply, 124
non-market activities: children, leisure, 16; failure of national accounts to measure, 2, 25, 28
non-official transaction, definition of, 82
normal good: definition of, 212; environmental quality, 207
North American Free Trade Agreement: government trade policy, 96; member countries, 97
Norton, W.E., 59, 220
Norway: government expenditure,

110; government outlays to
  GDP, 178–81
NSW Council of Social Services,
  water pricing, 163
NSW Dockyard, microeconomic
  reform, 164
NSW Environment Protection
  Authority, 209, 212
NSW Government Pricing
  Tribunal, 169, 219; water
  pricing, 163
NSW Water Board,
  microeconomic reform, 166

Oates, W., 121, 207–8, 214
O'Connor, J., 171, 220
OECD, see Organisation for
  Economic Co-operation and
  Development
office blocks, private investment,
  27
official transactions, definition of,
  82
offshore borrowing, growth in
  Australia, 166
oil crisis, effect on labour
  productivity, 29
Okun's Law, 70–1
One Nation Statement, 150–1
on-the-job training, 67
OPEC, see Organisation of
  Petroleum Producing Countries
open economy: Australia, 80;
  definition of, 4
open market operations, 128–9
Organisation for Economic
  Co-operation and Development
  (OECD), 220; Australian
  comparison to, 31, 50; capital
  adequacy ratio, 121;
  comparison of economic
  development, 32; deregulation
  trend, 184–5; government
  expenditure comparisons, 110,
  177–82; government size
  comparisons, 177; inflation and
  growth comparisons, 55;
  member countries, 97;
  microeconomic reform, 143;
polluter-pays principle, 196;
  productivity comparison, 148;
  public sector comparison, 170,
  176–82; public servants'
  performance, 185; role, xvi;
  sacrifice ratio comparison, 58;
  size of public sector, 13; state
  and market sector relationship,
  188; structural deficits, 116;
  System of National Accounts,
  176–82
Organisation of Petroleum
  Producing Countries (OPEC),
  xvii; member countries, 97; oil
  price increases in the 1970s, 48
Otto, G., 26, 220
output: business cycle, 18;
  interest rates, 127–8; Keynesian
  theory, 131; macroeconomic
  policy, 5; measures of, 15, 28
Owen, A.D., 191, 218, 220
Oxley, H., 110, 176, 180–1, 183,
  190, 220

Paasche Index, see Current
  Weight Index
Pagan, A.R., 219
partial equilibrium analysis,
  International trade, 93
participation rate: male, 68;
  Okun's Law, 70–1; pro-cyclical
  movement, 68–9; relation to
  labour force size, 68
payback period, effect of
  inflation, 53
Payne, T., 187, 217
Pearce, D.W., 220
Peng, Z., 218
perfect competition, international
  trade, 93–4
performance bonds, Australia, 211
Philippines: Australian exports to,
  152; manufacturing labour
  costs, 147
Pigou, A., 194, 196, 220
Pigouvian tax: environment,
  196–7; marginal social damage,
  200
Pitchford, J.D., 87–92, 100, 220

'Pitchford line': criticism, 91–4; defined, 90–1, 107–9
planning and urban development, 172–3
pollution (see environment, tradeable permits): carbon tax, 198–200; Coase theorem, 193–4; criticism of Coase theorem, 194; definition of, 192; fund pollutants, 195–6; noise and Sydney airport, 207–8; price mechanism, 196; social accounting, 16; stock pollutants, 195–6
population: aging, 175; growth, 15, 17, 19, 68; growth and output, 6, 25; labour force growth, 69–70; recent experience, 20
portfolio theory, 127
Portugal: government outlays to GDP, 178–81; public enterprise sector, 183
poverty, unemployment as a cause, 62
price index: effect of quality changes, 38; general price level, 37
Prices Justification Tribunal, 49
Prices Surveillance Authority, 152
prime assets ratio, 121
private investment, 6, 110, 174; Australia, 136; crowding out, 105; productivity, 35; recent experience, 26–7; role of interest rate, 105–6
private sector: capital expenditure, 39; consumption expenditure, 137; current expenditure, 48; deregulation of, 12; expenditure and output, 117; microeconomic reform, 143–4; 'new view', 88–92; offshore borrowing, 166; profitability, 167; public sector, cooperation, 172; savings, 174; structural deficit, 113–14
privatisation: Australia, 148, 183, 184; deregulation, 160; government business enterprises, 159, 185; in policy decisions, 3, 187; microeconomic reform, 12, 144; state banks, 160
product charges, 210
production, 2; contribution to growth, 33
productive efficiency, definition of, 143
productivity: Australia, 145–8; capital investment, 26; catch-up, 31; changes by industry group, 152; cyclical effects, 28; definition of, 28; effect on growth, 6; enterprise bargaining, 156; EPAC, 165; growth due to reforms, 34, 142, 144; growth in non-farm market sector, 29; Okun's Law, 70–1; labour market, 69–70, 158, 168; manufacturing, 151; microeconomic reform, 149, 168; port, 167; public investment, 26; reasons for slow down, 30; relation to inflation, 45; trend decline, 29; unit labour costs, 74
profit margins, 74
property rights: Coase theorem, 193–4; environment, 192; liability rules, 194; wealth effect, 194
proportional non-compliance fees, 210
prudential regulation, Reserve Bank, 120–2
public good: environmental quality, 194; OECD government spending, 179–81; user pays, 162–3
public investment: government accounts, 189; nature, 26; productivity, 35; recent experience, 26–7; relation to private sector productivity, 26–7
public policy, and business cycle, 18
public sector, 170–90; capital

expenditure, 39; current expenditure, 48; defence spending, 175; effect on market price, 45; expenditure, 170, 171; government enterprises, 167; investment, 6, 110; managerial reforms, 188; marketisation, 185–7, 188; microeconomic reform, 5, 9, 143–4, 164; 'new view', 88–92; outlays, 175; private sector cooperation, 172; privatisation, 160, 183; public programs, 179; range of reforms, 185; reform of, 159–64, 171; savings, 118; savings defined, 109; size in economy, 3, 12–13; structural deficit, 113–14; trends, 182–5; wages as pacesetters, 48

public trading enterprises: government spending, 175; standard of living, 173; System of National Accounts, 176

Qantas, privatisation, 148, 160, 183
quantitative lending restrictions, pre-deregulation control, 120
quantity theory of money, *see* inflation
quasi-markets, 186
Quiggin, J., 35, 216

Rao, B.B., 137, 220
rate of inflation, *see* inflation rate
rational expectation, *see* New Classical economics
Rayner, M., 217
Razin, A., 89, 217
RBA, *see* Reserve Bank of Australia
Real Gross Domestic Product, Australian experience, 47–52
Real Gross Domestic Product per capita: definition, 17; effect of inflation, 55–6
real income, quantity theory of money, 126

real transactions balance, effect of inflation, 54
real values, definition of, xvii
real wages, definition of, 74
recession: advanced economies, 19; Australia, 134; business cycle, 17; current account deficit, 109; effect on budget, 103–4; government spending, 179; hours worked, 23–4; investment, 26; labour force participation, 25; productivity, 29; structural deficit, 116; youth unemployment, 66
redistribution of income, as a cost of inflation, 53
redistribution of wealth, as a cost of inflation, 53–4
regulation, budgetary cost, 184
relative wages, definition of, 74
Repetto, R., 212, 220
research and development: government assistance, 98; microeconomic reform, 144; trade, 93
Reserve Bank of Australia (RBA), 220; assets and liabilities, 123–4, 140; Australia's balance of payments, 84; bank supervision, 121; bulletin, 14; charter, 119–20; check list, 138; exchange rate, 9, 80, 132; exchange settlement fund, 125; foreign reserve assets, 82; monetarist theory, 44; monetary aggregates, 135; monetary targeting, 131, 134; open economy model, 130; policy, 138–40; policy effect on economy, 127–8; pre-deregulation controls, 120; prudential regulation, 120–2; role in fixed regime, xv; structural deficit, 115; unemployment, 151
retirement, participation rate, 21, 68
revaluation, *see* appreciation
Ricardo, D., 92

INDEX

Richardson, P., 215
Riddington, C., 215
Roberts, M.J., 202, 220
Romer, P.M., 34, 35, 220
Rosovsky, H., 221
Ross, R., 187, 217
Rowthorn, R., 189, 221
rules, monetary policy, 131

Sachs, J.D., 221
sacrifice ratios: Australian estimate, 58–9; definition of, 58
Saunders, P., 13, 62, 176, 177, 180, 189, 190, 217, 221
savings, *see* national savings
savings gap: current account deficit, 108–9; fiscal policy, 117–18
Schelde-Andersen, P., 57, 58–9, 221
Schmidt, R., 68, 218
school retention rates, participation rate, 68
Schumpeter, J., 33
self-regulation, banking sector and criticism, 122
share market crash, 51
Sharpe, I.G., 122, 217
Sheehan, P.J., 34, 221
Shimada, K., 158, 221
short-term money market dealers, exchange settlement fund, 125
Siegloff, E.S., 137, 221
Simon, F., 215
Singapore: growth rate, 32; manufacturing labour costs, 147
small open economy: budget deficit, 143; definition of, 4; foreign inflation shocks, 47
Smith, A., 154
social accounting, and economic growth, 16
social alienation, unemployment cost, 62
social welfare: Australia, 110, 149; environment policies, 207–8; 'Green Paper', 77; New Zealand, 187; unemployment, 62, 103; United Kingdom, 187–8
South Korea, manufacturing labour costs, 147
Southern Bluefin Tuna fishery, individual transferable quotas, 206, 211
Soviet Union, government enterprises, 145
Spain: government outlays to GDP, 178–81; public enterprise sector, 183
Spence, M., 202, 220
spending ratio: definition of, 173; OECD comparison, 178–81
spillover effects: 'new' growth theory, 34; prudential supervision, 120
Srivastava, V.K., 137, 220
stance of fiscal policy: definition of, 103; structural deficit effect, 111
standard of living: Australia, 147, 168; catch-up, 31; comparison to Japan, 15; cost of unemployment, 61; economic growth impact, 2, 5; environment, 173; state intervention, 171
Statutory Reserve Deposit, pre-deregulation control, 120–1
Stegman, T., 8, 14, 74, 78, 79, 221
Stevens, G., 39–41, 46, 52, 58–60, 221
Stewart, M., 14, 100
Stiglitz, J.E., 129, 188, 214, 221
Stretton, H., 184, 221
strikes, 53
structural: data inference, 133; work practices, 168
structural change: history since 1880, 144–7; microeconomic reform, 166
structural deficit: Australia, 115–16; definition of, 10, 104, 111; estimated, 112–15; interest rate, 105

structural reform: labour market, 159; OECD countries, 172
structural unemployment, *see* unemployment
subsidies: effect on price, 45; EPAC, 165
Summers, L.H., 17, 19, 20, 21, 22, 25, 27, 32, 215, 221
superannuation, industry policy, 153
Swan Consultants, 222
swaps market, 132
Sweden: government expenditure, 110; government outlay to GDP, 177–81, 188; government revenue, 111; growth rate, 31–3
Sydney Water Board, 169, 222; environment, 163, 209

Taiwan: growth rate, 32; manufacturing labour costs, 147
Taperell, Q., 217
tariffs: Australian experience, 95–9; Australian policy, 150–3; EPAC, 165; lobby for imposition, 95; microeconomic reform, 149, 164; 'White Paper', 79
tax burden, definition of, 171
Tax Law Improvement Project, Australia, 153
tax policy, Australia, 153
taxation: aggregate demand, 101; budget deficit, 10; carbon tax, 198–200, 212; effect on investment, 12, 34; effect on investment composition, 27; environment, 192, 196–200; fiscal policy, 102–4; goods and services tax, 104; government financing requirement, 176; microeconomic reform, 144; need for reform, 12; 'new view', 90; public sector, 171; public sector savings, 118; reform, 148; savings, 109–10, 117; structural deficit, 116; tradeable permits, 202–6;

unemployment, 62; user pays, 163
Taylor, J., 140, 222
technical progress: average labour productivity, 69–70; business cycle, 18; contribution to growth, 33; definition of, 28; investment, 6
technology: economic growth, 16; spillover effects, 27; trade, 92
terms of trade: Australia, 48–51, 133; definition of, xvii; exchange rate, 132; exports, 12; foreign inflation effects, 47; inflation, 136
textiles, clothing and footwear, tariffs, 150–3
Thailand, growth rate, 32
Thurow, L., 169, 222
Tietenberg, T.H., , 194, 212–13, 222
Toronto Emission Target, Industry Commission, 153
trade gap, current account deficit, 108–9
Trade Practices Commission, 152
trade unions: and uncertainty, 53; enterprise bargaining, 35, 155
Tradeable permits: ambient permit system, 201; definition of, 200–2; emissions permit system, 202; examples of, 201–2; grand fathering, 200; Murray–Darling Basin, 210–11; pollution-offset system, 202; Taxes, 202–6
tradeables, 4
training: Australia, 146; contribution to growth rate, 28; enterprise bargaining, 156, 158; improve unemployment, 72, 78–9; microeconomic reform, 144, 164; on the job, 154; quasi-market reforms, 187
transaction costs, Coase theorem, 193–4
transport: deregulation, 184; EPAC, 165; microeconomic

INDEX

reform, 144, 148; public provision, 27
Treasury, 14, 140, 142
Trevithick, J.A., 60
Trivedi, P.K., 219
Turner, R., 220
twin deficits: criticism, 88; defined, 88, 108–9

uncertainty, as a cost of inflation, 52–3
underlying rate of inflation, definition of, 41–3
unemployment, (see long-term unemployed): as a cost of inflation, 55–7; Australia, 47–52, 61–79, 80, 112, 145; business cycle, 18; causes, 7, 71–5; composition of changes, 67–9; costs, 7, 61–4; current policy, 77–9; definition of, 62; discouraged workers, 21; duration of unemployment, 65; experience of social groups, 66–71; frictional unemployment, 7, 72–3; government influence, 94, 118; investment, 109; macroeconomic policy, 5, 10, 142; major cost of poverty, 62; market forces, 154; measurement, 7, 61–4; microeconomic reform, 154; natural rate hypothesis, 55, 59; 'new view', 90, 99; recent performance, 7; Reserve Bank policy, 139–40; role of demand, 71–2; role of wage levels, 73–5; sacrifice ratio, 58; social costs, 62; structural unemployment, 7, 72–3, 76–8; technological unemployment, 72
unemployment assistance, as automatic stabiliser, 174
United Kingdom: business cycle, 19; carbon tax, 199; enterprise bargaining, 157; government expenditure, 110; government outlays to GDP, 178–81; government revenue, 111; growth rate, 20, 32; manufacturing labour costs, 146; privatisation, 189; productivity, 145; public enterprise sector, 183; quasi-market reforms, 186–7
United States of America: carbon tax, 199; Clean Air Act, 203–5; effect of bank failures, 120; enterprise bargaining, 155; Environmental Protection Agency, 204; fiscal policy, 117; government expenditure, 110; government outlays to GDP, 177–82; government regulation cost, 184; government revenue, 111; growth rate, 31–2; international trade, 149; manufacturing labour costs, 146–7; microeconomic reform, 168; new classical model, 137; productivity, 145; productivity slow down, 31; public investment, 26; unemployment, 117; wheat subsidy, 95
US Clean Air Act, operation of, 203–5
user pays: arguments for and against, 162–3; environment, 209; government business enterprises, 164; Hunter Water Corporation, 209; marketisation, 185

velocity of circulation: Australia, 135; quantity theory of money, 126
vertical fiscal imbalance, definition of, 175
Victorian Commission of Audit, 222
Voss, G., 26, 140, 220
voucher, government services, 185–6

wage differentials, enterprise bargaining, 156

wage relativities: male–female, 74–5; youth–adult, 74
wages drift: effect on average weekly earnings, 47
wages policy, see Accord
Walsh, M., 105
Weiss, A., 130, 221
welfare: Australia, 189; economic, 16; economic growth, 5; programs and market mechanism, 185; user pays, 163
welfare state: composition, 179; OECD government spending, 181
well-being, measures of, 5
West Germany, manufacturing labour costs, 146
White, G., 140, 214
'White Paper', 78–9, 215
Whitfield, K., 79, 222

Whitlam government: microeconomic reform, 165; spending ratio, 173–4; trade policy, 96
Winston, C., 169, 222
women: employment growth, 74; labour force, 6, 34, 68–9
Wood, R., 185, 219
wool, effect on world economy, 4
work practices, microeconomic reform, 143–4, 165
working age population, effect on labour force size, 68
world economy, and Australia, 19

yield curve, definition of, 133–4; monetary policy indicator, 133
youth unemployment: Australian experience, 74–5; labour market experience, 66–8